Merengue and
Dominican Identity

Merengue and Dominican Identity

Music as National Unifier

JULIE A. SELLERS

Foreword by Stephen C. Ropp

McFarland & Company, Inc., Publishers
Jefferson, North Carolina, and London

LIBRARY OF CONGRESS CATALOGUING-IN-PUBLICATION DATA

Sellers, Julie A.
    Merengue and Dominican identity : music as national
unifier / Julie A. Sellers ; foreword by Stephen C. Ropp.
        p.   cm.
    Based on the author's thesis (M.A.)—University of
Wyoming.
    Includes bibliographical references and index.

    ISBN 0-7864-1815-X (softcover : 50# alkaline paper) ∞

    1. Merengue (Dance)   2. National characteristics,
Dominican.   3. Dominican Republic—Politics and
government.   I. Title.
GV1796.M45S45   2004
793.3'097293—dc22   2004017524

British Library cataloguing data are available

Cover image ©2004 PhotoSpin

Manufactured in the United States of America

McFarland & Company, Inc., Publishers
  Box 611, Jefferson, North Carolina 28640
  www.mcfarlandpub.com

To Mom, Dad, Denise,
Grandma, and Grandpa
for years of support
in all my endeavors

Acknowledgments

Ten years ago, I set off to spend the summer working in the Dominican Republic as part of a Kansas State University International Community Service project, little suspecting the breadth and intensity of the impact that experience would have on me and on the course of my life. My days spent working with the teachers and children in two preschools in Santiago were filled with constant glimpses into what it meant to be Dominican, although at the time I did not realize it. I spent many hours talking with my teammates, friends and constant companions of that summer, Jocelyn Viterna and Tom Lister, about the complex and often confusing elements of the Dominican culture that we experienced. Our Dominican friends taught us so much by answering our questions and offering their insights—it was like a hands-on course in Dominican identity, though I wouldn't have thought to call it that at the time.

From that point forward, there have been many individuals who have answered my questions and supported and encouraged my insatiable desire to understand and better know the Dominican Republic, what it means to be Dominican, and how to better dance the merengue.

In these few lines, I would like to thank those who have played a role in the making of this book, even when I didn't know that my random questions or life experiences were leading to it. The book would not have become a reality without them.

That first summer's experience in the Dominican Republic is central to the making of this book. Thanks to Dr. Doug Benson and Dr. Bradley Shaw of Kansas State University, and to Dr. William Feyerharm, former assistant dean of arts and sciences at KSU, for encouraging me to apply for the university's International Community Service Program in 1993 and helping me arrange all the fine points of that first trip to the Dominican Republic. And of course, to Jocelyn Viterna and Tom Lister, my community-service team members and friends, for an unforgettable summer in the Dominican Republic in 1993.

My Dominican friends have given me much to think about and answered an infinite number of questions. Thanks to them for the help, patience, and most of all, their *amistad*: Belkys Ikeda, *mi "hermana" dominicana*; Manuel, Magaly and Melisa Llaverías, my Dominican "family"; Víctor Crousset for his patience in teaching me to dance the merengue; José and Mapy Castellanos for the excursions in and around Santo Domingo; William Almonte for answers that always made me think of new things to ask; Jim McGowan and the late Teresita Pellerano McGowan for their contacts, enthusiasm for my topic, and answers to many questions; Apolinar Pérez for a number of insightful talks; and the children of CONANI with whom we spent the summer of 1993 playing.

The making of this book would have been impossible without the support and assistance of a number of other individuals. Many thanks go to my colleague, Dr. Stephen C. Ropp, for working with me on this project from its very beginning, for offering suggestions and for gently prodding me to revisit it and seek a publisher. I am indebted to Dr. Lewis Bagby, director of International Programs, and Dr. Oliver Walter, dean of arts and sciences, both of the University of Wyoming, for their financial support of my trip to the Dominican Republic in 2000. I am grateful to Tammy Timothy, Dr. Garth Massey (University of Wyoming) and Dr. Robert Hinton (New York University) for their proofing and editing suggestions, and to Patrick Eastman, UW Copy Center, for great copies and his interest in my progress. Many thanks to Dr. Klaus Hanson, head of the Department of Modern and Classical Languages, University of Wyoming, for the enthusiasm he demonstrates for all of my projects, and to Mrs. Joann Good, my high school Spanish teacher, for instilling in me a love for the Spanish language and Hispanic culture.

The photographs and illustrations that make this book come alive would not have been possible without the work and assistance of Miguel Gómez, Gina Aversano and Rocío Colón (Elvis Crespo World Fan Club), Rafael Zapata III and *Proyecto Uno*, Mary Katherine Scott, and Keith Joseph (Hispaniola.com). Thanks also to Andy Bryson (UW Ellbogen Center for Teaching and Learning) for his help in editing them.

A special thank you to Nelson Zapata for his personal interview and to Rafael Zapata III who arranged the interview and answered numerous other questions for me as well. I would also like to express my thanks to Dr. Gage Averill (New York University), Julia Álvarez (Middlebury College), Dr. Paul Austerlitz (Brown University), Dr. Silvio Torres-Saillant (Syracuse University), Sarah Aponte (CUNY Dominican Studies Library), Adolfo Valenzuela (*Listín Diario*), Donnie Linton (Hogland Records), Amber Fayyaz and Jason Chin (Jelly's Jamz), Jessica Morales (J&N Publishing), and especially Marti Cuevas (J&N Publishing) for their helpful suggestions and leads.

A number of friends encouraged and supported me throughout this endeavor: Alvaro Salas, Ross Vigil, Eric Atkins, Jim and Jan Garrett, Nancy Kipper, Nathan Hunt and Dr. Winberg Chai. I am especially grateful to J.D. Wallum, Dawn Carter, Sandy Garnett, Bonnie Henderson and Mary Richards for their friendship and constant prayers as I worked on this book. I will be forever indebted to my very dear friend, the late Agnes Farley, who wisely prayed for me when I first traveled to the Dominican Republic in 1993.

My family has been very patient with me through the years and their support has never wavered. Thanks to my grandparents, the late Helen and Benard Stromberg, for always being there for everything I did; to my big sister, Denise Sellers, who sends me great care packages and gives me good advice (like "Don't get lost"); and to my parents, Robert and Leah Sellers, who have always given me the freedom to follow my dreams.

And finally, I would like to thank God, who in His infinite wisdom sent me to the Dominican Republic in the first place instead of other places I might have gone that summer, and who has been with me every step of the way. This book would never have become a reality without Him.

Contents

Foreword

Stephen C. Ropp

When Julie Sellers asked me to write a foreword for her new book on the role of merengue in relation to Dominican identity, I felt deeply honored. We are colleagues at the University of Wyoming—she teaching Spanish in the Department of Modern Languages and I teaching courses on Latin America and the Caribbean in the Department of Political Science. For the past several years, we have team-taught the course "Identity in the Americas" that has been both a great pleasure to teach and a source of inspiration for both of us regarding how to think about the increasingly important topic of the relationship between national identities and the various modes such as music and language through which they are expressed.

At the same time, I suspected that Julie did not ask me to write this foreword because we are colleagues, but rather because I could bring a different perspective as a political scientist to the discussion of the topic covered in this book. From the standpoint of political science, what is of central importance in the formation and preservation of national identities is always the role of states, and this would appear to be the case in the Dominican Republic. As this book so convincingly demonstrates, the nineteenth-century musical form known as "merengue" was used by the dictator Rafael Trujillo to consolidate a sense of national identity which was not only generically anti-imperialist and anti-elitist in a classic Caribbean kind of way but also unique to the Dominican Republic.

Although there are many good books on the subject of Caribbean identity and the role of music in identity processes, I believe that you will find this book to be uniquely interesting and important for a number of reasons. First, it extends and deepens the ongoing debate between so-called "essentialists" and "constructivists" as to the basic nature of all national identities. From the essentialist point of view, identities are believed to be fixed and unchanging because they are seen as rooted in certain unchanging aspects of the nature of the group itself or in its most fundamental collective experiences. As such, these identities are viewed as natural and as existing quite apart from and independent of various actors who would seek to instrumentally use and or change them.

On the other hand, the prevailing view of national identities today is constructivist. They are seen as fluid and ever-changing because they are believed to be the product both of changing material conditions and circumstances as well as of the efforts of various actors (including state leaders) to manipulate them. Julie Sellers adopts a sensible middle-ground approach to this theoretical debate between essentialists and constructivists, suggesting that while merengue can be viewed as an essential aspect of Dominicans' sense of national identity, this inherently flexible musical form has been used by state leaders to maintain a sense of historical continuity and national unity in the face of compelling objective evidence (in racial and class terms) that such unity did not in fact exist.

A second reason that this book is important and interesting is that it introduces a new theoretical concept (filtering) into the debate over how various musical forms such as merengue and salsa change and evolve within their ever-changing domestic and transnational environments. To date, the concept of "crossover music" has been used to describe the process by which musical forms move from place to place and culture to culture. Julie Sellers discusses some of the weaknesses of this approach (for example, its implicit assumptions of hierarchy and linearity in musical exchange across borders), and suggests that this process can better be viewed as one in which a kind of multi-directional cultural and racial "filtering" is taking place.

Thirdly, readers should find this book to be of some interest because it is one of the very few that examines the role of music in the identity processes of Caribbean states from a broad comparative perspective. In Haiti, various musical forms have been used to reinforce rather than to "whiten" and thus dilute the country's attachment to its black roots. In Cuba, state-sponsored musical forms such as rumba have been used to reinforce the country's hybrid racial identity but also to reinforce the socialist ideal of egalitarianism under conditions where this ideal has been only imperfectly realized. And, in Puerto Rico, a number of musical genres serve complex purposes linked not only to the Commonwealth's racial mix but also to its ambiguous territorial status. From a comparative perspective, Julie Sellers argues that merengue has been uniquely important to the shaping and maintenance of Dominican identity because it is the *only* musical style that has been universally embraced as representative of the national identity and because it has few if any symbolic "competitors" for the allegiance of the Dominican people.

I can wholeheartedly recommend this book to those of you who are looking for a sophisticated theoretical discussion of the role that merengue plays in Dominican identity processes and of the similarities and differences between the Dominican Republic in this respect and other Caribbean countries. This is a pioneering work and one that the author has filled with vivid descriptions of both the music and of the people who have made it so central to their daily lives. Julie was raised in Kansas, but it will quickly become obvious as you read and enjoy this book that there must be a "merengue gene" somewhere in her family.

Introduction: In Our Blood

"Throughout the world music has been used to express and help create, contest or dissolve the identity of social groups."

(Seeger 1992: 451)

Before I first traveled to the Dominican Republic in 1993, I acquainted myself with the basics about the country: National Independence Day, February 27; colors of the flag, red, white and blue; current president at the time, Joaquín Balaguer; national music and national dance, merengue.

At the time, I suppose I considered the merengue to be something like the polka or other dances in the United States that are stored neatly in the closets and trunks of the national being and pulled out and displayed only on certain occasions such as festivals and parades. I quickly learned the error of my preconceived notions the very evening I arrived in the Dominican Republic. While wandering through the crowded streets of Sosúa, I was struck by the cacophony of motorcycles whose motors ground as they wound through the narrow streets, the scent of meat fried in the essential *bija* spice, bright laughter, lively conversation and the ever-present, relentless pulse of the merengue.

At first, I thought the festive atmosphere that filled not only the clubs but the streets as well would be unique to the beach resort of Sosúa. There was no doubt left in my mind about merengue's importance, however, after just one full day in Santiago de los Treinta Caballeros, the country's second largest city. Merengue, I discovered, was inescapable. It blared from huge speakers on street corners where cassette vendors displayed their wares. It enveloped passengers crammed sardine-style in inter-city buses and *conchos*, the tiny cars used for public transportation. It poured out of shops and small grocery stores (*bodegas*), and songs jumbled in the streets and patios of the countless houses where the music was played on cassettes, TVs and radios. And not only was the merengue played, it was danced as well—anywhere and at any time: waiting for *conchos*; in the aisles of buses; on the beach; by women doing housework; by preschool children at recess. Merengue was everywhere at once, joining Dominicans in some sort of common harmony amidst the honking horns, children playing baseball in the streets, the street vendors and neighbors chatting on the sidewalks.

"You must learn to dance the merengue," Dominicans of all shapes, sizes and walks of life told me. "It is our national dance."

After several attempts to learn to move my hips like the Dominicans around me, I was fairly convinced that the reason it was *their* national dance and not that of the United States was that there was something genetic involved. "A merengue gene: that must be it," I assured myself.

And Dominicans were quick to agree. "You mustn't be frustrated," they said. "Dancing the merengue is in our blood. It will just take you longer to learn."

And so I continued to attempt to move more fluidly while trying to avoid plodding and tromping like a veritable cow.

"*Cadera, cadera, cadera.* Hips, hips, hips," a Dominican friend who was attempting to teach me chanted to the beat. "Keep your shoulders still," he said, hitting me none too gently on the back. I was quickly learning that merengue dancing was serious business. "You're dancing like a Puerto Rican; *we* only move from the waist down." I vividly remembered that scolding several years later when a Puerto Rican friend insisted I loosen up because I was dancing like a Dominican.

Merengue can swiftly become an addiction. Its carefree nature and breakneck beat give it a magnetic draw that is impossible to resist, whether one seems to have been born with a merengue gene or not.

"It's in our blood," the Dominicans told me in complete earnestness. Yet the dance and music had not become such an ardent symbol of *dominicanidad* for merely primordial reasons. Since its humble origins in the mid–nineteenth century, merengue has changed and been changed, reacting to the historical, political and social situation of the time. Throughout its history, merengue has been believed to be "in the Dominicans' blood" while at the same time being subtly altered and manipulated to help solidify a collective view of the elements which constitute that blood.

A *merengue típico* band plays for tourists on the beach. Both nationally and internationally, merengue is considered the national music and dance of the Dominican Republic. Outsiders' expectations thus reinforce Dominicans' own notions about the central role merengue plays in their national identity. (Photograph: Julie Sellers)

Music and Identity

Studies of identity ultimately lead to the controversial debate about whether identity is primarily constructed or is inherent to a people. Proponents of the former position maintain that nations, and subsequently national identities, are created by intellectuals and those in power to meet their own goals. According to this paradigm, nations do not possess any essential character; rather, they represent ideologies or political projects. In contrast, essentialists or primordialists believe that nations and national identities have a common denominator. Essentialists center their argument on "[n]ational sentiment" which is believed to have a "real, tangible mass base" (Smith 1992: 107) instead of developing from the ideologies and political plans involved in nation building.

Rather than seeing these stances as mutually exclusive when studying questions of identity, it is most effective to consider the issue from a vantage point that combines the two. Certainly, nation-builders are adept at emphasizing certain aspects of the culture and life of the people they plan to unite, often at the cost of other elements. Nevertheless, as Smith points out, "nationalists cannot, and do not, create nations *ex nihilo*. There must be, at least, some elements in the chosen population and its social environment who favour the aspirations and activities of the nationalist visionaries" (1992: 108). As we shall see in the case of merengue's place in Dominican national identity, the dance was already a part of the culture of the island long before any sense of national unity was solidified. The elite from the north-central Cibao region, and the dictator Rafael Trujillo, both took advantage of this base at different points in history to help raise the merengue to its status as the national dance.

Although in reality merengue did not reach its height until the mid–twentieth century, the collective Dominican memory holds it as an inherent element of Dominican-ness that has always been. This histori-cal timeline is blurred as merengue is remembered as a part of *domini-canidad* since remote times. As Balibar comments, "it is not a line of necessary evolution but a series of conjunctural relations which has inscribed them after the event into the pre-history of the nation form" (1992: 133–4).

The link between music and identity is undeniable, for "[t]hrough-out the world music has been used to express and help create, contest or dissolve the identity of social groups" (Seeger 1992: 451). Part of music's ability to cement identities lies in the fact that "it offers, so intensely, a sense of both self and others, of the subjective in the collective" (Simon Frith, cited in Morris 1999: 194).

Regardless of a group's belief that its music is inherent to its being or in its blood, identification with that particular music is influenced by a number of outside social, political and cultural factors. It is impossible to study music as if it were held safely inside a vacuum, lacking any rela-tion to the historical and political situation and unaffected by elements such as race, social class, gender, and age. Music is inseparable from its historical context, so "[i]f we are to understand music we must understand the processes of which it is a part. If we are to understand those processes, we would do well to look to the music" (Seeger 1992: 459).

Changes in social, political and cultural life bring about changes to music. Likewise, music is capable of altering social, political and cultural aspects of a people, for "as social systems change the unique ways in which music is produced, distributed and consumed also change" (Campbell Robinson et al. 1991: 33). Music, then, does not simply mirror social changes: it is capable of effecting them as well.

So-called "national" musics are often seen as unaltered across the years and unalterable in the future. These forms are held up as a national symbol that has always existed. Likewise, groups express their identities in terms of antiquity and stability when, in truth, these identities shift and metamorphose according to the factors mentioned above. The key to understanding music's role in the creation of identities, therefore, is to remember that both music and identity are fluid and malleable; neither is fixed or unchanging.

Merengue, considered the national music of the Dominican Republic, exemplifies the constant interplay between outside processes and musical innovation. Although some work has been done concerning the topic of merengue and Dominican identity, insufficient emphasis has been given to the music's importance in unifying what had traditionally been an extremely fragmented and decentralized nation that lacked a sense of national solidarity, and by extension, of national identity. Not enough attention has been paid to the two-way influences between merengue and social, political and cultural contexts at different moments in Dominican history, nor has the question been raised of exactly why this single musical form has enjoyed such longevity. Additionally, Dominican-Americans' role and so-called "crossover" music have not been covered in any work to this point.

When studying questions of identity, it is necessary to remember that "[m]en and women make history but not under conditions of their own making. They are partly made by the histories they make" (Hall 1992: 340). For this reason, the mutual influences between merengue and Dominican historical, political, and social elements are at the heart of this study.

Fluid Identity, Fluid Music

Beginning with colonization, historic events within the Dominican Republic occurred in such a way as to necessitate a fluid identity that would represent the diverse elements within the nation while superimposing a sense of continuity and oneness. For example, during the Colonial period, the Spanish authorities began the practice of calling mulattos "white" in order to increase the numbers of freemen for reasons of security. This tactic reconfigured racial classification in the Dominican Republic, eliminating a strict division between black and white and replacing it with a fluid boundary that included more individuals in what was deemed the preferable category.

When merengue was later born, the syncretism inherent in the music resulted in differing interpretations of the genre by the country's diverse groups. Some believed the music's African elements to be predominant.

In turn, others emphatically maintained that merengue was primarily European-influenced.

In the twentieth century, this tradition of musical fluidity made it possible for the merengue to lend itself to complete and total dictatorial control. Rafael Trujillo appropriated the music not only for his own end of maintaining power but also as part of his plan to constitute a national, Euro-centric identity by embracing the variation of the dance from the whitest region of the country.

Merengue has also been an important symbol of identity in the Dominican Diaspora. Dominican immigrants to the United States and Puerto Rico have recreated in miniature their home nation by incorporating elements of Dominican culture, specifically merengue. In this way, they are better able to face the psychological stresses associated with emigration. Furthermore, merengue serves as a powerful marker of identity by separating Dominicans from North Americans and other Latino immigrants.

Merengue has become such a strong symbol of Dominican national identity partly because of its syncretism and flexibility. These elements allow it to represent not only the reality of Dominican identity but the perceived (or, to use Anderson's terminology, "imagined") and preferred elements that constitute it. Just as language is never static but constantly changing while still being the same language, merengue remains the same music while at the same time being subtly altered.

Dominican Identity in Opposition to the Other

Dominicans have long defined themselves by contrasting Dominican-ness with an "Other." This process involves defining the Self in contrast to that "Other" individual or entity. As Sander Gilman points out, "[b]ecause there is no real line between the Self and the Other, an imaginary line must be drawn" (cited in Aparicio 1998: 155). In the case of the Dominican Republic, national identity has historically been defined in contrast to neighboring Haiti. Dominicans insist on their Hispanophilic identity and accordingly, define only Haitians as black. Tensions concerning the border, trade and immigration have only served to strengthen this dichotomy with the passage of time.

Merengue as a defining element of Dominican identity is strongly linked to this concept of the "Other." Historically, support for merengue has grown most when Dominican identity has faced real or perceived threats from outside. Merengue has served as a cultural boundary between the Dominican Republic and Haiti by reinforcing Dominicans' belief that they are everything the Haitians are not. Furthermore, the music was also a strong marker of national identity during the two U.S. military occupations. For Dominicans in the Diaspora, merengue has served to reinforce the sense of group within a foreign setting.

The Whitening of Merengue

When merengue first appeared in the mid-nineteenth century, it was shunned by the Dominican upper class because of its association with the countryside and its African elements. Only in the early 1900s when established musicians disguised modified versions of the music as *danzas típicas* (typical dances) was merengue accepted in orchestras and salons. The dance was briefly embraced as a national symbol by the elite (a predominantly white group) of the Cibao region during the 1916–1924 United States military occupation; nevertheless, the music once again fell into disfavor following the U.S. withdrawal.

The most significant contribution to the growth in popularity of merengue was dictator Rafael Trujillo's appropriation of the dance as a method of control and propaganda. In order to make the music more appealing to the predominantly white upper class, Trujillo hired musicians to alter it to be more preferable to the elite. In this way, a split was made between traditional merengue and the new, orchestral version accepted by the upper class.

Post-Trujillo merengue was further whitened by the implementation of foreign (and specifically, North American) influences. Most recently, the merengue that has been most popular on the global stage has been that performed by white musicians, a trend that parallels the success of other Latin and Latin-influenced music in the North.

This Study

The structure of this work follows chronological lines to trace certain patterns in Dominican history. Generally, the historical context is presented first followed by merengue's specific role within that time frame. The primary exception to this format is found in Chapter 6, which deals with the Era of Trujillo, a time during which merengue and state were inseparable.

The centuries preceding the birth of merengue are discussed in order to situate the people, geography, and politics of the Dominican Republic. Despite being Spain's first colony in the Americas, the country

Traditionally a couples dance, the merengue step has often been compared to a cock wooing a hen, and in the past, a man used his fancy footwork to court a lady. (Photograph: Julie Sellers)

Merengue has served as a language specific to the Dominican Republic—a part of the culture that is the same yet ever-changing. (Photograph: Mary Katherine Scott)

was eventually abandoned by the Spanish Crown when riches were found in other colonies. Emigration from Santo Domingo (as the colony was then called) left it underpopulated and made it easy prey for the designs of other nations. This colonial legacy is discussed in Chapter 1.

Chapter 2 considers the role of the Haitian Other in the creation of Dominican identity. During the early nineteenth century, neighboring Haiti gained control of the Dominican Republic and ruled—brutally, as Dominicans maintain—for 22 years (1822–1844). This suppression under Haitian rule instilled in Dominicans a strong sense of "us" versus "them" and created the notion of the Haitian Other.

In defining themselves in contrast to this Other, Dominican national identity has traditionally been constructed upon the elements of race, language and religion. In the Dominican Republic, this translates to the image of a white, Spanish-speaking Catholic. Dominican identity has also been defined by what Dominicans maintain they are *not*, in relation to their island neighbor: not black, not speakers of a creole language, and not practitioners of voodoo. To further distinguish itself, it has been both state and individual policy in the Dominican Republic to highlight the contributions made by the European *conquistadores* while romanticizing the role played by the native indigenous people.

Both the affirmative and negative identity constructions arising from the view of the Haitian as Other reaffirm the imagined geography of the Dominican Republic.* As one might suspect of a nation squeezed onto an island with a neighboring country towards which it holds animosity, the geographical focus is on the border and geographies of identity become crucial. This arbitrary division of land has long been a source of contention between the two nations. While the border has officially been fixed since the 1930s, it has traditionally been fluid as both Haitians and Dominicans make their way across it and those who live along it switch easily between Spanish and Krèyol.

Chapter 3 focuses on the decentralization and creation of regional *caudillo* (strongman) rule that resulted from Spain's early lack of interest in and abandonment of the Dominican Republic. At this time, various small pockets of the population were each controlled by a different *caudillo* who exercised his power over the masses that in turn depended on his protection. The pattern of power and takeover was common; eventually, a stronger individual than the one in control would rise up and wrest power from the ruling *caudillo*.

National politics were run by whichever *caudillo* could retain power over all other contenders. Because of the *caudillo* tradition, nineteenth-century Dominican history and politics were marked by numerous uprisings and civil wars. This form of political rule ruined the nation's economy as constant wars devastated agriculture and prevented men from working the land. Furthermore, the *caudillos* began to co-opt political opponents with bribes, paid for out of state funds. The significance of the period of the great *caudillos* cannot be underestimated, due to the extreme fragmentation and regionalism that this form of government brought with it.

The longest period of continuous *caudillo* rule was under Ulises Heureaux (1882–1899). During this time, the Dominican Republic accrued an incredible foreign debt. As power was violently taken by one president from another in the years that followed, European creditors threatened to take drastic measures in order to be paid for the loans they had made to the Dominican Republic. United States President Theodore Roosevelt, fearful of European intervention in Latin America, had spearheaded the Roosevelt Corollary to the Monroe Doctrine. It was with this document that he justified his order to invade the Dominican Republic in 1916.

---

*Radcliffe and Westwood link the concept of the Other to such imagined geographies or "geographies of identity" which "can be defined as the sense of belonging and subjectivities which are constituted in (and which in turn can constitute) different spaces and social sites" (1996: 27). Nations are believed to be linked to specific places, and nationalities, in turn, are seen as pure within those delineated areas.

The merengue, as we shall see in Chapter 4, came prominently onto the Dominican social scene at the same time as *caudillo* rule was established in the mid-1800s. At this time, the upper classes opposed the dance and literary campaigns were launched that supported the *tumba* dance and staunchly repudiated the merengue. Opponents of the merengue were primarily concerned with what they considered the vulgar and inappropriate movements of what they viewed as a lower class dance. They were fearful that such a lascivious dance might replace the *tumba*, then considered the national dance.

Chapter 5 focuses on the U.S. marines' eight-year occupation of the country and how that event unified the Dominican Republic as it had never been unified under the *caudillos*. The U.S. forces confiscated all firearms to prevent revolts against them and created a National Guard to help keep order. They constructed roads and railroads that linked the various towns and cities and made possible a strong central government. The greatest resistance to the United States occupation was demonstrated culturally by an adherence to things Dominican, including the merengue in the Cibao region.

Although the merengue had been seen as a dance of the masses, the elite began to embrace it during the United States occupation. Dominican tradition holds that the merengue became such a vibrant symbol of national identity at that time because U.S. marines were unable to dance it correctly. A slower variation of the merengue, the *pambiche*, evolved at this time as Dominicans mimicked the marines' attempts to coordinate their hips and feet while dancing the merengue.

The United States' occupation of the Dominican Republic contributed directly to one of the bloodiest and most repressive dictatorial regimes in the history of all of Latin America. Through a series of personal connections, Rafael Trujillo, an uneducated telegraph operator, entered the National Guard formed by the U.S. By the end of the occupation, Trujillo had risen to the highest ranking military position, commander in chief of the National Police. By 1930 he had overthrown the elected president, Horacio Vásquez.

Trujillo was in essence nothing more than a post-occupation Dominican *caudillo*, with the only difference being that the marines had made it virtually impossible for him to be overthrown. They had rid Dominican citizens of their arms and created a National Guard that was completely loyal to Trujillo, and the country was well-connected thanks to the numerous construction projects.

Of all Dominican *caudillos*, Trujillo was by far the most astute. This strongman worked tirelessly to control the masses through various tactics, among them manipulation of the merengue. As we shall see in Chapter

6, merengue and the Dominican state became virtually one and the same during the 31-year era of Trujillo.

Trujillo was a great enthusiast of merengue, and he appropriated it to speak to the masses during his first presidential campaign. From a lower-class family himself, Trujillo held the Dominican elite in disdain. Embracing merengue at the expense of other musical styles was partly a maneuver to force the upper classes to do his will. A renowned dancer, Trujillo insisted that merengue be performed at all social functions. No one was allowed to leave before *El Jefe* ("The Chief," as Trujillo was called), and he often stayed at parties until the wee hours of the morning, dancing tirelessly while members of the elite were forced to endure a music they considered vulgar.

Merengue was a constant source of propaganda for Generalissimo Trujillo during his reign. Musicians were "asked" to compose merengues in his praise and for any occasionTrujillo deemed worthy: the construction of monuments in his honor, the celebration of the census or the border agreement, and the commemoration of his trip to Spain, to name but a very few examples.

Merengue was a perfect tool of control for Trujillo in every way. Its lyrics reiterated Trujillo's greatness and the country's need for him at its head. Merengue also allowed the poor masses to identify with the Generalissimo and, until the moment of his assassination, he held their support overwhelmingly. Because the elite disliked the music, it served as a constant reminder to them that the President dictated all aspects of political and social life.

Trujillo's pervasive and brutal power and his ability to weather any attacks made on his position kept him in control for over 30 years. When at last a group of conspirators succeeded in assassinating the dictator, merengue was also freed from his iron grasp. "*Mataron al chivo*" ("They Killed the Goat"), a popular merengue of the time celebrating the dictator's death, blared from radios across the nation.

Chapters 7 and 8 deal with post-Trujillo politics and music, respectively. As we shall see, a certain amount of stability, albeit under Trujillo protégé Joaquín Balaguer, eventually arose out of the chaos and civil war following the assassination of Rafael Trujillo. While Balaguer continued to practice many of the same methods to maintain power, manipulating the merengue was not one of them.

With the new leaders came an opening up of the country, and international influences poured in to reshape the national music. At this time, debates arose over the path the national music was taking. While some backed a traditional merengue, free of transnational influence, others supported incorporating such elements to reflect the modern Dominican Republic.

The 1970s also witnessed a debate originating in the Domnican *nueva canción* (New Song) movement concerning the ethnic origins of merengue. While adherents to *nueva canción* emphasized the African elements of the national music, the elite stubbornly maintained the long-held belief that merengue was essentially a Hispanic music.

With the fall of Trujillo, obstacles to obtaining visas were lifted, and Dominicans began to emigrate in unprecedented numbers. These emigrants, the majority of whom made their way to New York City, still considered themselves Dominican. They left for the United States with the clear intention of making enough money to be able to return to the island. For this reason, Dominicans became naturalized citizens in small numbers, even though many lived in the United States for decades.

Chapter 9 discusses how Dominicans of the Diaspora have recreated their home country in microcosm within their new settings. In New York City, the largest concentration of Dominicans can be found in Washington Heights, Hamilton Heights and Inwood. There, *bodegas* and other typical businesses line the streets. Dominican newspapers are sold, restaurants serve traditional foods, men play dominoes, and merengue can be heard. Nevertheless, the merengue that is playing is not always an import from the home country, for Dominican-American *merengueros* have risen to such levels of popularity that New York has become the focal point of the Dominican merengue music industry.

At the beginning of the twenty-first century, Dominican-Americans are poised to be a vital part of the growing and influential young Latin population in the United States. Dubbed "Generation Ñ" by Bill Teck (Figueroa et al. 1999: 53), this group of young Latin Americans has recently broken into the North American world of pop music with such "crossover" artists as Ricky Martin, Marc Anthony, and Enrique Iglesias. While studying the impact of these musicians, it is necessary to consider the terminology—"crossover"—used to label this music. As we shall see, the style coined "crossover" or even "Latino" is quite different from the same music produced and performed for Latino audiences. Ultimately, these questions lead us back to issues of race and the "whitening" of Latin music.

Chapter 10 briefly considers the question of music and identity in three other Caribbean nations: Haiti, Cuba and Puerto Rico. While some broad generalizations concerning the role of music in identity consolidation can be made, no other musical genre has been as central to identity process as merengue has been to the Dominicans.

Merengue and Dominican Identity

Merengue has become a truly transnational music. It has achieved international appeal in Europe, Asia and the United States and through-out Latin America as an easy (in comparison to other Latino styles) and enjoyable dance music. Merengue is inseparable from the Dominican Republic, for anyone who knows anything about it instantly associates the dance with that country. It is a symbol of *dominicanidad* for Dominicans and for the *dominicanos ausentes* (Dominican immigrants). What once was a music forced upon the masses and elite alike has become an integral element of their identity. Merengue, because it has so concisely encapsulated an essential and malleable base for identity while serving as a medium for communicating that identity, has been used for nation building and identity consolidation purposes as has no other music in the Caribbean.

In both the primordialist sense and the constructivist sense, merengue is in and of the blood of the Dominican people. As the pages of this work unfold, the complex interaction of music and dance, politics, history, economics, and social elements will reveal the story of a nation, its identity and its music.

1

Colonial Legacy

"They are, your Majesty, the most beautiful lands that human eyes have ever seen."
—Columbus to Queen Isabella,
cited in Aquino 1997:1

To the native peoples of the Caribbean, the island was known as Quisqueya; in the sixteenth century, Christopher Columbus would christen it Hispaniola and claim it for the Spanish Crown. From that point forward, it was destined to be a land of firsts in the encounter between Europe, Africa and the Americas:

> What is now Dominican land witnessed the first settlement of Europeans, the first genocide of aborigines, and the first cohort of African slaves in the archipelago. Santo Domingo initiated racial mixture, religious syncretism, linguistic nativization, and the overall creolizing process that typifies Caribbean culture [Torres-Saillant and Hernández 1998: 5].

Thus began some 300 years of colonialism on Hispaniola, the legacy of which would profoundly shape the island's political, social, and cultural future.

Encounter and the First Years of Colonialism

Approximately half a million Taíno Indians inhabited Quisqueya at the time of Columbus's arrival in 1492. The tribe, a peaceful people, lived

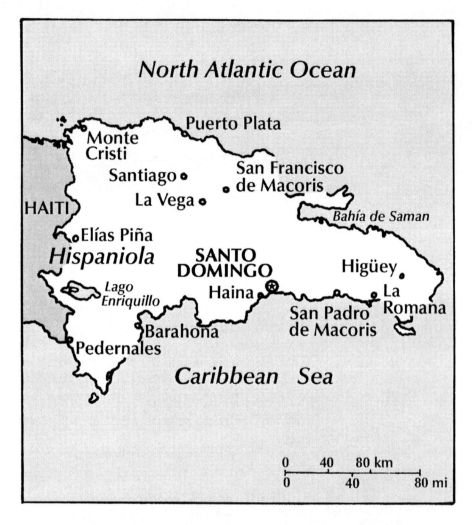

The island known as Quisqueya to the native Taíno people, christened "Hispaniola" by Christopher Columbus, and now known as the Dominican Republic, was a land of firsts in the encounter between Europe, Africa and the Americas. (*CIA World Fact Book 2002*)

and maintained power in the Greater Antilles. Unlike the cannibalistic Carib of the Lesser Antilles, the Taíno diet consisted of the numerous crops the people raised and what they could obtain by hunting and fishing.

Taíno stories of creation reveal that they considered themselves the original inhabitants of Quisqueya, having long forgotten their people's migration to the island from South America. A strong sense of solidarity, due primarily to a need for unity against the occasional invasions of the Carib, united the five different tribes of the island. Apparently, the caciques of those five tribes were close to forming an official confederation in 1492 at which time their efforts at consolidation were disrupted by the arrival of the Spanish (Moya Pons 1995: 22).

The people that Columbus encountered on Hispaniola were strikingly different from the Asians and Indians he had expected to meet. Nevertheless, Columbus was far from disappointed with the unexpected turn his voyage had taken. The golden ornaments and jewelry that some Taíno wore convinced Columbus that there were riches on the island. Enticed by the possibilities of fortune, Columbus ordered the construction of a permanent European settlement, beginning with a fort built from the wood of a wrecked ship. Thirty-nine men manned the structure, known as "*La Navidad*" (Christmas) to commemorate the December 24, 1492, date of the shipwreck, and the rest of the Admiral's men returned with him to Spain to deliver the news of their "discovery."*

Columbus, in addition to being a sailor and adventurer, also proved to be highly astute at marketing. His written and oral descriptions of the richness of Hispaniola emphasize the extent and abundance of exotic and unknown trees, flowers, fruits and plants as well as the beauty of the physical landscape (Chang-Rodríguez and Filer 1988:13–14). Of course, Columbus did not hesitate to mention that there was gold to be had and that the native inhabitants were quite docile: "They are the most fearful people in the world" [*Son los más temerosos que hay en el mundo*]" (*ibid.*, 13).† The island, he writes in a 1493 letter to the Spanish Royal Secretary, "is to be desired, and once seen, it is never to be left" [*es para desear, y vista, es para nunca dejar*] (*ibid.*).

When Columbus returned to Hispaniola in December 1493, he discovered that his perception of the Taíno had been fatally erroneous. Of the 39 men he had left at *La Navidad*, the admiral found that not one survivor remained. The natives Columbus had presumed "fearful" had attacked and killed all those who had stayed at the fort in retaliation for abuses committed against Taíno women.

Despite this setback, Columbus went forward with the establishment of a *factoría*, a commercial outpost, known as "*La Isabela.*" This system provided for a group of partners who would make their profits by trading

---

*Much debate has taken place concerning the terminology used to discuss the arrival of the Europeans in the Americas. This event has long been considered a "discovery," yet some groups have insisted it be referred to as an "encounter" while others (especially indigenous groups) maintain that the colonization of the Americas is best described as a "resistance" on the part of the indigenous peoples. In this text, I use the term *discovery* lightly, and in this case, to illustrate the point of view of the Europeans at that time.
†Unless otherwise noted, all translations are my own.

with the indigenous people; in turn, the partners would employ European artisans who were paid a set wage (Moya Pons 1995: 30).

La Isabela faced numerous difficulties from the start. The Europeans were unaccustomed to the tropical climate and its diseases and were also without medications and food. Many perished, and the *factoría* found itself far short of the laborers needed to make the system succeed. Columbus then ordered all men to work, regardless of class or rank, thus alienating many of the *hidalgos* (nobles). Following two military campaigns against the Taíno in 1494 and 1495, Columbus embraced the idea of giving captured natives to his men as slaves instead of paying them fixed wages. In this way, he not only saved money but alleviated at least some of the tensions with the *hidalgos* as well. These slaves labored in the gold mines under conditions of brutality and starvation.

In 1496, Columbus again returned to Spain, this time to report the "discovery" of Jamaica and Cuba to the Crown. The Admiral left behind his brothers, Diego and Bartolomé, to head the *factoría* in his absence. During the period of a little over two years that Columbus was gone, rebels under Francisco Roldán rose up against the Columbus family. Upon his return in 1498, Columbus was forced to accede to the revolutionaries to regain peace.

The chaos produced by Roldán's rebellion convinced the Spanish Crown to make drastic changes on Hispaniola. Francisco de Bobadilla was sent to the island as provisional governor in 1500, and Columbus returned to Spain disgraced and in chains. The practice of using Indian labor in the mines was legalized soon after on December 20, 1503; the only stipulation of this type of system known as the *encomienda* was that the Indians be taught the Catholic faith by their masters.

The *encomienda* definitively spelled the tragic end of Taíno society. Illness, hunger and work in the mines killed the Taíno rapidly and mercilessly. Many of those who survived the harsh conditions participated in ceremonial group suicides to escape the end of the world they had known. Likewise, mothers and soon-to-be mothers took their own children's lives to save them from the fate of slavery. By 1508, a mere 60,000 indigenous people remained (Moya Pons 1995: 33–4).

The numbers continued to decline; only 33,000 Taíno were left by 1511, and just six years later, less than 12,000 remained (Wucker 1999b: 65). In 1519, with fewer than 3000 indigenous people left on the island, a group of some 500 of them escaped to the mountains under the cacique (chief) Enriquillo, where they managed to evade the Spanish until a treaty was signed in 1533 that guaranteed peace. Enriquillo, in turn, agreed to return all escaped slaves he encountered to their masters. Over three centuries later, the cacique would become a national icon in Manuel de Jesús Galván's 1882 historical novel, *Enriquillo*. This novel, which depicts the cacique as the stereo-typical *buen salvaje* (noble savage) of nineteenth-century literature, is still required reading in the Dominican educational curriculum and reflects the racial hierarchy that yet exists in the Dominican national mentality.

During the first years of the sixteenth century, Santo Domingo, as Hispaniola had come to be called, was the central point of the Spanish presence in the region. When it became evident that gold deposits were not as plentiful as Columbus had thought them to be many of the colonizers abandoned the island for Mexico and South America in hopes of exploiting the gold and silver that had been discovered there.

This out-migration, coupled with the mass deaths of Indian slaves, resulted in a shortage of labor for which the remaining population could not compensate. At this time, Dominican friar Bartolomé de Las Casas arose as a spokesman for the rights of the indigenous people. A slave owner himself, Las Casas espoused the importation of African slaves who he considered better laborers than the Taíno. Furthermore, Las Casas believed that Africans were inhuman and therefore could not become Christians (Wucker 1999b: 65). Later in life, Las Casas would regret his earlier stance and role in initiating the importation of African slaves; he admitted regretfully that he had been mistaken for he had come to understand that Africans were human beings after all. But before then, his writings and other efforts were to be influential in bringing about the introduction of African slaves into the Americas. Las Casas's 1552 publication, *Brevísima relación de la destrucción de las Indias* (Brief Account of the Destruction of the Indies) as well as translations and intentional mistranslations of it done rapidly into other European languages in an attempt to discredit Spain, became known as the *leyenda negra*—the Black Legend. In addition to revealing the Spanish abuses against the Amerindians, the *leyenda negra* established internationally the concept of the *buen salvaje*—the noble savage of the Americas.

In the 1530s, landowners commenced the importation of African slaves to Santo Domingo. By that time, they had begun to plant sugar cane and laborers were needed to work the fields and harvest the crop. While the European population continued to leave the island in a steady flow, thousands of African slaves were brought to Quisqueya. By 1546, slaves outnumbered whites by a ratio of nearly 2.5 to 1 (Moya Pons 1995: 40).

The Spaniards were not naïve about the dangers posed by the numerical superiority of blacks on the island. What most concerned landowners was the possibility of a rebellion organized by the estimated 2,000–3,000 escaped slaves, or *cimarrones*. The Spaniards lived in constant fear of being attacked and they took the precaution of always travelling in armed groups of 15 to 20 men (Moya Pons 1995: 41).

In 1543, the Crown decided to take direct and immediate action against the *cimarrones*. When Alonso de Cerrato was appointed to serve as governor and president of the *Real Audiencia* (Royal Audience), he purposed to eliminate all possibility of black attacks or takeover. Thus ensued a bloody three-year war in which many *cimarrones* were captured, violently reprimanded, tortured or killed. By 1546, these measures had almost completely erased the possibility of a black uprising. The precedence of white power had been firmly established.

Contraband Trade and the Devastaciones

As the sixteenth century progressed, pirates and buccaneers became an increasingly dangerous threat for the people of Hispaniola. Previously, the Spanish Crown had established a monopoly dictating that Santo Domingo trade only with the Spanish port of Seville. Spain's waning interest in the island resulted in fewer and fewer ships being sent and the colonists suffered shortages of many supplies. The Crown refused the islanders' pleas to lift the monopoly to allow them to trade with other countries or even other ports of Spain. Continuing shortages pushed the inhabitants of the isolated Hispaniola to turn to contraband trade.

During the first years of the island's involvement in contraband trade, residents dealt only with Spanish smugglers. As time passed political obstacles to foreign contraband became blurred in the Dominicans' minds. Dominican trade boundaries widened when they began to sell their cattle hides and other goods to Portuguese, French, Dutch and English ships who gave them a better price. *Cimarrones* also joined in contraband trade and in parts of Hispaniola, smuggling became the mainstay of the economy.

The contraband trade infuriated the Crown and numerous orders were passed against it. Furthermore, smuggling began to be considered in terms of the infiltration of Protestant religious views in addition to a mere economic infiltration by other nations. In 1605, the Spanish Crown took more decisive steps to end the illegal trade, ordering the governor of Santo Domingo, Antonio de Osorio, to depopulate the main smuggling region, the western portion of the island.

The *devastaciones* of the primary smuggling centers left lasting effects on the people and history of Hispaniola. Economically, this act plunged the colony into extreme poverty. It was possible for the western inhabitants to rescue only a small percentage of the livestock raised in the smuggling areas when they were depopulated, and following the *devastaciones*, colonial production never again reached its previous levels. Despite its success in destroying the lucrative contraband trade, the Crown did not compensate by sending more Spanish trading ships to Hispaniola. Sugar production became almost nonexistent.

Politically, the *devastaciones* had been intended to keep enemies of the Spanish at a distance; nevertheless, European settlers filtered in to fill the depopulated areas in the wake of the Spanish retreat. The island was plagued by pirates and buccaneers, especially the Dutch, who were a menacing presence during the Thirty Years' War. Eventually, French influence from the island of Tortuga penetrated the western regions of Hispaniola, and by the late 1600s, that territory was occupied by French-speaking plantation owners who worked the land with black slaves.

Socially, the *devastaciones* contributed to continued out-migration. Since colonizers had stopped importing slaves even before the depopulation of the smuggling towns, the slave population simultaneously declined as well. Meanwhile, the number of foreign immigrants filling the western lands of the island continued to grow.

In 1662, slave importation to Santo Domingo began again in order to supply workers for the cacao plantations. Campaigns against the *cimarrones* were also launched, and those who were captured were returned to their former masters or sold. In spite of this increase in workers, the economy remained poor due to a series of natural disasters. The colony's population continued to shrink in light of the devastating economic conditions.

An Island Divided, an Island United

Once peace had been made between France and Spain in 1678, trade began between the western and eastern portions of Hispaniola. Relations were still fearful and suspicious as French settlers continued to push their way further and further inland into Spanish territory. Although the Spanish colonizers occupied more land, they were far outnumbered by their French counterparts of the west. The some 1500 families left on the eastern side of the island by the late 17th century were scattered sparsely across the landscape. By the late 1700s, Santo Domingo's population would be approximately a mere one-fourth of that of the western region, which had become known as Saint-Domingue (Wucker 1999b: 36).

Finally, the Spanish had begun the practice of protecting and freeing slaves who escaped from the French and reached Santo Domingo. Prominent Saint-Domingue rebel leaders such as Toussaint L'Ouverture, Jean François and Jean Biassou even received the assistance of Spanish border officials in their fight against the French.

Questions of where the border officially lay were ever present. Since the Spanish colonists were physically outnumbered by the French, they knew that securing the frontier by force was out of the question. Instead, authorities formulated a plan to re-populate the borderlands. This tactic offered land along the frontier to Spaniards from the Canary Islands. In this way, the settlers served as a living border even though they played no defensive role in the military sense.

Despite these efforts, Spain was unable to maintain its control on Hispaniola, and it waived its right of jurisdiction over Santo Domingo to the French in the 1795 Treaty of Basel. This treaty ended the war between France and Spain that had begun in 1793 and allowed the latter to recover all peninsular territories it had lost in return for the cession of the eastern part of Hispaniola to France. The Spanish colonial government then began the procedure of abandoning the island so that the colony could be officially surrendered. This was an extremely slow process that stretched across the next several years.

Meanwhile, in French Saint-Domingue, racial tensions were coming to a head. Saint-Domingue had experienced a high degree of racial mixing, due mainly to the lack of white women in the colony. Mulattos were officially considered equal to whites because of a 1793 law. This practice effectively split the population into three opposing groups: whites, mulattos, and blacks (Moya Pons 1995: 95). Although slavery was officially abolished in Saint-Domingue in 1793, whites there continued to discriminate against blacks and mulattos.

Following the abolition of slavery in Saint-Domingue, Toussaint L'Ouverture abandoned his shaky alliance with the Spanish and joined the French forces against the residents of the former Spanish colony that had opted to remain on Hispaniola. Toussaint, now made a general by the French, aimed to achieve complete and total unity of the island as a defense against Napoleon's plans to reinstate slavery. Even though the Spanish colony had not yet been formally surrendered and the French government had not granted authorization to Toussaint, he managed to gain approval for his plan from the governor of Saint-Domingue by threatening a massive slaughter of all white settlers if his designs against the Spanish were not supported. On January 26, 1801, Toussaint and his forces marched unopposed into the capital city of the former Spanish colony. He claimed Santo Domingo for the French and became its governor.

Toussaint immediately abolished slavery in Santo Domingo and began steps to integrate the eastern lands into Saint-Domingue's economy. Specifically, the general focused his efforts on agriculture. Toussaint believed that the Spanish dedicated too little time to hard work and too much to leisure activities, and he intended to radically change the current practice of small-scale, subsistence farming and ranching in Santo Domingo to improve production (Moya Pons 1995: 107).

Toussaint's rule in Santo Domingo was short-lived. In February 1802, French forces invaded the island. The citizens of Santo Domingo immediately allied themselves with the French against Toussaint. The general and his forces were driven from the east and the French re-established slavery soon thereafter.

The Spanish Dominicans' preference of being controlled by a European colonial power rather than a creole government is not surprising. Just as in Saint-Domingue, racial mixing had not been unusual in Santo Domingo. Nevertheless, this *mestizaje* (racial mixing) was seldom acknowledged by the citizens of that colony. In part, this denial can be attributed to the "practice of calling mixed-race residents white and Spanish" (Wucker 1999b: 75) that the colonial government had previously undertaken in an attempt to increase the sparse population of Santo Domingo. This action early established the practice of placing one element of Dominican ethnicity, the European, above the other groups represented (Taíno and black) in a racial hierarchy.*

It is telling that the inhabitants of Santo Domingo opposed French occupation only until they learned that the French had once again reinstated slavery. Dominicans' long-standing practice of claiming a white identity in the face of racial mixing made it impossible for them to consent to being ruled by people they considered black (Moya Pons 1995: 109). Despite abuses committed by the military government of French general François-Marie Kerversau, the residents of Santo Domingo "considered French rule a lesser evil than Toussaint's" (*ibid.*, 109).

Haitian Independence and Haitian Rule

The war between the French and the Haitian blacks was violent but short-lived. Aided by the British, the Haitian blacks soundly defeated the French and drove them from the island. On January 1, 1804, Haiti was declared an independent and sovereign state; it was the first independent black republic in the world. Nevertheless, the bloodshed continued even after the French surrendered. Haitian general Jean-Jacques Dessalines, first emperor Jacques I,

> ordered that all the French who remained in Haiti be killed. Some of
> the colonists tried to pass as Creoles who had grown up on the island

---

*As we shall see in the following chapter, black influences have historically received little to no recognition in the Dominican Republic.

and had African blood. Dessalines devised a test to weed out the ones who had not spoken Kreyol all their lives; they had to sing, "*Nanett alé nan fontain, cheche dlo, crich-a li cassé*" (Nanette went to the fountain, looking for water, but her jug broke). The French gave themselves away when they could not properly pronounce the Kreyol or duplicate the African cadences of the melody [Wucker 1999b: 37].

On the eastern side of the island, the French had finally gained full control of Santo Domingo. An 1803 decree made by Napoleon guaranteed that the French government would treat legal, cultural and social practices in the East with respect. Dominicans, though not pleased with the French presence, tolerated it as a lesser burden than Haitian rule (Moya Pons 1995: 113).

Ironically, it took events in Europe to stir up enough anti-French sentiment among Dominicans to bring about their rebellion. In 1808, Napoleon encouraged Spain's King Fernando VII to come to France by promising him his support. Once the Spanish monarch arrived he was made Napoleon's prisoner and forced to abdicate the Spanish throne to the emperor's brother, Joseph. In Santo Domingo, this insulting act was the last straw for many landowners and businessmen whose livelihoods had already been affected by French trading restrictions with Haiti.

One of these businessmen, Don Juan Sánchez Ramírez, built support both on the island and among Dominicans who had emigrated to Puerto Rico. Sánchez Ramírez called out to the people's Hispanic identity to unite them in a common cause against the French. Soon, Sánchez Ramírez had grouped together enough forces to face the French, and on November 7, 1808, he defeated them at Palo Hincado.

Following this victory, the British imposed a naval blockade that successfully prevented the French from receiving supplies. Eventually the French were forced to surrender, but they chose to do so to the British rather than to Sánchez Ramírez. The British then occupied the capital city, and it was up to Sánchez Ramírez to negotiate a settlement with them that allowed the colony to return to Spanish hands in exchange for rights of free entry for British ships.

The effects of the events of 1795–1809 on Santo Domingo were various. The population of the eastern lands continued to decline drastically: from a high mark in 1789 of some 180,000 inhabitants, Santo Domingo's population fell to less than half that number by 1809. Among those who had abandoned the island were many of its most educated. Economically, "[p]overty again became universal, and a deep pessimism fell on a people who perceived themselves as white, Hispanic, and Catholic, and who did not want to be abandoned by Spain" (Moya Pons 1995: 116). This firmly-established Hispanic identification coupled with the fear of black domination convinced the inhabitants of Santo Domingo to attempt to reinstate Spanish colonial rule precisely at the time when Spain's power and hold over its colonies had significantly weakened.

On the other side of the island, the fledgling Haitian nation feared that the Spanish colonial government would assist the French and allow them to regain their former colony. Haitian president Jean Pierre Boyer kept alive Toussaint's earlier goal of uniting all of Hispaniola under a single government. Boyer also believed that Santo Domingo was too weak to repel invaders and that it was in Haiti's best interests to consolidate power on the island. Haiti's interests in the eastern part of the island, then, were not solely racially motivated, as many believed and still maintain; they were also concerned with issues of national security and sovereignty (Balaguer 1994:12).

There were, at this time, three primary political factions in Santo Domingo: one supporting unity with Haiti, another desiring to remain a colony of Spain, and a third in favor of declaring independence from Spain and joining with Simón Bolívar's Gran Colombia. The first of these to take action was the pro-Haitian group who declared Santo Domingo's independence from Spain and its intention of placing Dominican lands under Haitian protection on November 15, 1821. The pro-Colombian group, led by José Núñez de Cáceres, immediately followed this proclamation with its own, declaring Santo Domingo free of Spain and part of Gran Colombia. Thus, the Independent State of Spanish Haiti was born.

Legacy of the Colonial Era

The colonial legacy of the nation then known as "Spanish Haiti" was multiple and complex. First, the encounter between three worlds had resulted in a multiethnic heritage. The effects of such *mestizaje* were also reflected throughout all aspects of life in Spanish Haiti, from language to the subtle syncretism that pervaded religious beliefs. Spain's early lack of interest in its colony and its subsequent progressive abandonment only served to encourage racial mixing between groups of disproportionate size. To maintain support and power on the island, a malleable ethnic identity was shaped and reshaped as mestizos and mulattos were proclaimed "Hispanic." The reverberations of this colonial practice would be felt across the centuries as Dominicans clung to the belief that they were predominantly a nation of European blood.

The Crown's disinterest in the colony also resulted in a severe lack of internal infrastructure to join its various population centers. Gone was the unity that had marked Taíno society and numerous and conflicting regional identities and allegiances developed that would haunt the country and impede its centralization for years to come. A further result of colonial abandonment was an economy that lacked diversification and relied on contraband trade.

The *devastaciones* of the seventeenth century and the loss of the western lands profoundly affected the course of history in the Dominican Republic. While fears of foreign invasion were ever present, even more significant was the strict division established between the Dominicans and their neighbor to the west. The first Haitian domination only served to reinforce the Dominicans' notion that they were a Hispanic people that contrasted markedly with the Haitians in terms of race, language and religion. Dominican distrust and dislike of its island neighbor began as "the product of the atrocities committed by Toussaint Louverture and Dessalines in 1801 and 1806" [*el producto ... de las atrocidades cometidos por Toussaint Louverture y Dessalines en 1801 y 1806*] (Balaguer [1983] 1994: 24). Furthermore, the Haitian invasions and encroachments set a brutal precedent of violence between the two nations and a fierce anti-Haitian sentiment was born among the inhabitants of the eastern side of the island. The practice of "Hispanisizing" the border first set into motion at this time would later be reinstated in a much more fanatical plan to "Dominicanize" the border during the era of Trujillo.

Despite the opposing viewpoints at the time of independence, Spanish Haiti clung to its imagined Hispanic identity by aligning itself in a Pan-American confederation, *Gran Colombia*. The new nation's place in this alliance as well as its independence was to be extremely short-lived.

2

Dominican Identity and the Haitian Other

"[Dominicans] had come to believe that only the Haitians were black."
— Moya Pons 1988: 245

Dominican identity has long been partly constructed by defining Haiti as the "Other." According to Tzvetan Todorov, "[i]dentifying the Other and asserting one's position relative to it involve three processes: a value judgement, an assessment of distance and ultimately identification or rejection" (Wucker 1999b: 242). In this case, Dominicans contrast their own perceived ethnicity and culture with that of the Haitians in terms of race, religion and language. Dominicans imagine themselves primarily as Hispanic—white, Spanish speaking, and Catholic, while they define Haitian identity as black, Krèyol speaking, and practicing voodoo.

As Sander Gilman notes, such stereotypes "'perpetuate a needed sense of difference between 'Self' and the 'object,' which becomes the 'Other.' Because there is no real line between the Self and the Other, an imaginary line must be drawn; and so that the illusion of an absolute difference between self and Other is never troubled, this line is as dynamic in its ability to alter itself as is the self" (cited in Aparicio 1998: 155). Long before two nations ever existed on Hispaniola, a first encounter with the Other took place when Europeans and Native Americans met on the island's soil. As Michele Wucker points out, this encounter was not only geographical

27

but psychological as well (1999b: 243). The Europeans considered the natives primitive while the Americans found the practices and appearance of the white man strange.

Since "the national 'self' is defined at any point in time by the Other" (Duara 1996: 163), each element of the stereotypical view of Haitian identity that Dominicans hold is judged to be inferior and backward compared to each corresponding component of Dominican identity. Thus, an enormous rift is created between two nations that share the same island and that are separated only by an arbitrary line known as the border. In spite of their insistence on the differences that divide them, Dominicans and Haitians share much of the same history of "brutal leaders, poverty, rejection by the outside world, and long episodes of violence (directed most often at those who have the least power to defend themselves)" (Wucker 1999b: 243).

Historical Origins of the Haitian Other

The identification of the Haitian as "Other" finds its roots in the early nineteenth century when Haiti first invaded its neighbor to the east. The violence of that time firmly established a sense of "us" versus "them" in the Dominican mentality. A second invasion later in that century only served to exacerbate and concretize that notion.

In 1821, the new nation of Spanish Haiti was born, but its independence lasted a mere two months. Boyer and his plan of island unity had continued to gain support among many that considered themselves mulatto or black in Spanish Haiti, and in February 1822 the Haitians were able to march unopposed into Santo Domingo where Boyer became president.

Once the capital was taken, Boyer immediately began to implement policies that alienated many Spanish-Haitians. His first move was to abolish slavery throughout the island. One of Boyer's most controversial policies was the Rural Code, a set of laws whose goal was to improve agricultural production, and thus, the economy. It became clearly evident that the unifying of the western and eastern parts of the island had been for both political and economic reasons. Not only did the Spanish side of the island serve as a buffer against attacks from the East, it was also a second source of income to finance Haiti's independence when that country acceded to reimburse France for lands lost as a result of the revoultion (Wucker 199b: 38–9).

In addition to these tactics, which were ill accepted on the eastern side of the island, limits were imposed on how much time could be spent on religious *fiestas*. Boyer also passed a law prohibiting cockfighting, the national sport of the Spanish Haitians, except on holidays; the new ruler believed that too much time was being wasted on leisure activities and too little being devoted to work (Balaguer 1994: 15).

Many of Boyer's policies went directly against the culture of the Spanish-Haitians and alienated Boyer from their support. Furthermore, a population that considered itself essentially European could not tolerate being ruled by a leader they saw as black. Rather than unify the island, Boyer's presence and his actions only served to emphasize the differences between the two nations that shared the island.

Several groups that secretly conspired against the Haitians began to form among the Spanish inhabitants of the island. One of these again sought the protection of Spain, while another favored British protection. A third group believed that the Haitians could be overturned with the help of the French, who would then be granted special privileges in Santo Domingo. The fourth group, *La Trinitaria*, was led by Juan Pablo Duarte, a young businessman whose father's business had been destroyed under Haitian rule (Moya Pons 1995: 138). Proponents of this faction supported independence without any strings attached.

Following a failed *Trinitario* attempt at rebellion in 1843, Duarte fled to Saint Thomas where he continued to build support for a revolution. In January 1844, tensions on the island escalated again. Those in support of French intervention acted first, declaring themselves independent from Haiti and asking for French assistance. On January 16, the *Trinitarios* produced a manifesto that cited specific grievances suffered during the Haitian domination and called for rebellion. These two documents are telling, for they reiterated the Dominicans' beliefs that they were markedly distinct culturally, religiously, linguistically and racially from their neighbors to the west (Moya Pons 1995: 151).

By this time, all of the rebellious propaganda had made its impression on the inhabitants of the east, and the *Trinitarios* successfully took the capital under the leadership of Francisco del Rosario Sánchez. On February 27, 1844, the rebels declared Santo Domingo's freedom from Haiti at the capital city's *Puerta del Conde* (The Count's Gate), the very site where that freedom had been relinquished 22 years before (Wucker 1999b: 40).

The Haitian rule would be recorded in the Dominican collective memory as a time of repression and brutality. Crassweller points to the history of violence between the two nations as surpassing issues of race as the source of continued conflict:

> Collective national memories are tenacious, and never more so than in countries where they are preserved largely by tradition and by folk tales

absorbed in the days of infancy. In the Dominican Republic, the
national memories of all things Haitian were grounded in the twenty-
two years of the Haitian occupation, from 1822 to 1844, and in the
decades of invasions and raids which followed [1966: 149].

The Haitian invasion was the "historical point of departure for an
understanding of contemporary ethnicity in the Dominican Republic"
(Duany 1994a: 66), for it fixed in the Dominicans' mind-set the view of
the Haitian as an evil opponent, a wicked and violent Other.

In his 1983 book *La isla al revés*, then–Dominican president Joaquín
Balaguer's comments underline the perceived antiquity and essential
nature of Dominican anti–Haitianism when he goes so far as to maintain
that "among the Dominicans there has always existed ... an instinctive
sense of antipathy towards Haiti" [*entre los dominicanos ha existido siempre ... un sentimiento instintivo de antipatía hacia Haití*] (1994: 24). In
truth, Dominican hatred of Haitians began as a result of the first Haitian
invasion at the turn of the nineteenth century and the brutalities suffered
at the hands of the Haitian army. The collective Dominican memory
depicts the occupation "as a brutal nightmare" (Manuel 1995: 98). Nevertheless, as Hartlyn notes, "the reality [of Haitian occupation] is more complex" for it established the idea of the Haitian Other by "[reinforcing]
Dominicans' perceptions of themselves as different from Haitians in 'language, race, religion and domestic customs'" (1998: 27).

Notions of Geographical Purity

In their study of Ecuadorian identity and nationalism, Sarah Radcliffe and Sallie Westwood link the concept of "Other" to what they term
"geographies of identity" which "can be defined as the sense of belonging
and subjectivities which are constituted in (and which in turn can constitute) different spaces and social sites" (1996: 27). By focusing on "imagined" (to use Anderson's term) geographies, questions of limits and purity
within those boundaries are raised.

In the case of the Dominican Republic, a nation that was destined by
history to share an island with another, more populous country, it is not
surprising that its geographical border with Haiti takes on a passionate
role in the collective imagination of identity. The border's importance
becomes even more symbolic given the two instances in which Haiti successfully invaded and occupied its neighbor for an extended period of
time. It is crucial to remember, as Anderson points out, that a "nation is
imagined as *limited* because even the largest of them ... has finite, if elastic

boundaries, beyond which lie other nations" (1991: 7). The relationship between the Dominican Republic and Haiti aptly exemplifies the simultaneous fixedness and flexibility of national boundaries, for as politicians struggled to officially establish a frontier, the people of both countries easily flowed back and forth across that imaginary line. Through trading and other interaction, these individuals absorbed elements of the culture and language of each nation.

In addition to the possibility of the loss of physical land through encroachment across a political border, Dominicans have long concerned themselves with the "intrusion" of all things Haitian: language, religion, culture and race. The self-proclaimed Dominican identity of a white, Hispanic, Spanish-speaking Catholic is contrasted with the way in which they define their neighbors: *negros*, speakers of Kreyol, and practitioners of voodoo. In this light, a definitive frontier is key to separating two peoples that Dominicans consider completely different, for "[t]he boundaries between nations reinforce territorial segmentation at the same time as they reinforce notions of purity and sameness within the territory, and difference and impurity outside the territory" (Radcliffe and Westwood 1996: 23). Accordingly, people and place become inextricably intertwined and locations serve as "'symbolic anchors' of identity'" (*ibid.*, 22) as national identities are commonly linked to "a sense of belonging to a specific territory" (*ibid.*, 16). This connection between nationality and locality results in "a hardening of boundaries" (Duara 1996: 169). Furthermore,

> [n]ot only do communities with hard boundaries privilege their differences, they tend to develop an intolerance and suspicion toward the adoption of the Other's practices and strive to distinguish, in some way or the other, practices that they share. Thus, communities with hard boundaries will the differences between them [*ibid.*].

One such "notion of purity" within strictly delineated boundaries is illustrated by the ties between " 'race' and place" (Radcliffe and Westwood 1996: 33). As has already been mentioned, Dominicans see their racial and cultural background as primarily Hispanic (read "European"), despite the fact that today "blacks and mulattoes make up nearly 90% of the Dominican Republic's close to eight million inhabitants" (Torres-Saillant and Hernández 1998: 143). Dominicans have long been able to take the elements comprising their ethnic identity and reconfigure them to fit their own collective vision of *dominicanidad*. In addition to the colonial practices adopted in attempts to increase Santo Domingo's population, yet another legacy left by the colonial rulers was a strong and enduring state

Statues representing each of the three races present in Dominican ethnicity grace the grounds in front of the Museum of the Dominican Man: Lembra, an escaped slave leader; Fray Bartolomé de Las Casas, the Spanish priest responsible for the *leyenda negra*; and Enriquillo, the Taíno cacique. Despite the supposedly equal representation of the three groups, the Hispanic element is still emphasized above the others, for the statue of Las Casas is set in the center and several feet in front of the other figures.

negrophobia that pervades Dominican society: "[a]ntiblack feeling has been promoted in the media, school textbooks, and speeches of some prominent political leaders" (*ibid.*).

Race and Identity

Racial mixture is acknowledged in the Dominican Republic, although "no other country in the hemisphere exhibits greater indeterminancy regarding the population's sense of racial identity" (Torres-Saillant 1998: para. 1). In other words, the importance of each of the three main ethnic heritages has been reconfigured. The European heritage is held to be strongest, while secondary influences are believed to have come from the early, extinct Taíno people. The latter were the perfect solution to explaining Dominican *mestizaje* without acknowledging Dominican blackness, for the Taíno "represented a category typified by nonwhiteness as well as nonblackness" (*ibid.*, para. 30).

The Museum of the Dominican Man in Santo Domingo offers keen

According to Dominicans, these traditional dolls are faceless because the Dominican is a mix of three cultures and has no single face. The ceramic dolls' skin is always a bronze color reminiscent of the pre–Columbian indigenous people. (Photograph: Mary Katherine Scott)

insights into the official Dominican mentality concerning race. Statues representing one man of each of the three races grace the grounds in front of the entrance to the museum: Lembra, an escaped slave leader; Fray Bartolomé de Las Casas, the Spanish priest responsible for the *leyenda negra*; and Enriquillo, the Taíno cacique. Despite the supposedly equal representation of the three groups, the Hispanic element is still emphasized above the others, for the statue of Las Casas is set in the center and several feet in front of the other figures. The placement is telling, considering the priest's influence on the depiction of the Taíno people as "noble savages" and his support of the importation of African slaves.

A tour of the museum is also revealing, for a majority of it is devoted to the pre–Colombian peoples that inhabited the island. Great pains were taken to include exhibits that depict every facet of indigenous life back to the first inhabitants of the islands. In contrast, African influence in the Dominican Republic is relegated to fewer displays, such as musical instruments, a drawing of the ships used to transport slaves to the island, and a mention of African influence in religion.

Another simultaneous attempt to both include and exclude certain

Angled view of a traditional Dominican doll. (Photograph: Mary Katherine Scott)

Displayed in the Museum of the Dominican Man and lining the shelves of tourist shops, these typical faceless dolls are a popular form of displaying and exporting a desired identity. (Photograph: Julie Sellers)

elements of Dominican ethnicity is found in a display of what are termed "typical" Dominican dolls. These ceramic dolls, which are an extremely popular item in tourist shops, are usually made with long flowing dresses, hats, and flowers or baskets. The most intriguing aspect of the dolls is that they are faceless. Dominicans are quick to explain that the dolls have no face because the Dominican as such has no single face—he or she is a mix of three cultures. Interestingly, the dolls' skin is always a bronze color reminiscent of the Taíno and never black. Though called "traditional," these dolls have only been in production since the 1980s. They are a popular form of exporting a desired identity through tourist consumption. Lining the shelves of tourist shops and displayed in the Museum of the Dominican Man to remind Dominicans of their official ethnicity, they give a subtle and unintentional glimpse of a people who desire to embrace a reality that does not exist.

Racial classification in the Dominican Republic is intricately stratified. For example, a study conducted by Dominican sociologist Daysi Josefina Guzmán in the 1970s found that Dominicans in the Cibao region could identify nine colors of hair and 15 categories of texture. Additionally, she discovered "ten facial structures, six physical types and five general racial types" (Wucker 1999b: 33). Even more interesting than this highly nuanced system of classification is the fact that those categories were not merely physically determined, for "[e]ach category could practically be used as a guide to where any Dominican stood on the social scale" (ibid.).

African elements are generally downplayed, silenced or renamed. In the nineteenth century, it became common for blacks to refer to themselves as blancos de la tierra—whites of the earth. Currently, individuals of mixed race refer to themselves as indios rather than using the term mulato. In the paradigm established in Guzman's study, hair texture defined as malo (bad) referred to "kinky Negroid hair" (ibid.).

Dominicans also tend to selectively ignore the fact that African influence had reached Spain some 700 years before Columbus arrived on Hispanolia, in the form of the Moorish occupation (711–1492). All African influence is relegated to a tertiary, almost non-existent place in the Dominican national ethnicity. As Moya-Pons so aptly states, "[o]ne of the great paradoxes of the Dominican national formation is that as the Hispanic population blackens, the Dominican mentality whitens" ([u]na de las grandes paradojas de la formación nacional dominicana es que mientras la población hispánica se ennegrece, la mentalidad dominicana se enblanquece) (1988: 238).

Joaquín Balaguer would go so far as to assert that "Santo Domingo is, by its instinct of self-preservation, the most Spanish and traditionalist people of America" [Santo Domingo es, por instinto de conservación, el pueblo más español y tradicionalista de América] (1994: 63). Dominicans insist that the Haitians' origin is predominantly African with few notable influences from other groups. In the collective Dominican imagination, what separates them from the western one-third of the island is not merely a border but blood, language, religion and culture: "Blackness ... continues to be relegated to the realm of the foreign in the land that originated blackness in the Americas" (Torres-Saillant 1998: para. 32).

Outsiders' perceptions of Dominican identity further served to reaffirm the aggregate sum of their imaginings. Mid–nineteenth-century documents illustrate that the United States considered the Dominicans to be of predominantly European descent. For example, when Secretary of State John C. Calhoun encouraged the acknowledgement of Dominican independence in 1844, his rationale was that the move would help halt the infiltration of black influence in Latin America (ibid., para. 2). Later, in one of several U.S. attempts to annex Samaná Bay and/or the country, a commission investigating the ramifications of such a move again emphasized a perceived white Dominican identity. Nevertheless, it must be admitted that a desire to convince U.S. politicians to back the annexation may well have altered the committees' perceptions. These views contrast sharply with the way in which the Spanish saw the Dominicans when the country was again annexed to Spain in 1865.

Cartographic representations of the Dominican Republic reiterate its physical limits and serve to remind the population that *dominicanidad* ends at the frontier. In the National Theater, lights arranged in the shape of the country illuminate the fixed boundaries of the Republic; the representation concludes at the western border, as if the western third of the island did not even exist. This type of depiction exemplifies Anderson's view of "the map-as-logo" in which each nation is represented "like a detachable piece of a jigsaw puzzle" (1991: 175), sovereign, whole and pure within its boundaries.

"The Haitian Problem"

Official histories further propagate the widely held belief that the border is an impenetrable boundary between two opposing elements. Balaguer maintained that "[t]he nearness of Haiti has been ... and continues to be the Dominican Republic's principal problem" (*[l]a vecindad de Haití ha sido ... y sigue siendo el principal problema de la República Dominicana*) (1994:99). Despite repeated claims that Haitian encroachment on and migration to Dominican soil has denationalized Santo Domingo, Balaguer upheld the commonly held belief that racial prejudice does not and has never existed in the country (*ibid.*, 163).

In addition to conflicts over the real or imagined encroachment of land, the strong presence of Haitian immigrant laborers in the Dominican Republic has further widened the chasm between the two nations. In the early twentieth century, a time when world sugar prices soared, Dominican sugar producers raced to increase production. However, there was a critical shortage of laborers for this type of work. The migrant laborers that had come in previous times from other islands and former colonies were not numerous enough to meet the new demand. At this time, sugar producers turned their attention to Haiti to find labor—cheap labor. For this reason, the 1920s and 1930s saw a rapid rise in Haitian immigration to the Dominican Republic. Unlike other black immigrant groups such as the *cocolos*—blacks that came from the former Caribbean colonies of France, Holland and Great Britain—the Haitians were never accepted in the Dominican Republic. Although they labor at jobs Dominicans will not accept, the country's economic problems are commonly said to stem from an excess of Haitian immigrant workers. As Michele Wucker points out, the situation is much like the tensions that exist between the Southwestern United States and Mexico where tensions arise based on the fears of illegal immigrants taking nationals' jobs when the jobs immigrants tend to fill are most commonly the ones that nationals would refuse (1999b: ix).

Within the overall "Haitian problem," questions of religion have historically been central as Dominicans point to their neighbors as "demonized" practitioners of voodoo (Manuel 1995: 98). In fact, religion has commonly been upheld as the primary motivator for Dominican antipathy towards Haiti: "[t]he only prejudice that has existed in Santo Domingo is of a religious nature" [*El único prejuicio que ha existido en Santo Domingo es de carácter religioso*] (Balaguer 1994: 96). In truth, voodoo is not foreign to Dominicans, although the form of the religion practiced in the western two-thirds of the island is different from Haitian voodoo. When I visited the Museum of the Dominican Man, my tour guide pointed to a few articles used in the practice of what he termed "white magic," but was quick to inform me that unlike Haitians, Dominicans do not perform black magic.

While some Dominicans practice magic and voodoo, most of those who do so still feel that they are officially Catholic (Torres-Saillant 1998: para. 13). In spite of the presence of voodoo in Dominican society, "the state-funded guardians of the official culture ... have vigorously rejected the trace of any 'pagan' forms of worship in Dominican society.... [T]hey have ascribed that predilection to unwelcome foreign influence" (*ibid.*, para. 14).

Issues of health and work ethic have often entered into the onslaught of accusations hurled at the Haitians as well. In addition to being blamed for weakening and corrupting the Dominican "soul," Haitians are also accused of setting a bad example with what is considered an inherent laziness (Balaguer 1994: 52). Furthermore, Haitian immigrants are held responsible for the upsurge of such diseases as syphilis and malaria in the Dominican Republic (*ibid.*, 40).

The creation of the Haitian Other, a process whose roots can be traced to the hatred resulting from years of foreign domination and subsequent invasions, has expanded to include any number of ills (if perhaps not all) that the Dominican Republic suffers. As will be seen, this "official vilification of Haitians" (Torres-Saillant 1998: para. 31) continued across the decades, serving as a type of identity cement for Dominicans by bonding them together against a perceived common foe.

It is also significant that Dominican Independence Day does not mark the nation's liberation from Spain in the 1860s; rather, Dominicans celebrate their independence from Haiti each February 27, the day the *Trinitarios* took back the capital in 1844. Likewise, the three statesmen responsible for that victory over Haiti—Duarte, Sánchez and Mella—hold a revered place in Dominican history. They are buried in the *Altar de la Patria* (the Altar of the Homeland), and their names are spoken as if they were contemporary friends. This serves to reinforce the importance that Dominicans place on maintaining a separation between themselves and neighboring Haiti.

Dominican attitudes of the 1840s clearly exemplify Anderson's claims that Latin American struggles for independence were partly the result of fears of black- or Indian-led revolts within the colonies (1991: 48). Though Dominicans might fear a Spanish invasion, they were terrified of the possibility of a slave uprising. With these common Pan-American attitudes in mind, it is not surprising that Dominicans emphasize and celebrate their independence from their western neighbor.

In contrast to earlier times, the political border between the two nations of Hispaniola has been officially set. Nevertheless, the boundary of greater concern for Dominicans is not geographical but rather religious, cultural, and racial. Dominican attitudes concerning its shared border with Haiti reiterate their imagined geography—that is, the fixed area within which is contained the pure essence of *dominicanidad*:

> What Santo Domingo wants is to conserve its culture and customs as a Spanish people and to impede the disintegration of its soul and the loss of its distinguishing characteristics. The only thing that is needed to advance this effort of national preservation is for both people to remain within the territorial limits fixed by the Treaty of 1936 and for Haiti to respect, accordingly, the boundaries and to renounce forever the old goals of Toussaint L'Ouverture [*Lo que Santo Domingo desea es conservar su cultura y sus costumbres como pueblo español e impedir la desintegración y la pérdida de sus rasgos distintivos. Lo único que se necesita para llevar adelante esa empresa de preservación nacional es que ambos pueblos se mantengan dentro de los límites territoriales fijados por el Tratado de 1936 y que Haití respete, en consecuencia, las fronteras y renuncie para siempre al viejo propósito de Toussaint Louverture*] [Balaguer 1994: 65].

The Border

Despite the imagined antiquity and apparent naturalness of anti–Haitian sentiment in the Dominican Republic, as well as the ardent claim that Dominicans merely desire to be left in peace within their geopolitical boundaries, the border is by no means a wall between the two nations. People, merchandise, language, religion and other cultural elements pass constantly and unobstructed between the two countries, as they have for centuries.

Somewhere in the shadows of history, various musical forms and traditions crossed such invisible boundaries unnoticed and fused in the Caribbean to form the dance that would become known by a variety of names. In Haiti, it was known as the *mereng* (also spelled *méringue*), and its African roots were emphasized and praised. In the Dominican Republic, the dance was commonly called the *merengue*, and it was originally despised because of the very African elements that were celebrated on the west side of the island. Later, as merengue's popularity grew, it was staunchly maintained that the music's origins were primarily Spanish with minor Taíno and African influences. As we shall see, merengue as an element of Dominican identity is every bit as fluid as Dominican ethnicity and has been reconfigured in the national imagination to support and strengthen a desired identity.

3

Fragmentation, Personalism, Violence and Economic Ruin: The Period of the Great *Caudillos*

> *"Santana and Báez ... held power in precarious coalition or active hostility for the better part of three decades.... [N]either of them during their long public careers ever performed a constructive act that could be regarded as disinterested."*
> —Crassweller 1966: 20

The 70 years following independence from Haiti were a period of intense political instability in the Dominican Republic. In truth, Dominicans had never ruled themselves for any significant amount of time, and national politics as such did not exist. The underdeveloped infrastructure resulting from Spanish abandonment kept the Dominican people regionally divided and without a true sense of national unity. Populations were fiercely loyal to regional strongmen known as *caudillos*. Indeed, the Dominicans' 1865 victory over the Spaniards that ended the nation's brief period of re-annexation to Spain was won not by a unified national army but rather by guerrilla units commanded by the *caudillos*. The ties of family, *compadrazgo*, and economics that bound individuals to those regional leaders would not be easily severed, and they consequently served as a formidable obstacle to the formation of a Dominican national identity.

Dominican sovereignty was also threatened during those seven

Juan Pablo Duarte, Matías Ramón Mella and Francisco del Rosario Sánchez, the *Padres de la Patria* (Fathers of the Homeland) are buried at the *Altar de la Patria* (Altar of the Homeland) in Santo Domingo. These Dominican heroes are honored for their role in the nation's independence from Haiti in 1844. (Photograph: Julie Sellers)

decades by the *caudillos'* schemes to attain foreign aid through the sale, lease or annexation of all or part of the country. Originally, the idea for such an arrangement resulted from the fear of foreign invasion. Later, the plan was undertaken in an attempt to acquire enough funds to pay off an increasingly insurmountable national debt that further threatened the country's sovereignty.

Together, the fierce regionalism and the campaign to lease the country further divided Dominicans and distanced them from a collective sense of national identity. These fissures would not be closed until they were forcibly joined decades later by a powerful dictator who would employ numerous tactics to create and impose national unity, among them, emphasis of the merengue.

Santana and Báez

The era of the great *caudillos* was in part a response to the continued threat of Haitian invasion. The Dominicans' neighbors to the west were not to be easily ousted by the February 27, 1844, coup. Haitian president Hérard saw the source of the money needed to pay off his country's debt to France slipping through his fingers, and he determined to put the Dominicans down with force, just as he had done in the past.

In light of the continued Haitian threat, the Dominicans appointed Pedro Santana military chief and he gathered troops to defend Dominican independence. Following several violent battles, further invasions into the east were halted by Haiti's own internal political struggles.

Soon thereafter, Juan Pablo Duarte returned from exile, eager to join in the defense. Tensions quickly arose between Santana and Duarte, as the former insisted that the Dominican army be defensive in nature while the latter pushed for it to assume an offensive stance against Haiti.

These differences of opinion were merely a reflection of the overall disagreements between the conservatives and the more liberal *Trinitarios*. Santana and the conservatives that headed the *Junta Central Gubernativa* (Central Governing Committee) were staunchly in favor of seeking foreign aid and protection from France. In contrast, Duarte and the *Trinitarios* opposed any sort of outside intervention, especially if it involved the rumors of leasing or relinquishing the Samaná peninsula.

This political crisis reached its breaking point in June 1844, when the *Trinitarios* acted swiftly to overthrow the *Junta* and replace its president, Tomás de Bobadilla, with one of their own, Francisco Sánchez. The situation in the foundling nation was further worsened by divisions within the *Trinitarios* themselves. In July 1844, the people of the Cibao region proclaimed Duarte president of the republic. Duarte accepted, even though Sánchez was still officially president of the *Junta*.

Although these internal divisions weakened the party, the greatest threat to the *Trinitarios* was Santana. In June, the military chief had requested to be relieved of his post for reasons of health. Nevertheless, when *Trinitario* Esteban Roca arrived to replace the general, Roca found that the troops would not follow orders from anyone but Santana. The army was nothing more than a conglomeration of intertwining personal ties between Santana and his family, friends and the poor men who worked his lands (Moya Pons 1995: 160). Furthermore, Santana loathed the idea of relinquishing his post to the liberals, so he agreed to continue in his position. Upon resuming his command, Santana vehemently accused the *Trinitarios* of not supporting the troops sufficiently to assure their success, thus widening the rift between the two sides.

On July 12, 1844, Santana marched into Santo Domingo with 2,000 troops loyal solely to him and overthrew the liberal government in a military coup. Santana intended to proclaim himself dictator of the Dominican Republic, but instead opted to follow the advice of the French consul and leave the *Junta* intact, minus all *Trinitario* members. In August, the new government formally declared several high-ranking *Trinitario* officials traitors and they were exiled for life. On September 10, 1844, Duarte himself fled the island, marking the end of the *Trinitarios*.

Although the new government intended to write a democratic constitution, the end product granted the president special military powers and control. Rather than the hoped-for democracy, the Dominican Republic had, in truth, fallen under the control of a political and military dictator. Santana was elected president for two four-year terms, the first of which began on November 13, 1844.

Following another attempted invasion by the Haitians in 1845, the Dominican conservatives who were in control became more certain than ever that it was necessary that the country have foreign aid and protection. Dominican diplomats began negotiations with Spain, England and France, though none of them officially recognized Dominican independence at the time.

Within the country, opposition to Santana was mounting, due partially to the severity of the economic situation and the dictator's repressive policies and actions. All of this took its toll on Santana; and ill and depressed, he resigned on August 4, 1848.

General Manuel Jimenes was chosen as president upon Santana's resignation. Unfortunately, Jimenes proved himself to be an inept ruler from the very beginning of his term. When France formally acknowledged Dominican independence, infuriating neighboring Haiti and sparking yet another invasion, Dominican congressmen lacked all faith in Jimenes's abilities to preserve the Republic. With the Dominican army's inability to halt the Haitian advance, Congress appealed to Santana to return to head the forces. Santana agreed, and with the crushing defeat of the Haitians, his political influence began to return.

Immediately following the war, Congress nullified Jimenes's presidency and returned its support to Santana. In May 1849, Santana's forces besieged the capital; and within less than two weeks, Jimenes surrendered and fled the country.

Santana opted not to assume power himself but instead called for presidential elections in July. Santiago Espaillat, Santana's hand-picked candidate, was elected but subsequently declined out of concern that he would be nothing more than Santana's puppet. Santana then backed Congressman Buenaventura Báez, who won the elections of the following month.

As president, Báez immediately began an offensive campaign against Haiti while simultaneously petitioning the United States, Britain and France to serve as mediators in the Dominican-Haitian conflict. The subsequent truce and the pressure exerted by the foreign mediators brought about a certain extent of peace in Dominican-Haitian relations during Báez's term.

Power passed into Santana's hands once again in the next elections. Ironically, Santana, the very man who had backed Báez as a candidate, undertook a slanderous campaign to force the former president out of the Republic because he feared Báez's popularity. Báez outmaneuvered his rival, leaving the country for Curaçao before he could be expelled. This marked the beginning of a violent 30-year struggle between two *caudillos* who were both power- and money-hungry.

Opposition to Santana's absolutism arose again not long after he had returned to office. At last, he was forced to accede to the demands for a new, more liberal constitution. But as the Constitution of 1854 was being written, many of its democratic elements were eliminated or modified in such a way as to guarantee Santana's absolute power. Democracy had been deterred once again.

Dominican exiles on Saint Thomas began to bond together in common cause against Santana as well. One of the greatest concerns of these men was a rumored agreement pending between Santana and the United States dealing with the sale or lease of Samaná Bay and Peninsula. Because Santana would have the protection of the U.S. military following the signing of such a deal, the exiles formulated a plan to invade the Republic and overthrow the dictator before a transaction was concluded.

Facing extreme opposition and pressure on several fronts, Santana opted to resign. Vice-President Manuel de Regla Mota then assumed the presidency of a nation that was in dire financial and political straits. Under these conditions, it was impossible to pay the army and troops were dismissed. The president was completely defenseless when the exiles invaded the Dominican Republic. Regla Mota unhesitatingly named Báez vice-president and then immediately resigned himself.

When Báez ascended to the presidency on October 6, 1856, he began his own vengeful campaign against Santana. Following several months of intense character assassination, Santana was sent into exile. Once the threat of Santana had been eliminated, the new president turned his sights towards the tobacco merchants of the Cibao region.

If Haitian agricultural policies had made an effect anywhere in the Dominican Republic, it was in the north central Cibao region, where tobacco production increased dramatically. Agriculture in this region was, as a whole, the most diversified in the nation. Infrastructure of any sort

in the Dominican Republic was almost nonexistent. With no roads to connect Santiago (the largest city of the Cibao and the second largest of the
nation) with the capital, the two areas were so isolated from each other
that they were two entirely different worlds. This bipolarity was commonly
reflected in the nation's political life, as residents of the Cibao often felt
that policies determined in Santo Domingo did not take them into consideration.

As president, both Santana and Báez had been faced with a disas-
trous economy that could not recover. The practice of printing new money
to pay off government spending became so common that by 1856 a total
of 23 issues of currency had been made (Moya Pons 1995: 191).

In the spring of 1857, not long after Báez assumed the presidency again,
the Dominican peso's exchange rate had improved slightly. Nevertheless,
the president ordered that another 18 million pesos be printed. Instead of
replacing deteriorated bills, as Báez had said he would do, the President gave
them to his political favorites. These men purchased Cibao tobacco and gold
before it was known that the nation had been flooded with new bills that
reduced the value of the peso (Moya Pons 1995: 191). Angered, the Cibao
tobacco farmers and merchants revolted. In July 1857, they established a
new provisional government with General José Desiderio Valverde as president. Although the rebels had planned to march on Santo Domingo, they
were wary of Báez's power and resources and they opted instead to allow
Santana back into the country to lead the army once more.

Not long after Santana returned to his previous post, the rebels realized they had made a grave error. The army continued to be Santana's personal force and remained loyal to him rather than to the provisional
government's military leader, General Juan Luis Franco Bidó. Soon, Santana had replaced Franco Bidó and held the power of the military securely
in his hands once again.

Even as the war raged on, the provisional government in Santiago
worked to create a democratic constitution. The Moca Constitution,
named after the Cibao city where it was written in 1858, strove to limit
the authoritarian abuses by which the country had been governed under
the Constitution of 1854. The authoritarian Santana fiercely opposed the
new constitution and, as soon as his troops defeated Báez, replaced it with
the Constitution of 1854.

Re-annexation and Restoration

Following the Revolution of 1857, the Dominican economy was in a
critical state. So devastating were the war's effects that Santana feared

another Haitian invasion. In light of the economic devastation and constant political upheaval, Santana again sought foreign assistance, focusing his efforts on Spain. At first, the president sought only the guarantee of Spanish protection, but as the negotiations continued, he began to push for a complete annexation of the country to Spain. Because of the strategic benefits of the annexation, the Spaniards were more than willing to comply.

Santana had kept his dealings with Spain from the Dominican people; and for several months before the annexation was officially proclaimed on March 18, 1861, he and his government took measures to ensure that the change would be made before Dominicans realized what was taking place. Various manifestos were forged so that the annexation would appear to be widely supported.

The annexation went unopposed on the international level as well. As Clayton and Conniff note, the motives for Spain's annexation of the Dominican Republic were "born of basically the same reasons as the French intervention in Mexico: instability in Latin America and the inability of the United States to invoke the Monroe Doctrine with force during the American Civil War" (1999: 228). Santo Domingo thus fell once more under European control by becoming a province of Spain with Santana serving as its "captain general." It was not long, however, before it became evident that Santana was virtually powerless under the new system he himself had helped to create.

The Spanish who came to the island to govern the new province were reaching certain realizations as well. Despite the Dominicans' claims of a Hispanic heritage and identity, the Spaniards found

> that the people they had come to govern were not as Hispanic as they had been led to believe. The majority of the population were mulattos, and their customs varied enormously from Spanish tradition because of the centuries of isolation during the colonial period, and particularly after 22 years of Haitian domination and 17 years of national independence.... [T]he race and color of the Dominicans ... was a constant topic of conversation among everyone because the Spaniards continually offended the Dominicans who were reminded that in Cuba or Puerto Rico they would be slaves [Moya Pons 1995: 206–7].

In addition to enduring the Spaniards' sense of racial superiority, Dominicans also suffered from economic, political and religious grievances. In February 1863, a group of rebels in Santiago rose up against the Spanish government, beginning the War of Restoration. In a strange twist of alliances, the Dominican rebels were aided by the Haitians who were uneasy at the prospect of having Spain, a formidable slave power, as a neighbor.

El monumento a los héroes de la Restauración (The Monument to the Heroes
of the Restoration) in Santiago celebrates Dominican independence from its
brief re-annexation to Spain from 1861 to 1865. (Photograph: Julie Sellers)

Although the Dominicans were united ideologically in the war against
the Spanish, it was impossible for them to form a truly national army due
to a lack of resources. The Dominicans instead resorted to guerrilla warfare, organizing themselves under local and regional leaders who cooper-
ated with the provisional government. Slowly, the Dominicans' tactics took
their toll. In addition to losses in battle, the Spanish soldiers fell to tropical diseases and other illnesses.

The Dominicans issued an Act of Independence on September 14,
1863, and a provisional government was established. Nevertheless, the
fighting continued for two more years until the Spanish capitulated. The
Dominicans at last had begun to realize that their national identity now
lay outside any connection to Spain:

> The War of Restoration consolidated the Dominican national identity
> in the sense that it showed the Dominicans that what they were being

for 300 years ... was an illusion.... The Dominicans took a great weight off their shoulders with the War of Restoration upon realizing what they were *not* and what they *didn't* want to be [*La Guerra de la Restoración consolidó la identidad nacional dominicana en el sentido de que mostró a los dominicanos que aquello que ellos estuvieron siendo durante 300 años ... era una quimera.... Los dominicanos se quitaron un gran peso de encima con la Guerra de la Restoración al saber lo que* no *eran y lo que* no *querían ser*] [Moya Pons 1988: 241].

Following restoration, the people of Santo Domingo saw themselves not as Spaniards but as Dominicans.

The two most serious consequences of the War of Restoration were a ruined economy and a continuing high degree of political fragmentation resulting from the traditional Dominican political system that operated around various regional and local strongmen known as *caudillos* (also called *caciques*). These strongmen "were very tough individuals who had clawed their way to local leadership and held it until someone a bit tougher came along. The central government was almost powerless to control caciques. Dominican politics consisted of several caciques periodically getting together to overthrow the government" (Espaillat 1963: 23).

This system of personalism dominated the country on one hand because the greater part of its inhabitants were illiterate and on the other, because the scattered populations were centered around one individual to whom others were tied through a series of personal links and loyalties such as the *compadrazgo* (godfathers). Additionally, because few roads existed to link the capital with other populations, different ways of thinking and governing developed.

Specifically, the differences between Santo Domingo and the Cibao of the north created a divergence in political outlook. In the southern regions around the capital, wealth was unequally distributed among the owners of great expanses of land and the peons who worked the land. In the Cibao the economy was more diversified and wealth was more equally distributed. This sense of equality pervaded northern political thought, and the Cibao provided fertile ground for liberal democratic ideas (Moya Pons 1995: 220).

Azules and Rojos

A constant struggle between the *Partido Nacional Liberal* (National Liberal Party) of the north, known as the *Azul* party, and the *Baecista* or *Rojo* party of the south marked the first 14 years of Dominican independence (1865–1879) following its brief time as a Spanish province. The *Rojos* and *Azules* were emblematic of two entirely contrasting political and economic views of the nation. The *Rojos*, with Baez at their head, sought power to make themselves rich. This party represented the southern interests of the ranchers and wood industry. In contrast, the *Azules* envisioned using power to improve the nation's economy and education and were proponents of the business men and tobacco growers of the north central region around the Ciabo Valley (Moya Pons 1995: 222).

Such political fragmentation, and the ensuing battles between the two parties, began immediately following the restoration of Dominican independence and lasted until 1879. During these 14 years, there were over 50 revolts and the government changed approximately 21 times (Hartlyn 1998:36).

This period also marked the beginning of a new series of intrigues that would continue through the years, involving the sale or lease of Samaná Bay to the United States. The United States considered the bay, located on the northeastern coast of the Dominican Republic, a strategic base. Negotiations concerning Samaná first began in 1866 with President José María Cabral, whose goal was to obtain military and economic aid from the United States in return for selling or leasing the bay. The discovery of the plan dashed the little popularity that Cabral enjoyed, and the *Rojos* rose up against him. By May 1868, Báez had returned yet again to become president.

Within days of assuming the presidency, the "Great Citizen," as Báez had been christened, was in the thick of new negotiations with the United States concerning Samaná. Báez first offered to sell the bay and peninsula outright to the United States but by the time Ulysses S. Grant had become president, Báez had changed his offer to a request for annexation. Grant was very much in favor of this action and Báez came close to success. The Dominican president forcibly obtained enough votes to make it appear that the populace was in favor of the move. In the United States the proposal met with greater opposition, to the extent that a senatorial investigative committee traveled to the Dominican Republic to determine whether or not annexation was viable and advantageous. Despite the committee's favorable report, the U.S. Senate remained split on the issue and eventually rejected the treaty of annexation.

With the failure of this project, Báez found himself in a dire predicament. The economy continued to suffer and the government desperately needed funds. Báez turned his attention at this point to the American adventurers who had first suggested that Samaná Bay be leased, sold or annexed to the United States. Accordingly, Samaná Bay and Peninsula were leased to a private company, the Samaná Bay Company, in 1873.

Opposition to Báez and the worsening economy eventually presented itself in the form of Ignacio María González, the governor of Puerto Plata, who rose up against the government later that same year. At that time, González formed a third party, the *Movimiento Unionista* (Unionist Movement, later known as the *Verde* party). The *Azules*, eager to rid the country of Báez, backed González and the provisional government set up by the *Verdes*. Nationwide support for the movement was overwhelming, and in the face of such a front, Báez formally resigned before fleeing the country with the illegal funds he had hoarded as president.

As the newly elected president, González acted to make the nation more secure. The president first focused on the agreement with the Samaná Bay Company. A clause in the contract allowed for the deal to be terminated if the company failed to make payments and as that was the case, González annulled the agreement. González also worked to improve relations with Haiti by calling for a treaty to resolve border issues and to establish trade between the two nations. Although this 1874 treaty was negotiated with good intentions, in reality the trade provisions resulted in Haitian encroachments of Dominican territory, an issue that created tensions down through the decades.

As González's term progressed, his policies became more and more permeated by authoritarianism, culminating in the writing of a new constitution that replaced the liberal document by which the country had been governed. The *Azules* were ripe for revolution, but in order to avoid another civil war, the dissatisfied *Azules* and *Rojos* reached an agreement by which González would resign and new presidential elections would be called.

The instability continued as Ulises Francisco Espaillat, Báez, González, and Césaro Guillermo each took power and were subsequently overthrown. The 1879 liberal uprising that brought an end to Guillermo's presidency marked the conclusion of an era of political instability that would never be equaled in the Dominican Republic (Moya Pons 1995: 241).

The country began to stabilize again under the liberals. As president, Gregorio Luperón undertook numerous measures to improve the economy. Also, a constitution was ratified in 1880 that was in essence a newer version of the more democratic Constitution of Moca.

At the conclusion of Luperón's successful presidential term, Father Fernando Arturo de Meriño served one term as president. In September, 1882, power passed to General Ulises Heureaux, a man who would significantly alter the course of Dominican history.

Ulises Heureaux and Economic Ruin

Although a trusted friend of Luperón, Heureaux sought to increase his power by displacing Luperón as head of the *Azules*. This created a serious and irreparable rift in the liberal party, as President Heureaux supported one set of candidates in the election while the party officially backed another. Although Heureaux's candidate, Francisco Gregorio Bellini, won the race, he quickly found he was nothing more than the general's puppet and resigned. Vice-President Alejandro Woss y Gil, on the other hand, knew that he had attained his position thanks to Heureaux and accepted the puppet presidency.

In the elections of 1886, Heureaux fraudulently defeated the *Azul* party's candidate, General Casimiro de Moya. Infuriated by the falsified election results, Moya rose up against Heureaux. Heureaux found himself on the losing end of the uprising but managed to put down the rebellion with bribes.

Heureaux was an "extraordinarily able and tireless despot ... [who] was controlled, brave, recklessly confident, possessed of the shrewd and suspicious nature of the savage, devoid of mercy, and gifted with a true genius for power" (Crassweller 1966: 21). Once in the presidency, Heureaux, known as "Lilís," implemented several measures to strengthen his hold on Dominican politics. Luperón was stripped of his place at the head of the *Azul* party, and the constitution was altered, changing the presidential term from two to four years. Finally, the president would no longer be determined by popular vote but rather by an electoral board.

Heureaux proudly proclaimed that he would bring an end to partisan conflicts by including individuals from all parties in his government. The *Rojos* could not have been happier with the changes the general made to the liberal *Azul* government, and upon their urging, the Dominican Congress proclaimed Lilís the "Pacifier of the Homeland."

Heureaux's rise to and maintenance of power was costly since the dictator depended on bribery and spies to crush all opposition. By the end of the war that brought the general to power, the government had little money at its disposal. To compensate for this deficiency, Heureaux sent General de Marchena to England and Holland to investigate the possibility of loans. In June 1888, de Marchena succeeded in reaching a deal with Westendorp and Company of Amsterdam for a loan of £770,000. In exchange for the loan, he mortgaged approximately one-third of Dominican customs revenues (Moya Pons 1995: 267).

Heureaux's money woes were lessened for the time being and he turned his attention to the upcoming October elections. *Azul* opposition and reaction to the dictatorship had been growing, so to pinpoint his competition, Heureaux feigned disinterest in reelection. With the path clear, Luperón declared his intentions to run; and not long thereafter, Heaureaux also announced his candidacy. Luperón's supporters were then systematically tracked down, persecuted, imprisoned and killed. The violence reached such a degree that Luperón eventually withdrew from the race for the sake of his followers and Heureaux was elected again.

Heureaux began to seek the assistance of foreign aid to help him retain his power. Upon reelection, the Samaná Bay and Peninsula plan was resurrected when Heureaux again offered the United States the opportunity to buy or lease the area. The treaty granted reciprocity to the United States by allowing certain U.S. goods to enter the country tax-free. This news brought about the immediate angry response of Germany, France, Holland and Italy who threatened not to purchase Dominican goods if the treaty were signed. Cibao tobacco growers and merchants clamored for rebellion, fearing the treaty would bring about the ruin of their livelihood by causing the Europeans to stop buying their product. In the face of such great national and international opposition, Heureaux was forced to withdraw his offer.

Heureaux's bribes and spies were dragging the country further and further into debt, and with the loss of the expected income from the Samaná Bay project, he sought another loan from Westendorp and Company in 1890. In financial straits itself, Westendorp and Company sold out its Dominican interests to a group of U.S. entrepreneurs (the San Domingo Improvement Company) not long thereafter. Loans and bonds issued by this company plunged the country so seriously into debt that the Dominican Republic owed a total of some 17 million pesos nationally and internationally by the late 19th century (Moya Pons 1995: 271).

The Improvement Company's power and influence over the Dominican Republic grew as the country's debt worsened. Most importantly, the company gained total control of customs receipts. By 1896, the Dominican Republic had entirely mortgaged itself to the company with dim prospects of regaining control of customs receipts (Moya Pons 1995: 274).

Cibao opposition to Heureaux continued to mount. When he finally obtained another loan, he decided to use the funds to pay off the southern sugar-plantation owners who had lent money to the government; none of the lenders from the Cibao were reimbursed, which only served to heighten existing tensions between the two regions. In another desperate attempt to gain funds, Heureaux agreed in secret to sell Haiti some of the borderlands that had been claimed by both nations for decades. As the sale was being negotiated, however, *Azul* rebels acted to end the oppressive rule of Heureaux. Jacobito de Lara and Ramón Cáceres assassinated the dictator on July 26, 1899, in Moca.

The country that Heureaux left behind him in 1899 was strikingly different from the one whose power he had assumed in 1886. His shady dealings and heedless borrowing, spending and embezzlements had financially devastated and further indebted the Dominican Republic.

The economic structure of both the north and the south was also altered. Sugar had become the predominant export of the southern regions while Cibao agriculturists had begun to produce coffee and cacao in addition to tobacco. In both cases, these products were aimed at United States markets, emphasizing the new direction that Dominican foreign policy had taken.

"Bolos" and "Coludos"

With Heureaux's death, Vice-President Wenceslao Figuereo assumed power, though his reign was short-lived. Another conspiracy arose, headed by Horacio Vásquez who ascended to the presidency upon Figuereo's August 30, 1899, resignation.

As provisional leader of the Dominican Republic, Vásquez was faced with the country's debt of more than $34 million. Various international groups of angry bondholders threatened to use force to recover their money by seizing control of Dominican customs. These drastic measures were avoided when Vásquez was able to arrange matters so that bondholders and the San Domingo Improvement Company would deal directly with each other rather than through the Dominican government.

Unlike former provisional leaders, Vásquez refused to stand as a candidate in the upcoming presidential elections. Instead, he supported Juan Isidro Jimenes and ran as his vice-president. Following the elections, the former *Rojos* began to conspire against both the president and the vice-president by playing them against each other. By 1902, Vásquez was so thoroughly convinced that his life was in danger that he rose up against Jimenes.

Vásquez's revolt marked the beginning of a 15-year power struggle between the two *caudillos*. In essence, it was the Santana-Báez conflict all over again, but with different *caudillos* at the head of the parties. Although many members of the *Rojo* and *Azul* parties had long since passed away, support for the new factions followed the old party lines: *Jimenistas* tended to be former *Rojos*, while *Horacistas* were often the more liberal *Azules*. As if to emphasize the violent nature of these political parties, each bore a nickname that reflected the national sport of cockfighting: *Jimenistas* were known as "*bolos*" (cocks with no tail feathers) while *Horacistas* were referred to as "*coludos*" (cocks with long tail fathers).

Vásquez's power lasted only a few months. Former Heureaux supporters opposed the president's negotiations and agreements with the San Domingo Improvement Company, and at the same time, Jimenes's support grew. On March 23, 1903, the numerous political prisoners who filled the Ozama Fortress in the capital revolted. Other opponents within Santo Domingo rose up simultaneously and overthrew the government. A violent one-month civil war erupted, but Vásquez was unable to regain the capital city; he resigned on April 23, 1903. Woss y Gil, who was elected after the war, lasted a mere three months in office before he, too, was brought down.

The leader of this latest conspiracy, Carlos F. Morales Languasco, had promised to assist Jimenes's return to power, but instead, he retained it for himself. From the beginning of his rule, Morales was in a more stable position because he had won the United States' support by honoring all former agreements made with the San Domingo Improvement Company.

Progress toward paying off the national debt was made under Morales. In June 1904, a board of arbitrators ruled that the Dominican Republic must use customs revenues to pay back the Improvement Company's investments. A financial representative of the United States would be responsible for collecting these funds.

Morales took advantage of every opportunity to try to strengthen his ties with the United States, believing that his neighbor to the north was his ticket to staying in power. The U.S. was very willing to become more deeply involved in the Dominican Republic. The 1904 Roosevelt Corollary to the Monroe Doctrine revealed the U.S.'s commitment to ensuring that Latin American nations would make good on their international debts (Wucker 1999b: 43). Roosevelt was particularly willing to back intervention in the Dominican Republic when European creditors went so far as to send warships in an attempt to collect their funds. In Roosevelt's eyes, the Europeans had overstepped their bounds and were treading in the United States' sphere of influence.

The alliance between Morales and the United States was strengthened by a subsequent 1905 agreement in which the government of the latter took responsibility of Dominican debts. In return, the United States would also control Dominican customs receipts through a General Customs Receivership, dividing the money so that 45 percent was given back to the Dominican government while 55 percent would be used for employees' salaries and to pay the country's debts. When this agreement reached the U.S. Senate, that body adamantly opposed its ratification, believing that it would make the Dominican Republic a U.S. protectorate. Therefore, the project was changed to function temporarily as a *modus vivendi*.

In spite of Morales's affiliation with the United States, his power had almost completely eroded by December 1905. When another group of rebels rose up under Ramón Cáceres, Morales resigned, as had numerous other Dominican rulers in the years since independence from Haiti.

Stability, Upheaval, and U.S. Intervention

Once Cáceres formally assumed the presidency on December 29, he began to battle the enormous debt of some $40 million. Later international negotiations adjusted the amount to $17 million. The United States then backed the country in its effort to receive a $20 million loan from a New York bank; in return for the United States' guarantee of its loan, the Dominican government would grant the U.S. control of Dominican customs until such time as the debt was paid. In addition to granting the United States total direction of Dominican funds and financial questions, this agreement also granted the U.S. the right to political intervention at any time that the country believed that customs receipts were compromised (Moya Pons 1995: 295). European domination of the Dominican Republic had been replaced by North American influence.

Cáceres's administration marked the first stable and peaceful Dominican government in years. Agriculture improved and with it, the country's economy. The sugar industry expanded when Cáceres removed taxes from the production and exportation of sugar and then allowed large foreign sugar companies to buy Dominican lands suitable for sugarcane (Wucker 1999b: 101). North American and Cuban entrepreneurs began to buy up uninhabited lands and to invest large amounts of money into new sugar *haciendas* as well as the construction of steam-operated sugar processing machines (Moya Pons 1988: 217). Funds were invested back into the country to improve roads, the railroad, communications, ports and to build new schools.

A new constitution was also promulgated under Cáceres. In the 1908 document, the presidential term was extended to six years. Most importantly, the constitution took military power away from provincial governments in order to put an end to *caudillo* uprisings.

Old political alliances, nevertheless, eventually eroded the stability, peace and prosperity experienced during the Cáceres administration. On November 19, 1911, the president was killed as he attempted to resist abduction by a group of conspirators.

An intense period of political jockeying followed Cáceres's death. For two months congress debated over who should be president and at length, Senator Eladio Victoria was chosen for the position. Soon thereafter, Vásquez returned to the country to organize a rebellion against the new president. Political persecutions and repression were widespread during the civil war.

United States intervention finally brought this rebellion—the first of three separate rebellions that were halted by U.S. involvement—to an end. The last of these conflicts was settled by the Wilson Plan, the terms of which were as follows:

> [T]he rebels were to lay down their arms and agree on the selection of a provisional president. If not, the United States would choose a president and keep him in power by force. The new president would then organize a government to hold elections that would be supervised by the United States. The government resulting from these elections was to be respected by all parties and would receive the support of the United States, which henceforth would not tolerate new rebellions [Moya Pons 1995: 311–2].

The Dominicans had little choice but to accept these terms; Dr. Ramón Báez, son of the former *caudillo*, was selected as provisional president in accordance with this document. Báez took office on August 27, 1914, and elections were organized and held on October 25, 1914.

Jimenes was chosen as the new president in the free election. Upon his assumption of power, the United States made further demands of Jimenes. He was asked to regularize the position of U.S. comptroller and to accept the formation of a National Guard to replace the armed forces. When Jimenes formally and flatly refused these demands, the U.S. responded by halting economic aid above and beyond the regular customs payments.

Despite having won his position freely and fairly, Jimenes was soon to be toppled by yet another rebellion. In the spring of 1916, Desiderio Arias, secretary of war, rebelled against the president and took the capital. The U.S. offered its support to Jimenes and he accepted arms and ammunition. Soon thereafter, Arias attempted to have Jimenes impeached, an action that violated the Wilson Plan. At this point, the United States government opted to send in the marines with the intention of guarding the safety of foreign residents in Santo Domingo. On May 7, 1916, Jimenes formally resigned as president and on May 16, U.S. marines occupied Santo Domingo. Occupation of the entire country was carried out during the following months and the U.S. declared that the marines would remain until earlier demands were met.

Dr. Francisco Henríquez y Carvajal, who had been sworn in as president on July 31, 1916, also refused to accept U.S. demands, declaring that they jeopardized Dominican sovereignty. The United States responded by halting the flow of customs funds to the Dominican government.

Eventually, Henríquez y Carvajal attempted to compromise by agreeing to accept the comptroller but still refusing the formation of the National Guard.

As the months of U.S. occupation passed and no agreement was reached with the Dominicans, United States officials had to decide whether to abandon the occupation or to continue it by formalizing its conditions. Internationally, officials deemed that in light of the imminent war with Germany, it was in the United States' best interests to remain, for many *Jimenistas*, including Arias, were pro–German. The United States opposed leaving the Dominican Republic under Arias's control because of the island's proximity to the United States. It was also feared that the Germans might establish a base there that would jeopardize travel through the Panama Canal (Moya Pons 1995: 319). Given this set of circumstances, the U.S. marines remained in the Dominican Republic and Captain Harry S. Knapp officially proclaimed the occupation on November 29, 1916.

The Era of the Great Caudillos in Retrospect

The effects of the period of the great *caudillos* would be felt through-out all aspects of Dominican life for decades to follow. Most importantly, the numerous and violent changes of power further fragmented the country politically. Although nationalism had served to join the diverse factors against the Spanish at mid-century, there was no true unifying factor to hold the nation together in the face of a system that placed personal loy-alties to individuals before loyalty to the nation. The absence of a politi-cally stable central government "meant that the country essentially lacked a national military institution that did not depend upon individual lead-ers or loyalties" (Hartlyn 1998:33).

The constant revolts not only divided the country politically but kept its various cities and regions physically separated as well. With almost all available funds being poured into the uprisings, there was nothing left to channel back into the creation of an internal infrastructure. Rather than working to create nationalizing centralism, the *caudillos'* actions only served to further decentralize the country. Regional identities that devel-oped in isolation from and generally in opposition to the capital proved to be stronger than any single national identity.

The era of the great strongmen ruined the Dominican economy. Costs of war and the high price of bribes, in addition to the crops left standing in fields when men went off to fight, devastated the country, and the loans that were eventually taken were negotiated without an infrastructure that would allow the Dominicans to make good on them. Furthermore,

Heureaux never concerned himself with the mounting debt, believing that he would never have to accept responsibility for the staggering debt in his lifetime (Moya Pons 1995: 270). The loans only served to endanger the Dominican nation's sovereignty, as it became inevitable that some foreign power would eventually intervene in order for the country's creditors to receive payment.

The Samaná Bay and Peninsula intrigues clearly illustrated the growing stereotype of the Haitian Other as well as the personalism that marked Dominican politics of the era. While the first negotiations could be considered nationalistic in nature because of Dominican leaders' fear of another Haitian invasion, later motives were purely financial as those in power sought the necessary money and weapons needed to retain their control.

Finally, the era of the *caudillos* established the precedence for the use of violence to gain power and eliminate opposition. Bribery and espionage became common mechanisms of control as well. At the time of the U.S. occupation, force and not democracy was the political norm.

The period of the great Dominican strongmen brought with it an increased tendency toward the regionalization of loyalties and thus of identities. Furthermore, the Samaná Bay deals reinforced the Dominicans' view of who they believed they were and were not. The legacy of this era of regionalism, political fragmentation, personalism, violence and economic ruin, would not be entirely erased even during eight years of United States military occupation.

4

Merengue's First Steps: 1844–1916

*"Cierto que la pasión del baile es común a todos
los pueblos de todas las edades.... Pero puede
afirmarse que es la nación dominicana una de
aquellas en que esa pasión ha sido más fuerte, viva
y dominante."* [It is certain that the passion for
dance is common to all people of all ages.... But it
can be affirmed that the Dominican nation is one
of those in which that passion has been stronger,
more alive and dominant.]
— Rodríguez Demorizi 1971: 65

Dominicans believe that dancing is inherent to their ethnicity—it is
"in their blood." Although it is probably not their intent to consider any
specific historical basis for this assertion, merengue certainly reflects
Dominican history, ethnicity and reality. Dance and music were an important ritual among the Taíno, though regional variations of pre–Columbian
music differed (Coopersmith 1949: 9). The Spanish *conquistadores* and
colonizers introduced European dances and musical forms. African slaves
imported to the Caribbean brought with them their own culture in which
music and dance were key elements. This latter group also introduced
what would become the main rhythmic instrument of merengue: the
drum.

Thus, the "pronounced passion for dancing" that del Castillo and
García Arévalo (1989:71) attribute to the Dominican people came from the

The definitive instruments of *merengue típico*: *güira*, accordion and drum. (Photograph: Miguel Gómez)

meeting of their ancestors. The influences of these different cultures combined to form new harmonies, rhythms and steps in a music that was not of any one world but rather represented the fusion of all three. Dominicans, however, are as likely to downplay or ignore the African influences present in merengue as they are to diminish them in their own ethnic makeup. We have already seen how Dominicans took advantage of the existence of the various ethnicities present to emphasize European and indigenous elements at the cost of African influences. In much the same way, merengue is a malleable element of Dominican identity. Proponents of a predominantly European Dominican identity focus on what they consider European tendencies of the music while those who support an Afro-Dominican identity point to its African characteristics. Still others point to the gourd used as a scraper as a Taíno contribution. Finally, those who view Dominican-ness as a blend of ethnicities see the merengue as a syncretic combination of contributions.

Questions of how, when and with whom merengue actually originated inevitably lead to questions of race. Studying merengue means looking critically at what it means to be Dominican on a personal and national level.

The Birth of Merengue

Throughout the colonial period, there were numerous regional dances in the Dominican Republic. In addition to these distinct dances, variations of each one also differed from region to region. Dancing was such a popular practice in the colony of Santo Domingo that in 1818 "the Governor of the colony published the following edict: 'Without a permit from the authorities, *dancing* in the streets and squares at night is prohibited. No *music*, or *songs to the accompaniment of the guitar* will be permitted after ten o'clock at night' " (Coopersmith 1949: 18).

On the eve of Dominican independence from Spain (1821), European dances were still extremely influential in the country. Forms such as the waltz, polka, fandango, cuadrilla, minuet, and mazurka were among the favorites (Batista Matos 1999: 1). The decline of group dances and the consequent rise in popularity of couple dances were almost simultaneous with Dominican independence from Spain. Of these, the *contradanza criolla*

The Dominican flag, designed by Juan Pablo Duarte, *Padre de la Patria* (Father of the Homeland) was first flown on February 27, 1844, when Dominicans regained their independence from Haiti. Legends of merengue's origins link it, like the national flag, to that important day in the national imagination. (Photograph: Mary Katherine Scott)

(later called the *tumba dominicana*) became one of the favorites. Over the years, the *tumba* came to be considered the national dance of the Dominican Republic. The *tumba* enjoyed great popularity until the mid–1800s at which time the merengue began to make its presence felt.

The exact origins of the merengue are unknown. Various dances that were similar existed throughout the Caribbean and in spite of the Dominican Republic's present-day status as the *cuna del merengue* (cradle, i.e. birthplace of merengue), Haiti, Cuba and Puerto Rico have all claimed to be the dance's country of origin. It is known that those fleeing Haiti during the Revolution brought with them a dance known as the *mereng,* a fusion of the European *contredanse* and African elements, to other Caribbean nations, in turn leaving its mark on the music there. For example, the Cuban *contradanza* (also called the *danza*) was strongly influenced by these refugees (Austerlitz 1997: 15–16).

Traveling bands carried a version of the Cuban *danza* to Puerto Rico in the early 1840s where it became known as the *upa* and sometimes called the merengue. There, the dance was outlawed in 1849 because the governor of the colony believed that the *upa* negatvely influenced the people of that island. This ruling brought about the eventual decline of the *upa* and within 20 years, it ceased to be performed in Puerto Rico (Austerlitz 1997: 17).

There is nothing certain that attributes the merengue to any specific country. Dominicans claim that it is a thoroughly Dominican creation, especially denying any ties the dance might have with Haiti:

> It doesn't appear that it [the merengue] … can be attributed a Haitian origin. If it had such a dark origin, it wouldn't have enjoyed any popularity at all in 1855, an epoch of bloody battles against Haiti; nor would those who repudiated the merengue have failed to mention such an origin as a sufficient motive for its definitive repudiation…. Nevertheless, it can be affirmed that the Dominicanness of the merengue is without doubt. It was born in the first years of the Republic, from 1844 to 1855, as a modality of the *danza [No parece que pueda atribuírsele origen haitiano. De haber tenido esa oscura procedencia no habría gozado de boga alguna en 1855, época de cruentas luchas contra Haití; ni los que repudiaban el merengue habrían dejado de señalar tal procedencia como suficiente motivo para su repudiación definitiva…. Sin embargo, puede afirmarse que la dominicanidad del merengue es indudable. Nació en los primeros años de la República, de 1844 a 1855, como una modalidad de la danza]* [Rodríguez Demorizi 1971: 125].

This emphatic denial of any possible Haitian influence in Dominican merengue emphasizes yet again the concept of the Haitian Other and reinforces the geographical boundary between the two nations. Merengue contributes to the imagined geography of the Dominican Republic. In other words, it helps "define the borders of a community—what it means to exist both inside and outside the community—which inevitably defines a dichotomy of 'us' and 'them'" (Mattern 1998: 140).

Legends of merengue's beginnings tie it inextricably to the nation's independence from Haiti, usually situating its origins around 1844. One of the most popular of such myths directly links the birth of merengue to the defeat of the Haitian invaders. Supposedly, the first merengue was invented following the Dominican victory in the Battle of Talanquera. According to the legend, Tomás Torres, the cowardly Dominican flag-bearer, ran from the battle with the national flag. That evening, as the Dominican troops celebrated their triumph over the Haitians, they began to incorporate the days' events into a traditional song. Sung with a new melody, the song was one of the first merengues:

Toma' juyó con la bandera	Thomas fled with the flag,
Toma' juyó de la Talanquera:	Thomas fled from Talanquera;
Si juera yo, yo no juyera,	If it had been I, I wouldn't have fled:
Toma' juyó con la Bandera	Thomas fled with the flag.

[Austerlitz 1997: 1; his translation]

Regardless of the popularity of this anecdote, there is no evidence of its historical authenticity. Nevertheless, the legend "links music and national identity in a bond that has endured through most of the merengue's history" (*ibid.*, 1–2).

Two of the oldest merengues, "*Juangomero*" and "*La Juana Aquilina*," have colorful, legendary beginnings as well. Interestingly, the lyrics of both songs reflect the musical form, mentioning the merengue intertextually. Ramón Emilio Jiménez relates the following tale about the origins of "*Juangomero*":

It is said that in the village of Juan Gómez, located in the Cibao region, an accordionist whose name is not remembered was being mocked and jeered by a group of young girls in response to the passes he was making at them. Afterwards, the girls entered into the yard of a nearby house, and began eating "cañafístola." These plants were called "elimina-tors" by the native Juangomeros, due to their vermifuge properties. As a result of the previously described incident, the aggravated accordionist improvised the offensive merengue "Juangomero" which due to its distinctive style and catchy rhythm has won overwhelming popularity [del Castillo and García Arévalo 1989: 74].

The lyrics of that vengeful song are as follows:

Las muchachas de Juan Gómez,	The girls from Juan Gómez
son bonita y bailan bien,	are pretty and dance well,
pero tienen un defecto:	but they have one bad trait:
que se ríen de to'el que ven.	they laugh at everybody they see.
Las muchachas de Juan Gómez	The girls from Juan Gómez
son bonita y bailadora,	are pretty and like to dance,
pero tienen un defecto:	but they have one bad trait:
que comen la sacadora.	They eat the "eliminators."

[del Castillo and García Arévalo 1989: 16; English translation 74]

"*La Juana Aquilina*" enjoyed great popularity in its time as well, probably, as Rodríguez Demorizi maintains, because the song was inspired by a true event. As the story goes, Juan Hernández attended a party at the house of one Juan Aquilino. Hernández was something of a rabble-rouser, and his loud and boisterous conduct created quite a stir at the party. In the midst of the chaos, Hernández smashed a guitar over the head of one of the musicians. Though only a fragment of this merengue survives, the song also folds back in upon itself intertextually:

Juana Aquilina	Juana Aquilina
va llorando	is crying
porque la llevan	because they're taking her
merengueando …	dancing the merengue …

[del Castillo and García Arévalo 1989: 16; my translation]

These lyrics may also make reference to the strong opposition to the merengue during that period. Although the composer of "*Juana Aquilina*" is uncertain, Dominican folklorists often attribute it to the first known composer of that musical form, Juan Bautista Alfonseca (1810–65). Bautista composed and performed merengues and other traditional styles of music and, for this reason, is known as the "Father of the Merengue."

Another merengue known to be sung around 1850 offers a contrasting view to that presented in "*Juana Aquilina*" by emphasizing the need to adapt to the new music:

Merengue, papá Camilo;	Merengue, Papá Camilo;
Merengue, papá Tomá.	Merengue, Papá Tomá.
Al golpe de la tambora,	To the beat of the drum,
O te compone o te va.	You best get your act together or go away.

[del Castillo and García Arévalo 1989: 16; English translation 74]

From these two examples, it is clear that merengue had met with mixed reviews in the Dominican Republic.

The first mention of merengue in print can be found in 1854. At this time, young Dominican intellectuals began a heated literary campaign against merengue in a series of articles that denounced the new music. The authors, who usually published under pseudonyms, were appalled by the fact that "the vulgar merengue was being danced in polite society" (Pacini Hernández 1995: 38). One article criticizes the rough and inappropriate movements of the dance and blames it for inciting generally sophisticated participants to mischief.

The merengue was also attacked because its growing popularity was displacing the *tumba* as the national dance. Manuel de Jesús Galván, whose *indigenista* novel, *Enriquillo*, would come to form such an integral part of the collective national imagination, joined in the battle against the merengue with a lengthy poem entitled "*Quejas de la tumba contra el merengue*" (Complaint of the Tumba Against the Merengue) in which the tumba bemoans its exile at the hands of the merengue, "Impure progeny of impure Hell/Child of the Devil and a Fury" (Austerlitz 1997: 19)

The way in which the merengue was danced, especially the swinging hip movement, also offended Galván whose poem calls on men to consider how they would feel if their sisters or daughters were dancing merengue and "[d]emonstrating the agility of [their] hips" (Austerlitz 1997: 21).

Although the intellectuals claimed reasons of decency and nationalism as the basis for their heated campaign against the merengue, it is also quite possible that questions of race entered into the battle as well. Hip movement in dance is a common characterisitc of African music and dance, and given the recent liberation from Haitian occupation, rejection of all things Haitian—and by extension in the Dominican mentality, all things black—would be natural. Nevertheless, no direct mention is ever made of Haiti nor its people in the articles, a fact, as we have seen, that Rodríguez Demorizi (1971: 125) points to as eliminating all possibilities of a Haitian origin for the merengue.

That the merengue could spark such a heated attack against itself reveals the central role of music in Dominican identity. Those denouncing the genre insisted that the *tumba* as national dance was the true representation of what it meant to be Dominican; the merengue, in their eyes, was not. This support of a more European-influenced dance and the subsequent attack by a syncretic African-influenced dance in competition for the status of "national music" reflects the long-standing Dominican tendency to define national identity in terms of whiteness versus blackness.

Additionally, the very fact that such a fierce literary campaign should

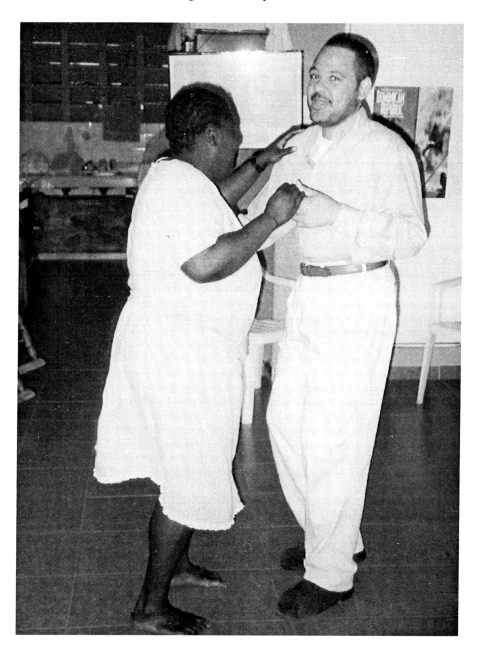

The first mention of merengue in print appeared in 1854 when a group of young Dominican intellectuals began a literary campaign against the dance, criticizing what they considered its lascivious steps. (Photograph: Julie Sellers)

be waged against merengue reveals that it was gaining a following within the country. Though physically separated from each other, people of the island's different regions were intensely embracing merengue at that time. The music's popularity was growing in the *campo* (countryside), despite the scorn that the intellectuals and the elite heaped upon the dance. This attraction to merengue is not surprising, given that the rural population far outnumbered that of the urban areas; in 1888, for example, 425,000 of the country's population of 435,000, almost 98%, lived in rural areas (Moya Pons 1988: 213). Furthermore, African cultural traditions were strong in those areas of the country.

Long a part of African-influenced religious practices, music and dance were an integral element of the culture of the *campesinos*. Dances were considered an important event in the countryside. Dressed in the finest they owned, the *campesinos* often danced outside under an *enramada*, a thatched construction with no walls whose dance floor was made of solidly packed earth mixed with lime and water. Musicians usually performed at these weekend events in exchange for liquor and food (Austerlitz 1997: 33). Given the popularity of the merengue in the countryside, some of the same aspects of the dance that "offended some Euro-Dominicans apparently appealed to others, a conflict inherent in the futile project of forging a Eurocentric identity in an African-American country" (*ibid.*, 22).

Choreography, Themes, and Instrumentation

The merengue step has often been compared to that of a cock wooing a hen, and according to Agustín Pichardo, in the past the man used his fancy footwork to court a lady (Austerlitz 1997: 34). The merengue, "like the male bird's dance ... has a sideways hitch and shuffle to it. The partners dance in a tight circle with the man leading on the outside, just like a rooster circling a hen" (Wucker 1999b: 12).

Merengues were made up of several different sections. Generally, each began with a short *paseo*. This march-style opening was followed by the "merengue" section whose lyrics centered around a theme. The *jaleo*, a section in a call-and-response format, followed. Although this was the common arrangement, the free nature of merengue allowed composers and performers to vary from it as well, thus enriching the genre.

Merengue's subject matter no doubt added to its growing acceptance. As has been seen in "*Juangomero*" and "*La Juana Aquilina*," the music commonly dealt with popular themes. Often, topics that would have been considered off-limits in polite society were worked into the lyrics of a merengue through numerous double meanings and plays on words.

Side view of *merengue típico* figures. (Photograph: Mary Katherine Scott)

In addition to local incidents, merengue dealt with national and international happenings. For example, Ñico Lora composed merengues that dealt with "*La libertad de Cuba*" ("Cuba's Liberty") (1899) and "*El aeroplano*" ("The Airplane") (1903). Merengue was often a key part of politics in the Dominican Republic as well, for *caudillos* and their policies might suddenly find themselves the subject of a merengue.

The regionalism that defined Dominican politics of the time was reflected in merengue's original instrumentation, which differed by region. Nevertheless, the most common organization of the bands reflected the blend of cultures inherent to the island. In its original form, merengue was performed by a group of musicians who played string instruments such as the *cuatro, tres, seis,* and the *tiple,* instruments that originated in Spain and were later developed in the Americas. The beat was kept on a goatskin drum known as the *tambora.* One drumhead was covered with billy goat skin and the other—the part beat with the stick—with that of the nanny; in this way "the bipolarity of the sexes—together with the symbolism of the stick beating upon the nanny goat skin—takes effect in the rhythmic cadence of the merengue" (del Castillo and García Arévalo 1989: 77). The final element of the ensemble was the percussive *güiro,* a scraper made from a gourd. Although this instrument is commonly attributed to the Taíno, there is no evidence to prove that it was used by the pre–Colombian people. The *güiro*, both in its original gourd form and it modern metal counterpart (*güira*), is considered to be an invention of the Dominican Republic or Puerto Rico.

Although band instruments such as the baritone horn and clarinet were introduced to merengue ensembles during the War of Restoration, the first major change to the instrumentation of the merengue came in the 1870s when the one-row accordion began to appear in the Dominican Republic as an import from Germany. This instrument began to replace the typical string instruments, especially in the Cibao region, since that area traded extensively with Germany. Although some critics felt the accordion would cheapen merengue because of its limited range, the instrument's popularity grew quickly because it was more sonorous (del Castillo and García Arévalo 1989: 78).

At this time, a second literary campaign against merengue was undertaken, headed by former president Ulises Francisco Espaillat. Espaillat,

Figures representing the three instruments of *merengue típico* are popular among both Dominicans and tourists as representative of a marker of identity that sets Dominicans apart: merengue. (Photograph: Mary Katherine Scott)

who referred to the dance as the *"fatal merengue"* (fatal merengue), believed that it "affected the nervous system too much and that it resulted in *the ailment of being unable to control the imagination"* [*afectaba demasiado el sistema nervioso, y que dejaba* el achaque de no poder dominar la imaginación] (Rodríguez Demorizi 1971: 136).

The accordion bore the brunt of the criticism in this new literary campaign for having replaced what were considered "typical" instruments of the Dominican Republic. Just as Galván had written against the merengue for displacing the *tumba*, another poet, Juan Antonio Alix, wrote *"El acordeón y el cuatro"* and later *"El cuatro y el acordeón"* in which the traditional stringed instrument condemns the accordion as a passing fad that will itself be replaced someday.

Y si hoy me dan con el pié	And if today they kick me out,
será poique me combiene,	maybe it's because it's fitting,
y ei que a ti amoi te tiene	and he who loves you so much,
aunque tu lo vea así,	though you might not see it this way,
te jará peoi que a mí	will do worse to you than to me
si otra cosa mejoi viene.	if something better comes along.

[Rogríguez Demorizi 1971: 160]

Opposition to the accordion grew to such an extent that the government of Santiago (the largest city of the Cibao) suggested placing a specific tax on accordions as a measure to decrease the demand for them, and thus the numbers imported into the country. The municipal government's reasoning was summed up as follows: "'Accordions are not necessary articles, and only serve to bring vagabonds together. They do not contribute to the edification of the country, as does the cuatro, which is more sonorous, more harmonious, more perfect, and thus, more useful'" (Austerlitz 1997: 26–7). In addition to these arguments, an underlying antipathy towards the accordion might well have been found in the rejection of all things African, since the accordion tended to emphasize "the music's African and percussive elements at the expense of the Hispanic and harmonic elements" (*ibid.*).

Another innovation important to merengue was the later inclusion of the saxophone. As the story goes, this change was merely the result of chance. One night a band's drummer was ill and unable to perform, and the only instrument available to replace him was a saxophone. The performance was such a hit that other musicians began to include it in their ensembles as well.

Merengue circa 1915

Merengue continued to gain an audience in the Dominican Republic in its numerous regional variations. Of these, the style that would eventually be elevated to "the" national dance, the *merengue cibaeño* (merengue of the Cibao region) was taking shape in its modern form in 1915 and 1916, just as national sovereignty was compromised by the U.S. occupation. With the marines' invasion, the man about whom the United States was most wary, Desiderio Arias, avoided confrontation with the North American forces by leaving the capital. A merengue was composed to commemorate Arias's retreat, and its lyrics reveal that his refusal to fight was believed to be based in the Biblical principal of turning swords into plowshares: "The weapons he now prefers/Are the weapons of planting" (Austerlitz 1997: 36).

Although the merengue was not wholly embraced by all Dominicans in 1916, the U.S occupation would provide the dance with an opportunity to unite Dominicans against yet another foreign "Other," thus strengthening a sense of *dominicanidad* and initiating the merengue's role within it.

5

U.S. Occupation and Dominican Nationalism

"Schools, roads, bridges, and hospitals were con-
structed. Unification of the country through these
infrastructural improvements had the effect of neu-
tralizing the power of the caudillos, that is, the
local political leaders, and literally paving the way
for political centralization."

—Georges 1990: 27

The United States marines' eight-year occupation of the Dominican Republic was to have profound and long-lasting economic, political, social and cultural effects on the nation. The Dominican Republic became oriented away from Europe and towards its neighbor to the north, and U.S. influence spread throughout all realms of Dominican life, including its music. Nevertheless, as the occupation continued, a sense of Dominican nationalism arose and began to grow, especially in the Cibao, the nation's most densely populated region. Alongside the image of the Haitian "Other," a second "them" arose in the form of the United States. While the military government of the occupation would undertake numerous public works projects and highway construction to unify the country geographically, its presence would also serve to join the Dominicans as a people.

Stabilization and Development

Captain Harry S. Knapp imposed several decisive measures immediately following the United States' official proclamation of occupation. First, in an attempt to stabilize the political situation within the Dominican Republic and prevent revolts, Dominicans were prohibited to carry firearms. The press was also censored to eliminate written opposition to the occupation. Finally, the former president's cabinet was dissolved on December 8, 1916, and United States officers filled those positions.

Actions to improve the financial situation within the country were also set into motion. To win support for the occupation, Knapp used the funds formally held by the Customs Receivership to pay public servants whose wages had been withheld. Some of these monies were also channeled back for government use and to fund public works projects.

The military government's steps to disarm the entire Dominican population were at times violent. Individuals who resisted these measures faced the possibility of arrest, prison time and even torture. The thorough disarmament was soon followed by the creation of a National Guard in April 1917. The Dominican guardsmen were taken under the tutelage of U.S. officers and trained with the intention of pacifying those who opposed the occupation. The long-term goal of the National Guard was to provide a military body composed of Dominicans that would be able to put down regional rebellions once the occupation had ended.

One of the young men who enthusiastically joined the National Guard in 1918 was Rafael Leonides Trujillo de Molina, a poor telegraph operator from the town of San Cristóbal near the capital. An uncle of Trujillo's was a close friend of Colonel McClean, an officer of the occupying forces, and thanks to this friendship, it was not long before Trujillo was named an informant. During the years of the United States occupation, Trujillo would rise swiftly through the National Guard.

The occupying force undertook various measures in an attempt to increase the country's internal revenue. One of these, the Land Registration Act of 1920, was intended not only to increase revenues but also to modernize the country by eliminating the land tenure system that had been in place since the colonial era. Additionally, the Land Registration Act "effectively facilitated and reinforced the expansion of U.S.-owned sugar plantations" (Georges 1990: 27) by offering more incentives to those companies to expand their operations.

The sugar companies' increased holdings were soon to pay off. Following World War I, sugar prices soared due to the devastation of sugar-beet fields in Europe. Although foreign owners of sugarcane plantations enjoyed the greatest benefits, the Dominican economy as a whole was bolstered by

The U.S. intervention of 1916–1924 unified the Dominican Republic geographically through the construction of highways that joined its cities and towns. (Copyright and Courtesy of Hispaniola.com)

this sudden economic boom. Cane workers' salaries increased, small cane-farmers enjoyed more economic freedom, and exports of other crops also grew. During this time of economic prosperity known as the "Dance of Millions," population centers that had been mere towns exploded into thriving urban centers and money poured back into the national infrastructure.

Soon after the official proclamation of the occupation, the military government began numerous public works projects such as schools, hospitals, highways and bridges. With the increased funds made possible by the "Dance of Millions," the government undertook the completion of three highway projects that had previously been suspended. The government believed that these highways were essential to unifying the country and would decrease the likelihood of further revolts in isolated locations where the population's loyalty belonged to regional *caudillos*.

Opposition to Occupation

In spite of the improved economy and the public works projects, both Dominican and international opposition to the occupation was growing. These tensions were partly due to a new set of U.S. officers who replaced those who had originally run the government. These newcomers, and most significantly Knapp's replacement, Rear Admiral Thomas Snowden, were less familiar with Dominican realities and culture than had been their predecessors (Moya Pons 1995: 327). Furthermore, the military government's policies and abuses lent themselves to the growing hostility. The sense of nationalism that always seemed to arise when the Dominican Republic was threatened from outside surfaced once again:

> Dominicans did not like being governed by U.S. soldiers, as they had not liked when they were ruled by Spanish soldiers at the time of the annexation, by Haitian soldiers during Boyer's rule, or by French soldiers. ... A long tradition of independence had made a foreign government intolerable. On many occasions, Dominican politicians and intellectuals let it be known that they preferred a free country with rebellions to an occupied country living under an imposed peace. Moreover, the censorship, the obligatory use of passports, the military courts of justice, the arrests of innocent persons, and the torture of prisoners accused of opposing the occupation created an atmosphere of patriotic resistance in the country [ibid., 328].

This "patriotic resistance" was staged on diplomatic, military, and cultural fronts. Diplomatically, elite Dominicans began a war of propaganda, aimed at swaying international opinion against the occupation. Worldwide opposition began to be voiced, pressing the United States to withdraw.

Militarily, campesino guerrillas in the east known as gavilleros resisted the marines from 1917 to 1922. Captain Fred Merckle, the officer sent by the military government to fight the guerrillas, met the threat with unrestrained violence and torture. Merckle's brutality, which had been neither ordered nor approved, was not reserved solely for the gavilleros, however; civilians were subject to them as well at Merckle's will. One of the soldiers under Merckle's command was Rafael Trujillo who, "acting first as an informant and later as an officer, actively participated in these campaigns of repression against the general population" (Aquino 1997: 18). Trujillo served under Merckle from 1919 to 1922, and during that time he participated and adapted the colonel's brutal tactics.

Culturally, the people of the north-central Cibao region began a campaign against the influence of North American culture. Todo lo dominicano—

all things Dominican—were embraced. Most importantly, merengue, which had been practiced in its various forms in the different regions of the country, was claimed as a symbol of resistance. The Cibao version of merengue, the *merengue cibaeño*, was celebrated as a national symbol of *dominicanidad* that contrasted with a North American "Other."

Prior to the occupation, music from the United States had been growing in popularity among the members of the upper class while merengue was a dance of the *campo* and the poor barrios. Nevertheless, merengue began to come into vogue among the elite under the military government. A portion of the merengue's acceptance at this time is due to the modifications made to the music. In 1918, the first concert merengue, "*Ecos del Cibao*," was written by Juan Francisco "Pancho" García. This composition was not presented as merengue when first performed in 1919 at the Teatro Colón in Santiago. Rather, García claimed his work to be *danzas típicas* (typical, or folk dances) to make the form more palatable to the upper classes. Other composers followed in García's footsteps with compositions based in local music.

The works of this group of composers, later known as the national school of Dominican music (Coopersmith 1949: 22), slowly but surely made their way into the elite circles, in large part because nationalistic sentiments were strong at the time. The Dominican school of music was yet another form of resistance to U.S. occupation. This school of musical composition was a clear statement of non-support that united Dominicans against the North American Other.

Although merengue was held up as a national symbol, it should be noted that the nationalistic cultural campaign was waged primarily in the Cibao.

Ironic as well is the fact that it was "not the Cibao peasant's most Hispanic music ... which ... [was] taken as a symbol of identity, but rather his recreational music, the *merengue*, a hybrid with regard both to style and instrumentation. The selection of this genre represents a sort of reinterpretation of *hispanidad* as a creole identity" (Davis 1994: 146). While the sense of oneness created among Dominicans during the Haitian rule had been based upon the rallying cry that Dominicans were Hispanic and white while Haitians were African and black, the spirit of nationalism that arose in the Cibao during the U.S. occupation embraced the syncretic merengue.

Such a selection might also have been made to better show the gulf that separated the cultures of both nations. While Dominicans themselves might minimize all African influences in their culture, the passion for dance could probably find its origins in the "deep rooted legacy and the importance of dance" in the African cultures (Hanna 1992: 183). The

Americans' inability to fluidly dance the merengue no doubt lent itself to a sense of superiority in the Dominicans, who were at that time submitted to unwanted foreign rule. As Judith Hanna points out, "[i]f one has … little power … the body and its use are likely to become particularly important" (*ibid.*, 187). Therefore, dancing invoked a sense of self-governance in individuals who had been forcibly disarmed and were required to comply with the imposition of foreign domination.

As in the past, merengue chronicled political happenings. For example, Ñico Lora's "*La protesta*" ("The Protest") condemns the U.S. occupation while supporting the guerrilla warfare of the *gavilleros*: "We'll attack them with machetes/We'll make them leave" (Austerlitz 1997: 37).

Just as the merengue's origin is tied to the nation's independence from Haiti, the development of a variation of the dance known as *pambiche* is linked to the United States' occupation of the early twentieth century. According to national legend, the occupying marines in Puerto Plata danced the merengue poorly and essentially had to make up their own step, a mix of the merengue, one-step and fox-trot, to be able to keep up with the music. The Dominicans mocked the marines by imitating them, and thus a new step was born. This dance, originally called Juan Ester and *merengue estilo yanqui* (Yankee-style merengue) was later given the name *pambiche*, "a mispronunciation of Palm Beach, a fabric with the name of the Florida summer beach, which was newly acquired in the country and had become fashionable" (del Castillo and García Arévalo 1989: 73). It is very possible that this variation of the merengue existed prior to the occupation and was only named during the U.S. presence. Nevertheless, as the *pambiche* legend illustrates, Dominican musical nationalism was based once again on the construction of a foreign invader, an "Other," with whom Dominican-ness could be contrasted.

The various campaigns waged against the U.S. military occupation eventually began to make their impact. Internationally, the action was called into question as no end to the occupation appeared to be in sight. Therefore, President Wilson ordered that freedom of the press be reinstated and that Dominicans be allowed to gather to petition for an end to the occupation.

Economic conditions also convinced the United States to reconsider its position. The European sugar industry was beginning to recover and consequently, Dominican sugar prices dropped, leaving the government without sufficient funds to continue its various public works projects. A loan of $6.7 million was necessary merely to finish the construction of highways and to pay public workers their salaries (Moya Pons 1995: 323).

In light of the financial crisis and mounting international opposition to the occupation, United States president Warren Harding sought to evacuate the marines from the Dominican Republic. In May 1922, a prominent Dominican lawyer, Francisco J. Peynado, traveled to Washington to encourage the negotiation of a settlement that would be agreeable to both nations. Peynado and Secretary of State Charles Evans Hughes eventually reached an understanding. This agreement, the Hughes-Peynado Plan, provided for the creation of a provisional government that would organize elections. It also established that the United States would continue to supervise Dominican customs until such time as all Dominican debts to foreign creditors were fully reimbursed.

Within the Dominican Republic, the Hughes-Peynado Plan met with opposition from those who, like ex–President Henríquez, supported a "'pure and simple'" total evacuation with no strings attached (Moya Pons 1995: 332). Nevertheless, Dominican political leaders accepted the plan, and Juan Bautista Vicini Burgos was named provisional president.

As preparations were being made for the eventual withdrawal of U.S. marines, Brigadier General Harry Lee arrived to replace Rear Admiral Samuel S. Robinson (Snowden's replacement of 1921) and to train the police force that would maintain order in the country once the marines had pulled out. The United States had a vested interest in this body that had been created as a national police force to be used by the Dominican president (Moya Pons 1995: 334). The Haina Military Academy was established for this formal training, and among those attending was Rafael Trujillo. Having risen at an amazingly rapid rate through the ranks, Trujillo was now an officer.

While the provisional government carried out the steps necessary to bring about U.S. withdrawal, the old political parties began to reorganize in preparation for the upcoming elections. The former *Horacista* party became known as the Partido Nacional while the *Velazquistas* assumed the name of the *Partido Progresista*. Two new parties also arose, the *Alianza Nacional Progresista* and the *Coalición Patriótica de Ciudadanos*. The elections that were held on March 15, 1924 were truly free and former *caudillo* Horacio Vásquez won a decisive victory.

The Occupation in Retrospect (1916–1924)

The United States military occupation of the Dominican Republic ended on July 1, 1924, and the last of the marines were off the island by the following month. The effects of the almost eight years of U.S. presence in the nation were diverse and long-lived. Politically, the nation was better unified geographically and politically by the construction of highways that joined its various urban centers and de-emphasized regional power.

The complete disarmament of the Dominican people marked the end of the constant uprisings and coup attempts. For the first time, there was a military body, the National Guard, which was at the service of the Republic, rather than an army whose loyalties went first to a single *caudillo*.

One of the less desirable effects of the U.S. occupation was its model of violence and repression:

> [T]he military government had been a government of occupation and, as such, had taught the advantages of repressive methods, especially to the members of the police who were now in charge of maintaining order in the country. With the population disarmed, whoever controlled the National Police could easily exercise enormous power over the rest of the population [Moya Pons 1995: 337].

While the military government had intended to leave the country safely in the hands of a police force loyal first to the president and the Republic, in truth what was left was a body that, in the hands of the wrong individual, could become a dangerous tool. At the time of U.S. withdrawal, the commander of that force was Rafael Trujillo, a man who would profoundly alter every aspect of Dominican life in the decades to follow. Trujillo, tutored under the repressive measures of the occupational government and specifically by the tactics of Captain Merckle, had already begun to follow the old patterns of the *caudillos* by using his position to accumulate a small fortune. It would not be long before he conformed to their model of personalism as well, but in a way which had never before been seen in the Dominican Republic.

Culturally, the occupation "left behind a very marked taste for the consumption of North American ... articles" [*dejó un gusto muy marcado por el consumo de artículos ... norteamericanos*] (Moya Pons 1988: 222). Americanisms were adapted into the language and baseball replaced cockfighting as the national sport. Although some developed a taste for North American music, merengue also gained popularity among the elite as a national symbol, though admittedly for a relatively short time and primarily in one region of the nation, the Cibao.

Following the marines' withdrawal, merengue lost its symbolic status as the national music and once again was considered a marker of class and a music linked to the *campo*. The rise and fall of merengue emphasizes the link between the music's rising popularity in the face of foreign threats present in Dominican history. Nevertheless, this popular musical form had made inroads into the Dominican consciousness through its political uses, and it would not be long before merengue would once again play an influential role in national politics.

6

In Step: Merengue in the Era of Trujillo

"[T]he Trujillo Era was also the era of the big bands, the recordings, radio broadcasting, the arrival of the small screen with its magical force, of the graceful entrance of merengue in the ballroom, of the social legitimation of the merengue and its virtual legalization as a national dance. This would be the era of the merengue's apotheosis."
—del Castillo and García Arévalo 1989: 81

What foreign occupation did not completely do for merengue's popularity, 30 years of brutal dictatorship did. During the long and violent period known as the Era of Trujillo, the dance was raised from the lowest rungs of society to the uppermost cultural echelons, where it became an unquestionable symbol of Dominican national identity. Nevertheless, this profound change did not occur without coercion on the part of the national government and resentment on the part of the elite.

Understanding the process by which merengue came to be at the center of *dominicanidad* is inseparable from a knowledge of Trujillo and his 30-year rule, for merengue was but one of the dictator's numerous tools. Although merengue had often incorporated political themes and personae, the development of the music had been to that point only parallel to that

81

of the Dominican government. During the Era of Trujillo, merengue and state were inseparable.

The Vásquez Presidency and Trujillo's Rise to Power

Before Trujillo came to power, Horacio Vásquez governed the Dominican Republic. Peace, prosperity and order marked the first years of Vásquez's return to the presidency following the United States occupation. The first seeds of modernization that had sprouted under the military government continued to grow under Vásquez. The government undertook various new public works projects and transportation continued to improve; human rights and liberties were respected as well.

The new sense of organization, peace and democracy was not to last, however. Despite the trends toward modernization, Dominican rulers clung to the *caudillo* view of politics as a means to personal gain. As early as 1926, some politicians were claiming that Vásquez had been elected under the 1908 constitution and that his term should be six years rather than four. A movement known as "*La Prolongación*" organized to make an extension possible by altering the constitution. Vásquez complied with the plan and in 1927, his term was officially lengthened. Vice-President Federico Velázquez, who had vehemently opposed these actions, was removed from his post by the president in August 1928 and his position was filled by Vásquez's hand-picked replacement, Dr. José Dolores Alfonseca.

Rafael Trujillo, now brigadier general and head of the former National Police that had become the

Dictator Rafael Trujillo, a product of the U.S.-instituted National Guard, centralized both the Dominican government and Dominican national identity during his 31 years at the head of the Dominican government. Trujillo named or renamed geographical sites after himself, ordered the construction of statues and busts, and created awards and medals (such as those adorning his uniform in this photo) merely so that they could be bestowed upon him. (Photograph: Picture Quest)

National Army in 1927, was one of President Vásquez's political favorites. The general demonstrated only the utmost respect for and loyalty to Vásquez and in return received the president's unquestioning faith. Trujillo's true motives were far from rendering unfailing allegiance to the president, however. Even as the general was publicly supporting Vásquez, he was putting into practice tactics used by the nineteenth-century *caudillos* by transforming the army into his personal military force which would help him achieve his own goals. Methodically and systematically, Truijllo solidified his officers' support by ridding the military of his personal and political enemies, silently biding his time. In spite of rumors, the elderly President Vásquez refused to believe that Trujillo was anything but loyal to him, making it impossible for anyone to speak or act against the commander of the army.

As the 1930 elections approached, Vásquez appeared not to plan to run for reelection and instead supported Alfonseca as his party's candidate. Alfonseca had many personal enemies, among them Trujillo. Later, President Vásquez opted to back his nephew, Martín de Moya, as a candidate instead, in a move that created a rift within the party. In truth, this was a political strategy that worked greatly to Vásquez's favor. Only by supporting Vásquez in a bid for reelection could the party overcome its internal divisions. As the campaigns continued, Vásquez, old and in poor health, fell ill. In October 1929, he was flown to Johns Hopkins Hospital for emergency surgery.

Vásquez's opponents were concerned about the very real possibility that their rival party would continue in power for six more years. Astutely, these politicians approached Trujillo and began to play upon his personal antagonism for Vice-President Alfonseca, who had made it clearly known that he did not believe Trujillo's show of loyalty to Vásquez. Alfonseca was convinced that the chief of the army was plotting against the president. Trujillo knew that, should Vásquez die and Alfonseca assume the presidency, Alfonseca would not hesitate to act against him.

Trujillo took advantage of the president's 10-week absence to begin to plot against the unsuspecting Vásquez. Trujillo conspired secretly with Rafael Estrella Ureña, a Santiago politician, to plan a coup that would force Vásquez to resign. Trujillo would not execute the coup himself, believing that he might receive the support of the United States if he were apparently to rise to the presidency through elections rather than violence (Hartlyn 1998: 40). The conspiracy instead called for Estrella Ureña to lead a rebellion in Santiago that would take the San Luis Fortress. Following this uprising, Estrella Ureña would march on Santo Domingo and force the president's resignation. Estrella Ureña's troops were guaranteed to face no interference, as the army would refrain from counterattacking in a feigned desire to avoid bloodshed (Moya Pons 1995: 353).

Although Vásquez had received numerous warnings that his trusted army chief was plotting against him, he refused to believe that Trujillo would betray him. Not until Estrella Ureña and his revolutionary troops entered Santo Domingo on February 23, 1930, did the president realize his grave error.

The United States was outraged to see that the Dominican Republic, which they believed to have achieved a certain level of stability, was in the throes of another revolution. Nevertheless, the U.S. did agree to allow Estrella Ureña to be sworn in as provisional president of the country, provided that Trujillo would never run for president (Galíndez 1973: 15). Yet although Estrella Ureña assumed the presidency upon Vásquez's March 2 resignation, Trujillo was without a doubt the true force behind the uprising.

The Foundations of the Regime

Despite the agreement reached with the United States, Trujillo and his vice-presidential candidate, Estrella Ureña, appeared as candidates in the May 16 elections. Opposition to the general was strong, and a common motto of the time was "*¡No puede ser!*" (This cannot be!) On election day Trujillo was reported to have won with 45 percent of the votes. This number is deceiving for, in the true spirit of *caudillo* politics, Trujillo had employed terror and violence against supporters of the opposition, forcing the other candidates to withdraw from the race. The politics of brutality, terror and coercion had returned to the Dominican Republic, this time with the added danger of a disarmed population at the mercy of an efficient, U.S.-trained army. Thus began the regime of a modern Dominican *caudillo*, a rule that would end only with the death of the dictator himself in 1961.

Although the United States had objected to Trujillo's candidacy, they accepted his victory in the elections. In fact, the United States supported Trujillo throughout most of his rule, despite the reported incidents of human-rights violations, for the U.S. considered him a lesser evil than his national and international political enemies (Moya Pons 1995: 357). Some U.S. State Department officers did not agree with such tolerance, but others, including Secretary of State Cordell Hull, were strong proponents of a lenient stance towards Trujillo. President Franklin D. Roosevelt probably best summed up the sentiments of the time by pointing out that Trujillo "'may be an S.O.B., but at least he's our S.O.B.'" (Wucker 1999b: 143).

Trujillo's dictatorship differed considerably from others of history and of his contemporaries in that it entirely lacked a clear political ideology.

In this way, he was adhering to the long-standing Dominican tradition of the great *caudillos* by seeking power for power's sake and the personal wealth that power could bring him. Although Trujillo clearly articulated his stance on certain issues—he was anti–Communist and pro–economic nationalism—he never specifically stated any one ideology (Hartlyn 1998: 49). Trujillo's government centered around the exploitation of the nation as a private business to amass a great fortune. Above all, the Trujillo regime revolved around the imposition of the dictator's will upon an entire people. The Trujillo government was a neopatrimonial regime characterized by

> centralization of power in the hands of the ruler who seeks to reduce the autonomy of his followers by generating ties of loyalty and dependence, commonly through complex patron-client linkages; and, in the process, the blurring of public and private interests and purposes within the administration [Hartlyn 1998: 14].

Trujillo organized the government as "a regime of plunder" (Moya Pons 1995: 359) whose purpose was to place economic control in his own hands. He began with the sugar industry, and using his own funds as well as those of the state, he bought up the majority of the mills owned by foreign companies. Within a short time Trujillo had become the country's largest producer of sugar, the Dominican Republic's main source of foreign trade (Gramsuck and Pessar 1991: 28).

El Jefe (The Chief, as Trujillo was known) systematically bought numerous enterprises, creating monopolies of basic products such as rice, milk, livestock, salt and shoes. In order to solidify these monopolies, numerous laws that might now seem absurd were passed. For example, a law was enacted that forbade the manufacture of sea salt, thus forcing the Dominican people to use salt from Trujillo's mines in Barahona. These measures brought about a drastic increase in the price of salt, from $.60 to $3 per 100 pounds (Moya Pons 1995: 359).

Another such measure involved the production of shoes. To encourage the purchase of shoes from his factory, Trujillo created a law that forbade individuals to go barefoot in Santo Domingo and other Dominican cities. Trujillo was not the only entrepreneur to profit from this measure, as some clever individuals set up businesses at the city limits to rent shoes to the poor *campesinos* who went to town for a day (Aquino 1997: 93).

The economic life of the Dominican Republic was intimately tied to its political life which in turn was synonymous with the president. At the time of his death, almost 80 percent of industrial production was under Trujillo's control. A full 45 percent of the nation's labor force was employed by the president's firms, and 15 percent more worked for the state (Moya Pons 1995: 365; Hartlyn 1998: 50). The economic legacy Trujillo would leave behind in 1961 was that of a country severely divided between a small group of very rich individuals and an enormous lower class.

As Trujillo's economic and political powers increased over the decades, so did his ego and need for self-aggrandizement. As Crassweller points out, this tendency grew into pure megalomania (1996: 74). This need in the dictator can perhaps be partly attributed to his lowly birth and the way in which he was shunned by the elite, even as an army officer. Once in power, Trujillo thrived on humiliating the members of the upper class. The elite resented Trujillo, but had no choice but to conform to his complete power. Thus, those who most detested the president were forced to praise him and his regime while he took every measure possible to denigrate them.

Trujillo's megalomania presented itself most conspicuously in the geographical sites named after him and the numerous monuments constructed in his honor. For example, the dictator changed the name of Duarte Peak, the highest mountain in the Caribbean, to Trujillo Peak. Wucker relates that the geographer who measured the height of the peak was afraid that its 10,128 feet might not be enough to impress Trujillo, so he took it upon himself to record the peak at 10,417 feet instead (1999b: 45). In January, 1936, the dictator decided to rename the capital after himself, and Santo Domingo thus became "Ciudad Trujillo."

In addition to these geographical alterations, Trujillo had countless statues and busts of himself constructed around the country. At one point during his rule, the dictator was even "listed in the *Guinness Book of World Records* as the world leader who built the most statues in his honor" (Wucker 1999b: 69).

Trujillo also coveted medals, and various distinguished awards were created merely so that they could be bestowed upon him. Although his flamboyant military dress uniforms were covered with these, he "was proudest of a faded, threadbare medal attesting to his service with the Marines," for he "always thought of himself as basically a Marine Corps officer" (Espaillat 1963: 24). Trujillo continued to feel a personal tie to the United States, and he strove throughout his reign to remain on good terms with the U.S.

Also notable are the numerous titles granted the president. A Congressional resolution of 1932 conferred upon him the title of "Benefactor of the Fatherland," and in 1933, Trujillo was awarded the rank of generalissimo. One year later, this man, who had almost no formal education whatsoever, was granted an honorary doctoral degree. Perhaps the most honest title, granted to Trujillo in 1940, was that of "Restorer of

Financial Independence" since the national debt was truly paid off at last during his rule.

In 1955, the president was named the "Father of the New Fatherland," a title that revealed his belief that he was the "forger of the Dominican nation" (Hartlyn 1998: 49). While Trujillo's tactics for keeping peace and creating a sense of oneness were certainly questionable, it is undeniable that a national sense of *dominicanidad* developed and grew throughout the Era. As Trujillo worked to create an official Dominican identity, he reverted to the historical argument that Dominicans were white, Spanish-speaking Catholics. In other words, the dictator told the people what they had always heard and wanted to hear, and because this ethnicity was at least based in reality—even though it was not the entire truth—the people believed it (Moya Pons 1988: 245). This was certainly an efficient means by which to create a solidified Dominican identity, for "nationalists cannot, and do not, create nations *ex nihilo*. There must be, at least, some elements in the chosen population and its social environment who favour the aspirations and activities of the nationalist visionaries" (Smith 1996: 108).

Trujillo and Anti-Haitianism

Trujillo returned to the historical antithesis between the official Dominican identity and the Dominican stereotype of Haitian identity. Playing upon the Dominicans' smoldering hatred of Haitians, Trujillo pointed to them (especially Haitians along the border and Haitian immigrants) as the source of all Dominican ills. In this way, the president created an even stronger sense of "we" among the Dominicans, widening the chasm between the two countries. Trujillo took an aggressive stance against the Haitians and their culture; for example, the practice of voodoo was strictly prohibited.

Ironically, for all his tirades against the neighboring nation, its culture and religion, and black ethnicity, Trujillo himself carried Haitian blood; his maternal grandmother was a full-blooded Haitian woman. In spite of the law against voodoo, Trujillo was known to consult spiritualists and on occasion to resort to curses. The Benefactor, however, masked this reality psychologically as well as physically. Throughout his rule, Trujillo wore pancake make-up to lighten his dark complexion.

One of the most gruesome events of the early years of the Trujillo regime concerned a massacre of Haitians. During an October 1937 visit to the border, Dominican *campesinos* complained to the president that Haitians had been stealing their livestock. On October 2, at a party held at the border town of Dajabón, Trujillo proclaimed that such abuses would no longer be tolerated.

In truth, the dictator was motivated by more than the reported thefts. According to Wucker, Trujillo hoped to divert the Dominican public's attention from the troubling state of current sugar prices to the matter of the numerous Haitian immigrants who worked the cane and the perceived strain they placed on the Dominican economy. As Trujillo saw it, as long as "Dominicans directed their anger at foreigners, he would become a hero fighting to keep the intruders out" (Wucker 1999b: 103).

At the time of the massacre, Trujillo was also involved in a Haitian plot to overthrow the current Haitian president. Some sources maintain that on the evening of October 2, Trujillo learned that his secret agents in Haiti had been found out and killed, and that his decision to undertake the massacre was made in a resulting fit of violent fury (Crassweller 1966: 154).

Whatever the reason, the day following the party Dominican soldiers singled out Haitians to be made examples of, killing them and showing their bodies to other Haitian immigrants with the warning that they had precisely 24 hours to leave the Dominican Republic. The next day the massacre began as the Dominican army thoroughly searched the border area for Haitians. Just as the Haitians had done to their European masters in their fight for freedom over a century before, the Dominicans singled out Haitians from mulatto Dominicans by means of a pronunciation test. All suspects were made to say the word "*perejil*"—Spanish for "parsley." This tactic of dividing dark-skinned individuals into two groups, Dominian and Haitian, reveals the central role that language plays in the creation of ethnicity since it is "immanent in the people" (Balibar 1996: 141). Haitians, who were distinguished by their inability to pronounce the Spanish flipped "r" in the test word, were brutally killed with machetes, knives and shovels; guns were not used, in order to make the massacre appear to be a peasant rebellion rather than a government-sanctioned killing.*

To this day the exact number of Haitians massacred in October 1937 is unknown. Basing his estimates on the tallies kept by Francisco Espinal in the Dajabón post office, Miguel Aquino notes that along the border alone 18,000 deaths were reported. This calculation does not include the numbers killed in the inland cities of the Cibao where the massacre also spread. Aquino offers an estimate of 20,000 to 25,000 Haitian deaths.

In spite of Trujillo's attempts to disguise the massacre as a spontaneous peasant revolt, international reaction was strong. A special commission that had been formed to take action on the case required Trujillo

---

*Haitian workers on U.S.-owned plantations were untouched.

to pay the Haitian government $750,000. This amount was never paid in full, though Haitian officials hardly seemed to notice. The lack of an angry denunciation on the part of the Haitian government was probably due to the fact that President Sténio Vincent feared losing the support he had been receiving from Trujillo (Wucker 1999b: 54).

Soon after the massacre, Trujillo attempted to silence international tensions and opposition to his rule by arranging the election of Jacinto Peynado, the first of three puppet presidents who would wear the title while Trujillo pulled all the strings.

Trujillo also tried to calm the international waters by offering the Dominican Republic as a home to German-Jewish refugees in 1938. The goals of this proposal were twofold: Trujillo aimed to present a kind face to the global community, while at the same time he desired to integrate more white blood into the Dominican population. It is telling that limitations on the number of married refugees were strictly held in place. Although some Jewish immigrants did come at that time to settle in the north around Sosúa, the majority abandoned the island soon after (Wucker 1999b: 57).

The Dominican government undertook "an intense propaganda campaign defending Trujillo" as the country's savior (Moya Pons 1995: 369). Against the backdrop of conflict with their neighbor to the east, Dominicans did not see the massacre in the same light as foreign outsiders who considered the act to be unfounded (Crassweller 1966: 159). Trujillo had taken advantage of the Dominican mentality concerning ethnicity as well as the medieval notion of *limpieza de sangre* (cleansing of blood) inherited from the Spanish to viciously assassinate thousands of innocents. Once again, this "official vilification" (Torres-Saillant 1998: para. 31) of the Haitians and the intensified stereotype of the Haitian Other united Dominicans in a common identity.

Trujillo exacerbated these tensions by proclaiming his intentions to Dominicanize the border. This program reiterated the image of Trujillo as the defender of the Dominican Republic in general and specifically of its Hispanic culture and Catholic tradition (Moya Pons 1995: 369–70).

"Even the Walls Have Ears"*

Trujillo's use of violence was not limited to the perceived foreign enemy. In September 1930, only a month after he assumed the presidency, a hurricane devastated the country. Trujillo took advantage of the natural

*Aquino 1997: 73

disaster and the people's dependency on the government to strengthen his position. It was also convenient for the new president to dispose of the opposition by adding their bodies to the piles of those killed by the hurricane; the piles were burned in its aftermath (Aquino 1997: 34).

Forcible compliance with the regime was a common practice. Within a little over a year, the disarmed nation was almost entirely subdued. Soon thereafter, the "conversions" of any opposing individuals commenced. Trujillo's tactics were completely thorough, and he successfully eliminated any other individual who might threaten his power.

According to his biographer, Robert D. Crassweller, Trujillo had "a complete absence of scruples" (1966: 77). He was "[c]alculating, ice-cold … a formidable and brutal opponent" (*ibid.*) who possessed a certain element in his character that both drew people to him and frightened them away.

A cornerstone of Trujillo's repressive tactics was *La 42*, a group of terrorists that he had formed during his presidential campaign. *La 42's* sole purpose was to coerce the Dominican population with violence and terror. This band of thugs, named after the 42nd Marine Company, whose job had been to control the people of Santo Domingo during the occupation, traveled through the country in a red Packard that became known as the "Death Car." Dominicans from all walks of life died mysteriously or disappeared without leaving a trace at the hands of *La 42*.

Later in the regime, an intricate spy network, the *Servicio de Inteligencia Militar* (Military Intelligence Service) or SIM was formed. Created in 1957, the SIM was first headed by Arturo Espaillat. Thousands of secret agents known as *calies* worked for the SIM to report real or suspected anti–Trujillo activities. No one was safe from being accused, and even the poorest wretch of society feared that he might find the SIM upon him at any moment, prepared to kill him or carry him off to the interrogation center known as "*La Cuarenta*" or to one of the dreaded prisons.

The SIM became even more feared when Espaillat was replaced by Johnny Abbes, a vicious, heartless man—a kindred spirit of Trujillo. Within two years of taking over the SIM, Abbes, a "latter-day Himmler" (Diederich 1978: 32) was second in power to only the president. Abbes, a man that Trujillo described as " 'a fellow who knows' " (*ibid.* 33), worked diligently to increase both the size and reputation of the SIM. Soon, the spy network was one of the largest and most thorough in all of the Americas.

Every Dominican felt it was possible that he might be the next victim arrested for disloyalty or crimes against the government because of the most innocent statement or action. Often the *calies* would make a seemingly innocent comment, known as a "hook," just to see how another individual would respond to it. This method was used to "catch the fish"— to trap enemies of the government (Aquino 1997: 73).

The worst aspect of the Dominican situation was that one needed not directly criticize the government to be arrested. Insufficient praise of the Benefactor or the regime was deemed unpatriotic and suspicious. Furthermore, the SIM network was so well extended that no one knew if his best friend or relative might be part of it. It was commonly known at the time that "'even the walls have ears'" (Aquino 1997: 73).

A sense of inescapable terror based on true accounts of bloodshed and unimaginable tortures created a pervasive state of panopticism among the Dominican people. According to the model for the Panopticon, Jeremy Bentham's proposed design for the ideal prison, cells with windows should be built surrounding a tower. The tower and cells are constructed in such a way as to allow the observer in the tower to watch the individuals held in the cells, but to keep them from seeing the observer. The prisoners cannot communicate with each other, yet the observer is capable of knowing what each prisoner is doing at all times. Even should the tower observer leave, the prisoners would not know that they were not being watched. It is this uncertainty that makes Bentham's model so effective:

> Hence the major effect of the Panopticon: to induce in the inmate a state of conscious and permanent visibility that assures the automatic functioning of power…. [T]he surveillance is permanent in its effects, even if it is discontinuous in its action…. Power should be visible and unverifiable. Visible: the inmate will constantly have before his eyes the tall outline of the central tower from which he is spied upon. Unverifiable: the inmate must never know whether he is being looked at any one moment; but he must be sure that he may always be so [Foucault 1995: 201].

A personal anecdote related by Miguel Aquino clearly illustrates the panoptic atmosphere of those times. Aquino was riding through the capital city of Santo Domingo in a public transportation car with a group of strangers years after the fall of Trujillo when he heard the following exchange:

> As the vehicle in which we were traveling drew near to the Duarte Bridge, which joins the east and west parts of the capital, one of the passengers exclaimed, "Every time I go across this bridge I am afraid; they haven't repaired it for a long time and I think that one day it will collapse in pieces. […]" That exclamation initiated some comments on the part of others who were basically in agreement with the apprehension expressed by the skeptical passenger. The comment also served as a spark for a lively discussion among all of us who shared the public transportation vehicle.
>
> At that point the driver burst out laughing, noting, "How much things have changed since the death of Trujillo. […]"

> Then he told how a few months before the death of Trujillo, a passenger had made quite a similar comment as the vehicle approached the bridge....
>
> The driver noted that in the time of Trujillo, a comment like that constituted an open criticism of the government which supposedly "didn't maintain the bridge" and the passengers immediately suspected that a calie was tossing out a "hook" to detect those hostile to the regime, and the "suspicious one" alone kept talking, totally ignored by the other passengers....
>
> "The others gazed out the window of the vehicle 'distractedly' and I began to count my coins [...] also pretending not to have heard anything," the driver concluded [Aquino 1997: 74].

No one ever knew who was watching whom or who might arrest whom. No one was safe, for the dictator could turn on even his favorites without notice. The omnipresence of Trujillo was undeniable.

Trujillo did not rely solely on brutality, terror and violence to retain his power. Just as Heureaux had done, Trujillo made use of money, gifts and promotions. The generalissimo believed that everything and everyone had a price, and he was not afraid to dole out any amount needed to achieve his ends. Trujillo needed not only to know he had money with him but to feel it as well, and he carried enormous sums of cash with him wherever he went (Crassweller 1966: 74).

Likewise, politically ambitious individuals were rewarded with positions and promotions if they met with El Jefe's approval. These posts were never certain, for the smallest mistake, the vaguest accusation from some political enemy, or no real reason at all could leave the aspiring politician demoted, without a job, or worse yet, imprisoned or killed.

Those closest to the president were kept under control through any number of psychological games. Trujillo held weekly Sunday luncheons to meet with his chiefs of staff and the secretaries of the armed forces. None of those in attendance knew when El Jefe might call on him to render an account of his recent activities or projects. Commonly, Trujillo would discover some minute loophole in the report and unleash an angry tirade against that individual to humiliate him. Likewise, "Trujillo delighted in playing one aide or officer against another ... [t]o guarantee that the most powerful officials and army officers would never trust each other. They could never unite in common front" (Espaillat 1963: 40–1).

In addition to the tactics used to instill total compliance among the officers and politicians, Trujillo adopted numerous measures to assure the loyalty of the masses. In truth, what El Jefe accomplished during his 30-year rule was a thorough brainwashing of the Dominican people. Textbooks that presented a re-imagined national history lauding the achievements of the dictator began to shape citizens' thoughts at an early age. Trujillo even wrote a textbook for the elementary grades whose themes were primarily patriotic; total loyalty and devotion to the president were also emphasized (Crassweller 1966: 119–20).

Another method that was popular with both the people and Trujillo was the use of various slogans to make the masses feel they identified with the president. Two of the best-known of these were his famous "'And I will remain on horseback ...'" and "'There is no danger in following me ...'" (Aquino 1997: 70). The former hinted at the continuity of the government while the latter served as a reminder that the only danger lay in not following the dictator. Within homes, families often hung pictures of the dictator along with the slogan, "God and Trujillo." The dictator's use of propaganda stretched so far into the depths of Dominican life that "even in front of the Nigua city insane asylum, a sign proclaimed, 'We owe everything to Trujillo'" (Manuel 1995: 102).

Trujillo also gained the support of the populace through his exploitation of the system of *compadrazgo* (godfathers). *El Jefe* offered to baptize any Dominican child, thus becoming his godfather and extending his ties to "relatives" throughout the nation. This tactic, which mirrored the *caudillo*'s system of personal loyalties, allowed Trujillo to strengthen his following by baptizing literally thousands of Dominican babies.

Merengue and the State

Without question, one of the most effective methods of mass control was Trujillo's use of the merengue. So thorough was his appropriation of the dance that by the end of his 30-year rule, it had risen from being a lower-class dance of the *campo* to the hallowed position of the national music of the Dominican Republic. A decree issued in 1936 officially gave merengue that status (Manuel 1995: 102). While various authors have commented on the role of merengue in the Trujillo Era, insufficient emphasis has been placed on the repressive motives behind Trujillo's use of the dance. Commonly, studies emphasize the propagandistic nature of the music (i.e., Austerlitz 1997: 61, 69; del Castillo and García Arévalo 1989: 81; Pacini-Hernández 1995: 42; Wucker 1999b: 45–6). Other arguments point to Trujillo's obsession with humiliating the upper class and maintain that his appropriation of merengue was to antagonize the elite he despised. Finally, Trujillo's own personal preference for the dance as well as his ability to dance the merengue well are considered motives for his use of it (del Castillo and García Arévalo 1989: 81). Austerlitz states that "[h]is talent as a merengue dancer perhaps brought some small solace"

(1997: 68). Incháustegui also points to Trujillo's ego and need for praise and self-aggrandizement since the dictator's merengue abilities are said to have left people commenting on them following dances (*ibid.*).

Although each of these motives may have existed, Trujillo's ultimate reason for imposing the merengue was to more thoroughly control the population and solidify Dominican nationalism over regional identities. It is inconceivable to think that a man who would resort to violence against fellow countrymen of all ages and both genders would impose his will upon the population through music merely to irritate, prove his superiority, or advertise. I agree with Bernarda Jorge's statement that "music was one of the principal ideological means that contributed to reproducing and perpetuating the Trujillo regime" [*la música fue uno de los principales medios ideológicos que contribuyeron a reproducir y perpetuar el régimen trujillista*] (1982: 76).

As we have seen already, Trujillo was sharply astute in matters of human, and particularly Dominican, psychology. The mind games *El Jefe* played on those involved in the regime, including his favorites, reveal that he believed he was completely capable of manipulating even peoples' thought, and the sense of panopticism created by the terror in the nation proves he was correct.

According to Batista Matos, the idea to associate Trujillo with merengue and by extension with the masses belongs to Rafael Vidal, a political strategist who "had done some studies on the merengue and even published a brief essay, and glimpsed the powerful effect that having typical merengueros accompany Trujillo would have" [*había hecho algunos estudios sobre el merengue, e incluso publicado un breve ensayo, y vislumbró el golpe de efecto de hacer acompañar a Trujillo de merengueros típicos*] (1999: iii). Trujillo himself was well aware of the possibilities merengue presented for unifying the Cibao, the whitest region as well as the one where the most members of the upper class resided (Austerlitz 1997: 64). Trujillo had already witnessed firsthand the nationalistic sentiments that arose during the U.S. occupation. Having seen for himself how even the U.S. military government of the occupation was weakened by the nationalistic cultural movement built around merengue, he no doubt knew that the music, if left uncontrolled, could be a threat to him. As John Fiske comments,

> Anything out of control is always a potential threat, and always calls up moral, legal, and aesthetic powers to discipline it.... The signs of the subordinate out of control terrify the forces of order ... for they constitute a constant reminder of both how fragile social control is and how it is resented; they demonstrate how escaping social control, even momentarily, produces a sense of freedom [1989: 69].

Merengue, traditionally subversive and by nature critical of any number of themes, could have easily posed a threat to Trujillo's power.

Judith Hanna notes that "[d]ance is an intimate and constitutive aspect of cultural identity, and like language, is a window to a person's world view" (1992: 179). Since dancing had always been a popular pastime in the Dominican Republic, Trujillo took advantage of his people's world view by identifying a common and favorite practice with the regime. As Averill points out, "[t]he powerful appeal of music—its engagement with human emotions—is the reason it serves effectively as an instrument of politics and a medium of power" (1997: 19). Although some Dominicans realized the propagandistic nature of the lyrics, they could still find the music itself aesthetically pleasing (Austerlitz 1997: 61). Dominicans were able to enjoy a popular social practice as a means of dealing with the oppression under which they lived—a momentary "sense of freedom" (Fiske 1989: 69) from the harsh and terrifying reality of their daily existence.

The dictator was also well acquainted with the rhetoric of the Dominican Hispanophilic identity to which the nation had so long ascribed. Nevertheless, as his use of light-colored makeup and the occasional voodoo curse illustrates, he found within himself the inherent contradictions in Dominican ethnicity. As Duara points out, "nationalists always have to engage with their many histories, even when they are manipulating them for their own purposes" (1996: 156). Trujillo found in the Creole creation known as the merengue a symbol with flexible boundaries that could be representative of all his people and communicate with all of them, despite their differences in ethnicity, class and livelihood.

Just as he had centralized a government that had been based on regional loyalties, Trujillo adopted one version of merengue, the merengue *cibaeño*, as representative of the entire Dominican Republic. This practice is not uncommon to groups with varying identities, for "political actors can take advantage of the disagreements within different communities about claims of authenticity, selectively choosing one voice and calling it paradigmatic" (Mattern 1998: 20). By imposing one specific version of the dance that had already enjoyed some popularity, Trujillo was able to overcome the diversities of the Dominican Republic—regional, social, and ethnic—to join all in an apparent commonality.

Becoming a proponent of merengue won Trujillo popularity with the masses through the populist musical symbol because they saw that their leader was dancing their music and that he was forcing the elite to dance it as well. For the dance to appeal to the upper class, Trujillo chose the variation of the dance from the Cibao, the whitest region of the country, and emphasized the music's use of the *copla* and the *décima*, traditional forms of Spanish poetry, to strengthen the notion that merengue was a primarily European musical form. As we shall see, musical alterations made to merengue helped it to eventually gain a following among the elite as well. Trujillo's choice was astutely based on questions of ethnicity, class, and history, and elements of everyday Dominican life.

Merengue was an integral part of the Trujillo political machine even before he assumed office. During his first bid for the presidency, merengue bands accompanied Trujillo on his campaign, performing merengues that assured the crowds of great days to come under Trujillo's leadership. "*Se acabó la bulla*" ("The Racket Is Over"), written by Isidoro Flores in 1930, commemorated the political change that had taken place with Trujillo's election and proclaimed a glorious future. The song's lyrics are obviously propagandistic in nature, for they support a single-party totalitarian state:

Horacio salió y ahora entra Trujillo.	Horacio left and now Trujillo is in.
Tenemo' esperanzas en nuestro Caudillo;	We have hope in our Caudillo;
todo cambiará en marcha caliente,	everything will change with great speed,]
pues ahora Trujillo es el Presidente	because now Trujillo is President
[repite].	[repeat].
Se acabó la bulla, se acabó;	The racket's over, it's over;
se acaba'n los guapos, se acabó;	The bullies are finished, it's over;
ni "Co'lú" ni "Bolo";	No more "*Coludos*," nor "*Bolos*";
se acabó eso de partidos, se acabó	The political parties are finished,
[repite].	it's over [repeat].

[Rivera González 1960 vol. 3: 10–11]

Certainly the "racket" was over, for the former parties—the *Coludos* and the *Bolos*—had been efficiently eliminated and permanently silenced, and no one would dare raise a contradictory voice under the new regime. This example from the beginning of the Trujillo Era reveals that the very nature of merengue had changed as the music "lost its subversive character to openly support the established regime" (Duany 1994a: 73).

To make the music more appealing to the upper class as well as to "better reflect his new social context and ... turn it into a symbol of the power and modernity of his regime" (Pacini-Hernández 1995: 39),

Trujillo hired musician Luis Alberti and his ensemble, *La Lira del Yaque*, as his personal band in 1935. When merengue music was first performed in the capital, the city's residents were appalled to hear it, but no one was brave enough to question *El Jefe*'s musical preferences, so they endured.

Alberti brought about several innovations to merengue. As other composers had done at the time of the U.S. occupation, Alberti incorporated aspects of Dominican folk merengue into his compositions. He also replaced the accordion and guitar with the saxophone, clarinet, or trumpet in order to distance the music from its rural origins (del Castillo and García Arévalo 1989: 82). A new, introductory *paseo* section was added as well, which allowed couples to "model their glamorous attire across the entire ballroom" [*modelar su glamorosa apariencia por todo el salón*] (*ibid.* 32).

Alberti and his band soon became Trujillo's favorite, an honor that carried with it some difficulties, as the bandleader often had to break previously scheduled engagements when the dictator suddenly took a whim to hear the group perform. Alberti was no fool and "to the raging demands of the organizers of ruined dances, maestro Alberti gave only one intelligent answer: 'reasons of a higher force'" (del Castillo and García Arévalo 1989: 82). In 1944, Alberti and his *Orquesta Presidente Trujillo* were "convinced" to move to Trujillo's hometown, San Cristóbal, which he had made into "the mecca of music" [*la meca de la música*] (Batista Matos 1999: 36). At this time, the orchestra was renamed *la Orquesta Generalísimo*.

Despite the discomfort no doubt created by such changes in schedule, location and name, Alberti was in the fortunate position of having Trujillo's support and backing. For this reason, the leader and his band became extremely popular and well known throughout the nation. Musical historians now point to Alberti as the musician who played the greatest role in establishing the merengue as the Dominican national dance.

While this new style of merengue made it somewhat more palatable to the elite, the innovations created a division in the music that followed class lines. The traditional, accordion-based merengue was known as *merengue típico cibaeño* while the salon version was called *merengue de orquesta*. The former remained popular among the lower class while the upper class preferred the sound of the latter. With its variations, salon merengue was somewhat like the generalissimo himself: in essence, a dance of the *campo* with African elements covered over with lighter make-up.

In spite of this cleft, both styles of merengue were performed at public concerts held outdoors, which brought the elite and the lower classes into common company. Even though the two classes might be divided at other times, these concerts created at least one setting where a sense of *dominicanidad* could reach across such boundaries. The theme of things

Dominican and the communal experience of all classes listening to both merengues solidified a sense of a shared Dominican existence. As John Dewey points out, "'Works of art that are not remote from common life, that are widely enjoyed in a community, are signs of a unified collective life. But they are also marvelous aids in the creation of such a life'" (Mattern 1998: 15).

Trujillo's participation in the musical life of the nation extended even to instruction. Various musical academies were opened, as well as a musical conservatory. The dictator founded a symphonic orchestra and a national choir. Several new auditoriums were opened for musical performance during the Era, and the state also sponsored composition contests (Jorge 1982: 76).

Music, like the numerous statues, monuments, bridges and other structures built in Trujillo's honor and the many sites named after him, was an omnipresent reminder of the dictator's power. Composers were expected (and at times forced) to write merengues extolling the many great qualities of the Benefactor and his policies and actions. Panopticism was also a motivator, for composers feared what might befall them should their works not contain enough themes about *El Jefe* or the state. This same fear was present at parties or performances. Trujillo's favorite merengue, entitled "*Canto a San Cristóbal*" after his hometown, became a required piece wherever any musical group might play (Batista Matos 1999: 40).

Since "[d]ance requires the same underlying brain faculty for conceptualization, creative expression, and memory as verbal language" (Hanna 1992: 177), the multitude of merengues comprised a constant musical message about Trujillo—his power, his greatness, and most importantly, his very presence. Because of its pervasiveness, merengue invaded the very psychology of the Dominican people, reminding them that even leisure activities such as parties were under the ultimate control of the state. Keeping in mind Hanna's assertion that an individual's body and how he uses it become his one source of power in circumstances when he has "few material possessions and little power," it is clear that Trujillo in essence stripped his people of that last realm of self control. "Society," writes Judith Hanna, "inscribes itself on the body, the body incorporates social meaning, and the individual minds the body" (1992: 191). The themes of the official music—in fact, the mere existence of an official music itself— reminded the population that even its dancing body was controlled. In this way, the threat of imprisonment, torture, and death—loss of power over the body—was reinforced.

At the same time, Trujillo astutely chose an activity that served handily as an escape valve for any tensions that might arise among the people.

Dance's sense of "spontaneity, freedom … [and] sensuality" provided the illusion of momentary liberation even as Dominicans danced to an official state music in a totalitarian state, thus adhering to a "structured form and set order" (Daniel 1995: 147).

Certainly, the different themes of merengues functioned as tools of propaganda for actions, policies or works of the time, speaking to all Dominicans whether literate or illiterate. Numerous compositions sang the praises and glory of the Benefactor and his policies. If Trujillo built a new monument, a merengue was composed to commemorate the occasion. Likewise, his honorary title of Doctor Honoris Causa became both the subject and title of a 1934 merengue by Luis Horacio Payán:

The formation of the official state party, the *Partido Dominicano*, merited yet another composition that reiterated that all "good citizens" should join:

Partido se ha formado	A party has been formed,
el que debemos seguir	the one we should follow
con fé, honradez, y altura,	with faith, honor and nobleness,
sabiéndolo mantener.	knowing how to maintain it.
Partido que es como un credo	It's a party that's like the creed
de todo buen ciudadano	of every good citizen,
pues que Trujillo es emblema	for Trujillo is the emblem
de todo dominicano.	of every Dominican.
Partido Dominicano	*Partido Dominicano*
nuestra única razón	our only reason
pues Trujillo lo ha fundado	for Trujillo has founded it
para bien de la nación.	for the good of the nation.
Todo el que es buen ciudadano	May everyone who is a good citizen
y tiene gran corazón,	and has a big heart
que se inscriba en el Partido	become part of the party
para el bien de la nación.	for the good of the nation.

["*Partido Dominicano*" by Julio Alberto Hernández, in Rivera González 1960 vol. 2: 16]

When it came time for reelection, merengues begged the general to run again since "if another President takes over, the nation is lost" [*si viene otro Presidente, pues se pierde la nación*] ("*Le Reelección*" by Toño Abreu, cited *ibid.* vol. 1: 24). Pedro N. Pérez's 1947 composition "*Y seguiré a caballo*" helped to immortalize and spread the popular slogan:

"*Y seguiré a caballo*"—	"I will continue on horseback"—
eso dijo el General.	that's what the General said.
"*Y seguiré a caballo*"	"I will continue on horseback"—

le dijo a la comisión.	he told the commission.
Y ella muy orgullosa	And the commission is pleased
interpreta la expresión	as it interprets the saying
porque siguiendo a caballo	because, by continuing on horseback,
sigue salva la nación.	the nation remains safe.
Y el pueblo orgulloso	And the proud people
aclama al Benefactor	applaud the Benefactor
insiste en que él acepte	and insist that he accept
la nueva postulación.	the new nomination.
Y lleva en su alma	And the people carry in their soul
la frase del inmortal	the phrase of the immortal leader
dice "y seguiré a caballo"—	who says "I will continue on horseback"—
Gloria, gloria al General.	Glory, glory be to the General.

[Rivera González 1960 vol. 3: 86–87]

Some of these compositions had a limited life due to the immediacy of their themes. Others were more enduring. Among those that remained popular from the time it was composed in 1945 until Trujillo's death was the aforementioned *"Canto a San Cristóbal"* by Rafael Colón. All questions of musical preference aside, this merengue, written in honor of Trujillo's hometown, was a constant at any party or gathering, whether the general was in attendance or not. No one wanted to be accused of lack of loyalty to *El Jefe* by not including it in the evening's repertoire.

San Cristóbal, cuna de nuestro Caudillo,	San Cristóbal, birthplace of our Strongman,
el gran hombre que ha salvado la nación:	the great man who has saved the nation:
gloria eterna de todo dominicano	eternal glory of every Dominican,
pues le ha dado a su pueblo el corazón.	for it has given the people their heart.
San Cristóbal hay que admirar tu grandeza	San Cristóbal, one has to admire your greatness,
como bien te lo mereces—marchas ya	as you well deserve it—you're already marching
muy delante de toda ciudad moderna	far ahead of all modern cities,
y esas glorias te las dio el General.	and the General gave you this glory.

[Rivera Gonzalez 1960 vol. 1: 76–77]

The border with Haiti was a merengue theme on more than one occasion. In 1935, Julio Alberto Hernández penned *"El acuerdo fronterizo"* ("The Border Agreement") to mark the establishment of the border:

Dominicanos, ya se arregló el problema,	Dominicans, the problem has been fixed,
ese problema que nadie osó arreglar,	that problem no one dared to fix,
pero Trujillo, capaz de grandes cosas,	but Trujillo, capable of great things
con gran inteligencia lo pudo remediar.	was able to remedy it with great intelligence.
Una obra, Patria, el acuerdo fronterizo.	A great work, Homeland, the border agreement.
Ahora vivimos con gran tranquilidad,	Now we live in great tranquility,
pues para el bien de la Patria sí lo hizo	Because for the good of the Homeland, yes, he did it
con sabia inteligencia y con toda integridad....	With wise intelligence and all integrity....

[Rivera González 1960 vol. 2: 32–33]

Five years later, Julio Eladio Pérez would compose "*Trujillo en la frontera*" (Trujillo at the Border). This merengue, written in the form of a thank-you note from the inhabitants of the border, emphasized that Trujillo's policies (no doubt including the brutal massacre of 1937) had allowed the *fronterizos* (people of the border) to live in peace and had brought progress to the region.

While some merengues dealt with new monuments in honor of the dictator and with his great acts, a composition of the mid– to late–1950s celebrated the new product, *Pega Palo*, a Dominican vine that supposedly increased virility (Espaillat 1963: 45–6). Still others commemorated extending the vote to women ("*El Voto y la mujer*" by Cármen Ariel, in Rivera González 1960 vol. 3: 60–61) and the country's self-sufficiency in the production of rice ("*Arroz dominicano*" by Julio Alberto Hernández, *ibid.* vol. 2: 42–43). So numerous were the merengues composed during the 30 years of the Trujillo Era that Rivera González's *Antología musical de la era de Trujillo, 1930–1960* contains some 300 of them alone. For this reason, special attention has been called to but a few.

These merengues were a form of propaganda to convince the people of the numerous "good" things the government was doing for them and to bombard them with the "necessity" of preventing any change that might disrupt such peace and prosperity. More importantly, merengue's main role was that of extending the iron-fisted control of a single man over the entire Dominican population. Merengues dealing with such numerous and various themes could only reinforce and communicate the truth: that Trujillo was involved in every imaginable aspect of Dominican life.

Merengue and Mass Media

The modern inventions of radio and television were an added benefit that the *caudillos* of olden days had not had at their disposal, and Trujillo became a master at exploiting these forms of mass communication. As Batista Matos points out, "the greatest determining factors in the national turning towards the merengue, at the beginning of the decade of the 1940s, would be: the new orchestral paradigm, the radio, the record, and above all, the frightening will of Trujillo" [*Los factores más determinantes en el repunte nacional del merengue, al inicio de la década de 1940, serían: el nuevo marco orquestral, la radio, el disco, y sobre todo, la temible voluntad de Trujillo*] (1999: 33).

It was especially helpful to the dictator that his brother José "Petán" Arismendi Trujillo was a music enthusiast who launched his own radio station, *La Voz del Yuna* (The Voice of the Yuna, named after a Dominican river), in 1942. Although Trujillo had his own state-sponsored station at the time, Petán's quickly became the leader of all mass media in spreading official propaganda. In 1945, Petán moved the station to Ciudad Trujillo and changed its name to *La Voz Dominicana* (The Dominican Voice). In truth, *La Voz Dominicana* was the government's voice, transmitting the official view of national and international news, dictating the choice of music and other leisure programs, and spreading propaganda.

Petán was an avid fan of music. His preference was for live music, and he employed numerous bands to play live on the radio. One of these, the *Super Orquesta San José*, became extremely successful because of the North American big-band influences present in its style. This ensemble, whose merengue was spicier and faster than that of Luis Alberti, showcased Joseíto Mateo, "The King of Merengue," as lead vocalist. Another member of the orchestra, the young Johnny Ventura, was just setting out on the path to what would be a tremendously successful musical career.

La Voz Dominicana transmitted both *merengue típico cibaeño* and *merengue de orquesta*, thus exposing radio listeners to both styles. One of the most successful *típico* groups was the *Reynoso Trío*, one of the first ensembles to bring that style to the capital. Presentation was central to this group's performances: band members went barefoot to project a rural image and omitted the saxophone for the same reason (Austerlitz 1997: 62).

Radio access also allowed the Dominican people to experience Latin musical forms, and these became popular on the island as well. It became common practice for *merengueros* to remake foreign hits as merengues that were quite successful.

In 1952, *La Voz Dominicana* expanded into television broadcasting. This new medium opened other doors for merengue. Since bands could now be seen, a new emphasis was placed on appearance and choreography. The most recent dance steps became the latest rage, and Joseíto Mateo was among the leaders in this type of innovation. As del Castillo and García Arévalo admit, "[t]hose of us who were young men then practiced the new steps introduced by Joseíto in order to show-off later in the ballrooms of the clubs or private parties" (1989: 83).

Another television station, *Rahintel*, was founded in 1958, thus creating even more opportunities for *merengueros*. One of the most popular *Rahintel* programs, "*La hora del moro*," was hosted by Rafael Solano. This program highlighted aspiring performers of various styles of music. Solano, who would go on to achieve international fame for his own compositions, also used the program to showcase his own talented orchestra.

As in all forms of media, the content of radio and television programs was closely monitored and was determined by the state. All media were careful to keep their programming in line with the regime. Nevertheless, the most effective form of censorship was self-censorship, for panoptic fear was quite sufficient to frighten broadcasters into transmitting nothing but praise for the dictator and his regime. In this way, Trujillo effectively manipulated all forms of mass communications and used them to the benefit of the state.

It was the possibilities afforded by modern media that differentiated the Trujillo regime from those of the nineteenth-century *caudillos* who had preceded him. Santana, Báez and Heureaux held power through pure force and personal loyalties. Mass media made possible the psychological manipulation of the greater population. By transmitting the new forms, the improved communications also dictated culture, and these imposed patterns upheld the regime. In addition to the official news and other praises, the numerous merengues written in honor of and about *El Jefe* efficiently diffused word of his greatness throughout the country.

The use of mass media to spread merengue and its various messages also contributed to the growth of a Dominican national identity by creating a conception of simultaneity and a sense of the larger group. As in Anderson's example of newspapers and journals, an individual listening to merengue on the radio or seeing it performed on television was subconsciously aware of the body of other Dominicans listening to or watching those same programs. In this way, " '[m]usic seems to be a key to identity because it offers, so intensely, a sense of both self and others, of the subjective in the collective' " (Simon Frith, cited in Morris 1999:194). The sense of collectivity occurs "within 'virtual' time, outside the flow of time associated with day-to-day living" (Averill 1997: 20), thereby creating a sense of unity with Dominicans of all times and locations.

Truijllo's isolationism extended even to the music industry. By limiting Dominicans' exposure to many forms of outside music, Trujillo succeeded in intensifying the practice of merengue; this solidified the genre's place as the national music of the Dominican Republic in the political discourse as well as in the Dominicans' hearts.

Television and radio programs, like the newspapers in Anderson's study, are a "cultural product" (1991: 33). Therefore, including songs with certain themes (praise of the Benefactor, nationalism, need for the generalissimo, the end of political party tensions, etc.), while excluding others whose attitudes contradict these topics, re-enforced those songs' place within the nation.

The Dominican recording industry had a slow start because of Petán's preference for live music. The first recordings were made at *La Voz del Partido* radio station on a homemade recording machine designed and built by Juan Sálazar Hernández that incorporated "a steering wheel, sewing machine parts and watch parts" (Austerlitz 1997: 72). This contraption was used to record a handful of merengues in 1936.

The first real step in the Dominican recording industry was made at sea in 1941 when Leopold Stokowski was visiting the Dominican Republic. The national music interested Stokowski, and he invited Luis Alberti and his *Orquesta Presidente Trujillo* aboard his personal ship, which had its own small recording studio. Stokowski invited Alberti to make a recording at sea, and Alberti accepted the offer. The release, which consisted of 20 songs of which some five were merengues, was first produced on Columbia Records.

Petán eventually got into the recording business himself when he purchased a Fairchild system in 1947. Once Petán had founded the Dominican Recording Company and the label Caracol Records, Trujillo immediately passed a law prohibiting the importation of foreign records. The Trujillo family's involvement in the music industry spread the terror of the regime to that realm as well. Others who might have been interested in recording were frightened away, and for this reason the Dominican Republic did not follow the same path of development in this area that other countries did (Austerlitz 1997: 72).

Merengue Abroad

Because of Trujillo's policy of isolationism, merengue developed very differently outside the country. Very few Dominicans were allowed to travel abroad, and likewise, musicians were seldom permitted to make foreign performances or tours. Some musicians immigrated to other countries where they began their own bands. Of these, one of the most popular and successful was *Conjunto Típico Cibaeño*, an ensemble established by Angel Viloria in New York. Contrary to what its name suggests, the band did not play *merengue típico cibaeño*. Its music was a combination of the two styles of merengue, with its instrumentation resembling that of *típico* ensembles and its style similar to that of salon merengue. Viloria's New York releases grew to be the most popular merengues outside of the homeland. Viloria and the *Conjunto Típico Cibaeño* did not achieve much popularity back home in the Dominican Republic because of the Trujillo family's control of the music industry as well as the censorship of external elements (Austerlitz 1995: 74–75).

Various other orchestras spread merengue around the world. Napoleón Zayas and his orchestra carried the sound of merengue internationally, playing in prestigious locations in the United States and throughout Europe; Zayas even performed with Duke Ellington. A duet composed of Simón Damirón on piano and vocalist Negrito Chapuseaux was presented live as well as on radio and television around the world. Dominican Billo Frómeta and his ensemble, Billo's Caracas Boys, became the most sought-after dance band in Venezuela (*ibid.*).

Trujillo, always the great propagandist, recognized the success that the emigrants' merengue was achieving internationally. For the 1955 *Feria de la paz y la confraternidad del mundo libre* (Fair of Peace and Brotherhood in the Free World), he hired Xavier Cugat and his New York City Latin band to cut a record of more-cosmopolitan merengues (*ibid.*).

The Beginning of the End

The 1955 *Feria de la paz y la confraternidad del mundo libre*, organized with the purpose of demonstrating to nationals and internationals alike what 25 years of Trujilloism had done for the Dominican Republic, turned out to be the first chip in the foundation of the regime. The numerous construction projects carried out for the fair cost the country dearly, and the event produced only a small portion of the anticipated revenue. The financial stability of the nation was often touted by the regime, but following the Fair, that same level of stability would never again be reached during the Era of Trujillo (Crassweller 1966: 298).* A chain of events slowly

*A 1942 merengue by Pedro Nestor Pérez ["*Pueblo libre* (Free People)"] celebrated this erasure of the nation's debts, crediting Trujillo for this achievement. (Rivera González 1960 vol. 1: 56–57)

began to unleash long pent-up tensions, setting in motion a plan that would bring the decades of a violent dictatorship to a violent end.

By 1955, "[m]any things invisible and intangible had reached their plateau. Among them was the attrition of the Dominican soul, a process which often left the outer walls intact, like those beached sea shells whose inner substance has departed upon out-flowing tides. With the deep essences lost, Dominicans were mere reflections" (Crassweller 1966: 289). Trujillo had successfully accomplished the complete manipulation of Dominican thought, and though his rule was entering its final stages, on the eve of the fair he was still in total control of the government as well as the people.

The Trujillo Era would be remembered for its peace, prosperity, and stability, as well as for its cultural contributions. Ironically, one of the bloodiest dictatorships in all of Latin American history coincided with the golden age of the national music; it was a time when merengue was synonymous with repression.

Trujillo was highly conscious of his role as forger of a Dominican national identity. No longer were there regional or party identities that were held as more sacred than identification with the nation. Furthermore, the Dominican people were solidly self-defined in opposition to their neighbor to the west, and national territory was imagined as safe within Dominicanized borders. Trujillo's address at the dedication of the 1955 fair emphasizes these achievements:

> I received in 1930 a Republic which lacked some of its essential attributes as a sovereign entity; today I present it to history as a nation without the ties which limit its actions, with full financial autonomy and standing on a basis of equality with the freest nations of the world.
>
> There was delivered to me a people with a weak sense of identity, with their territory still undefined, and today I offer to my fellow-citizens a country the demarcation of whose frontiers has been completed with a fruitful human achievement through religion, culture and work....
>
> That is, in summary, the patriotic achievement of the Era which national gratitude has baptized with my name.... I submit myself today to history. The verdict of posterity does not worry me because I have not failed the hopes of my people in the exercise of my duty and in the force of my will. The increasing greatness of the nation will be my best witness in the hour of the final judgment of history [cited and translated in Crassweller 1966: 295–6].

Trujillo, such an accomplished manipulator of the thoughts of others, himself believed that which he told the public. Some truth can be found in his claims to greatness, for it is certain that Trujillo achieved what none of the previous *caudillos* had been able to do. He centralized Dominican politics and consolidated a national Dominican identity. Nevertheless, the blood with which that identity was purchased is read only between the lines of the generalissimo's emotional discourse. It was but a matter of time before the outrage over that spilled blood would rise to the forefront and force recompense.

7

Post-Trujillo Politics: Continuity and Change

"On the night of May 30, 1961, Rafael Leonidas Trujillo Molina, Generalissimo of the Dominican Republic, ruthless assassin of hundreds of enemies, absolute dictator of more than three million people, was shot to death on a highway in the southwestern outskirts of Ciudad Trujillo."
—Diederich 1978: xiii

A series of events that began soon after the 1955 fair caused silent yet strong opposition to Trujilloism to mount. Various groups whispered among themselves of overthrowing the government, either with or without assassinating the dictator. Although most of these conspiracies were nothing more than mere talk that was hushed by fear or definitively silenced by the government, one band of conspirators eventually succeeded in bringing *El Jefe* and his 30-year reign of terror to a bloody end.

When news of Trujillo's death spread, the Dominican people "asked themselves: does this mean the end of the era of Trujillo, all we have known for thirty-one years, or will the same old merengue continue without the band losing a beat, even with the bandleader dead?" (Diederich 1978: 173).

Politically as well as musically, both change and continuity were in the air. The national music would embark once again on a separate yet parallel path to politics as it had in the decades before Trujillo inextricably joined merengue to the state. Trujillo's successors did not share *El Jefe's* passion for the music and were uninterested in controlling the genre or its production and distribution. Although merengue would still be influenced by national and local political and social matters, the music was at last free to enter again into a two-way exchange of influences with history.

Some elements of both politics and music would remain the same in the decades following the Era of Trujillo, yet others would change dramatically, and the passage of time was to reveal that liberty was to become much more of a reality in the latter elements.

Silent Opposition

The first link in the chain of events that led to the end of the Era of Trujillo involved a Spanish loyalist, Jesús de Galíndez, who had fled to the Dominican Republic in 1939. Galíndez served for a while as an instructor in the Diplomatic School and was also the Labor Department's legal advisor. In one way or another, he eventually fell into disfavor with Trujillo, and in 1946 he fled again, this time to New York. There, Galíndez was involved in various activist groups while teaching at Columbia University and working on a doctoral degree in history. As part of his degree program, Galíndez made the fatal mistake of choosing to write his dissertation on the Era of Trujillo. Trujillo was thoroughly outraged and far from honored, in spite of the fact that Galíndez actually concluded his dissertation by acknowledging what he considered to be some of the positive aspects of the regime. What most infuriated Trujillo was that Galíndez planned to defend his dissertation on February 27, Dominican Independence Day.

Although nothing has been proven to this day to link the events of March 12, 1956, to Trujillo, it is certain that Galíndez entered a New York City subway station that night and was never seen again. Numerous clues abounded, but they were conflicting and led nowhere. Prior to that night, Galíndez, fearing violence of some sort against himself, had given a final copy of his dissertation to a Chilean friend who passed it on to a publisher in his home country. The revealing manuscript was printed in spite of Galíndez's unexplained disappearance and probable murder. The book enjoyed tremendous success, so news of the Galíndez case spread and created an "international clamor against the tyranny and turned into a cause célèbre which, over the long run had much to do with the demise of the regime" (Aquino 1997: 47).

One of the most crucial events of the late 1950s was the attempted invasion of the Republic by Dominican rebels in Cuba. Although Castro had received aid from Trujillo in the revolution, he intensely disliked the Dominican dictator and was more than willing to aid the rebels. The invasion was no secret to Trujillo, and it was easily put down when the rebels struck on June 14, 1959. Nevertheless, the attempt inspired a highly secret underground movement in the Dominican Republic, and from this failure the movement took its name: *Catorce de Junio* (1J4), or "June 14." Encouraged by the determination of the rebels, numerous conspiracies against the dictator's life began to be planned both within and outside the borders.

Trujillo's involvement in a 1959 plot to kill Venezuelan president Rómulo Betancourt brought intense international disapproval. Betancourt was an active supporter of Dominican exiles in his country who were planning an invasion and the subsequent overthrow of the Trujillo government. After Betancourt was wounded by a Dominican secret agent's attack on his life, a commission was convened by the Organization of American States (OAS) to decide what measures should be taken against Trujillo. Venezuelan representatives clamored for a break of diplomatic relations with the Dominican Republic by all member nations and the imposition of harsh economic sanctions. The United States, however, feared that any extreme measures taken, while tending Trujillo's rule, might also pave the way for communism in the form of Castroism (Crassweller 1966: 418). The final OAS decision called for diplomatic relations with the Dominican Republic to cease and for partial sanctions to be implemented against the nation. The traditionally cordial relations Trujillo had enjoyed with the United States cooled after this, and the Dominican Republic was left in isolation in the New World, condemned by sister nations of Latin America as well.

A pastoral letter signed by the Dominican Republic's six bishops and read in Sunday masses throughout the country on February 5, 1960, marked the first time in 30 years that the Catholic Church dared to oppose the dictator. The letter took an official stance against the government's violence and repression. Given the Church's influence over the Dominican population, this proclamation was a daring move. Other such pastoral letters had been responsible for the fall of at least three dictatorships in Latin America, but Trujillo responded with an iron will, refusing to be the fourth. Eventually, he forced the Church to write another letter that stated its regret for the "ecclesiastical imprudence" (Crassweller 1969: 389) that the first epistle had demonstrated. Once angered, Trujillo was not one to forget or forgive. He plotted his own revenge by hiring someone to kill the Pope by giving him the evil eye (*ibid.*, 393), and on May 30, 1961, the very night of *El Jefe*'s death, an order went out to take prisoner the six

Joaquín Balaguer, left, priest Luis G. Posada, center, and Rafael Trujillo smile in a photograph whose date is unknown. Trujillo, who ruled from 1930 to 1961, enjoyed almost the continuous support of the Dominican Catholic Church. In 1960, a pastoral letter condemning the regime's atrocities was read in churches nationwide. Although Trujillo quickly squelched the sentiments behind it, this temporary show of disapproval was one in a series of events that eventually led to the downfall of the regime. (Photograph: AP)

bishops. Vice-president Balaguer revoked the order the next day before it could be put into action.

Meanwhile, a gruesome crime brought about what was perhaps the greatest reaction among the Dominican people: the brutal murder of the Mirabal sisters. These three women had been involved in 14 activities and had also spent time as political prisoners, enduring atrocities and tortures. Their husbands, three of the movement's leaders, were arrested. Eventually, two of the sisters' husbands were transferred to a prison in Puerto Plata near where they lived. The Mirabal sisters were allowed to visit, and they made the trip from Santiago to Puerto Plata daily. The SIM took advantage of this predictable routine and ambushed their vehicle on their trip home. The three sisters were separated and dragged off to be killed, along with their driver. Once the vile job was finished, SIM agents pushed their jeep over the mountainous road and threw the bodies after it in an attempt to make the brutal murders appear to be nothing more than a motor vehicle accident.

Trujillo, so convincing in his theatrical lies, called in the acting chief of the SIM the next morning. "'Don't you know what happened last night?' he asked. 'Do me the favor of investigating the matter at once, before they begin to accuse the government of doing it'" (Crassweller 1966: 403). Two months later, on a visit to Santiago, Trujillo took an evening walk along the road where the women had been slaughtered. As Crassweller relates,

> [w]ith him was an intimate associate who knew the details of the Mirabal assassinations. Trujillo paused, gazing silently over the precipice and down the deep slope. Then, to the eerie surprise of his companion, he said, "This is where the Mirabal women died—a horrible crime that foolish people blame the government for. Such good women, and so defenseless!" [*ibid.*].

The cold-blooded murder of the Mirabal sisters struck the Dominicans as none other of Trujillo's crimes had. Resentment grew, though fear of *El Jefe* and the SIM still prevailed.

The Conspiracy

Of the numerous groups that considered the overthrow of the government in hushed tones and uttermost secret, almost none would have been able to bring about the dictator's downfall or to initiate a new government (Diederich 1978: 43). One group, however, was able to establish ties with a United States contact living and working in the Dominican Republic. This band of dissidents consisted of upper-class individuals, many of who had once or still occupied positions in the Trujillo regime. They did not espouse any single political stance, for in truth,

> [t]his was a plot in which *compadrazgo* ..., not ideology, would bind its members. Ideology was exactly what the conspirators lacked. Conserva-

tives, they had no definite political theory. They feared communism and Castroism as much, if not more, than Trujilloism. All had personal scores to settle, or fears of Trujillo's wrath to come [*ibid.*, 63].

Once the United Stated had ceased to view Trujillo as "our S.O.B" during the Eisenhower administration, the prevailing attitude was that it would be best to accelerate the end of the Trujillo regime in hopes of preventing the fall of another Caribbean nation to communism. In 1960, a United States force known as the Special Group, formed to oversee covert CIA actions, began to investigate the possibility of supplying aid to Dominican dissidents (Diederich 1978: 40).

Through carefully guarded relations, the CIA promised the conspirators weapons to be used to end the dictatorship. The group began to discuss possible plans in earnest then, for although each of its members was allowed to possess weapons because of his privileged position, the promised North American arms provided them with the psychological assurance of support. After all, there was still the rest of the Trujillo family to consider upon the death of the dictator.

Eventually, the conspirators settled on a plan to follow Trujillo on his usual weekly visit to his home in San Cristóbal. Convinced of the powerful grip of terror he held on the nation, *El Jefe* always made the trip alone with only his driver. This would be the easiest time to take Trujillo by surprise. Once the act was done, General José René "Pupo" Román, secretary of the armed forces, would use his position and troops to proclaim a civilian-military junta that would rule until elections were held. Román was wary of involving himself in the plan, however, and insisted that he see the corpse of the dictator before proclaiming a coup; it would not do to take any risks.

As the plot became better articulated, the conspirators lost the U.S. support they had been counting on. Following the failed Bay of Pigs invasion, President Kennedy feared that should the assassination attempt go awry, conditions in the Caribbean might be such as to usher in another Communist regime. Kennedy believed that "'The United States should not initiate the overthrow of Trujillo before knowing what kind of government would succeed him'" (Diederich 1978: 92).

By this time, the conspirators were too deeply involved to halt their plans. They watched and waited tensely for the perfect moment, and it came at last on the night of May 30, 1961. Trujillo's vehicle was ambushed as planned, though he engaged his attackers in an intense exchange of gunfire and wounded several before crumpling at last to the pavement, dead.

Although the plan succeeded in ending the brutal dictator's life, the rest of its pieces slowly began to fall apart in the next few hours. Arturo Espaillat, a member of Trujillo's cabinet, was on his way to a nearby restaurant when he heard gunshots and remembered that Trujillo had just passed in his vehicle. Espaillat sped down the highway, and upon seeing the carnage on the road, went directly to the second most powerful man in the nation, General Román. As Espaillat himself admits, Román "should have shot me. When we walked out of his house he doomed his coup and himself. I was the only one who knew Trujillo had been assassinated" (1963: 20).

But at that crucial moment, Román was unable to overcome the intense psychological control that Trujillo had established over the Dominican people. So Román did not shoot Espaillat; instead, he followed him to the scene of the assassination, and when his fellow conspirators arrived at his home with the corpse of Trujillo, the man who had ruled the Dominican Republic for 31 years, in their trunk, Román was nowhere to be found. The coup never occurred, and with each passing moment, the conspirators' likelihood of escape diminished.

Peruvian writer Mario Vargas Llosa, in his 2000 historical novel *La fiesta del chivo* (The Death of the Goat), summarizes General Román's seemingly illogical actions in this way:

> From that moment, and in all the following minutes and hours, a time in which he decided his fate, that of his family, that of the conspirators, and in the end, that of the Dominican Republic, General José René Román always knew, and with complete lucidity, what he should do. Why did he do exactly the opposite? He would ask himself this many times during the following months, without finding an answer [*Desde ese momento, y en todos los minutos y horas siguientes, tiempo en el que se decidió su suerte, la de su familia, la de los conjurados, y, a fin de cuentas, la de la República Dominicana, el general José René Román supo siempre, con total lucidez, lo que debía hacer. ¿Por qué hizo exactamente lo contrario? Se lo preguntaría muchas veces los meses siguientes, sin encontrar respuesta*] [419–420].

Certainly, Vargas Llasa's work is an historical novel and not a biography or history. Nevertheless, as the author was quick to point out in interviews following the controversial publication of the work, "there is much more fiction than history, but any one of those fabrications could perfectly well have occurred" [*hay mucha más invención que historia, pero cualquiera de esas invenciones pudo ocurrir perfectamene*] (Méndez 2000: n.p.).

The conspirators' plans and fate were so bizarre that they almost seem the plot of an espionage novel. They had given so much attention to the details of the assassination itself that no backup plans had been made to allow the men to escape should the coup not take place as planned. Furthermore, the conspirators left a sloppy trail of abundant clues behind them. The first conspirator to be captured was Pedro Livio Cedeño, the worst wounded in the exchange of gunfire between the *ajusticiadores* (executioners) and the dictator. Taken to the International Clinic for treatment, Cedeño mentioned General Román's name in his pain and delirium. As the days passed, the SIM made short work of the conspirators. All but two of them—Antonio Imbert and Luis Amiama Tió—were captured or killed. Those who were taken prisoner were alternately tortured and revived with medical care to be tortured again for months. They were then slaughtered by Trujillo's son, Ramfis, before he fled the country with the rest of the Trujillo family in November, when military officers rose up. In the same spirit with which his father had hidden countless violations of human rights behind theatrics, Ramfis arranged the conspirators' murders so that it appeared that they had attacked and killed their guards to escape as they were being transported from a re-enactment of the crime for supposed judicial purposes.

Meanwhile, Dominicans across the country were mourning Trujillo's death, some truly lamenting the passing of the dictator and others too uncertain of the nation's political future to risk celebrating. The poor rural and urban masses in particular wailed in the streets, and puppet president Joaquín Balaguer lauded the fallen tyrant:

> I present to you, ladies and gentleman, felled by the breeze of a gentle gust of wind, the sturdy oak that, during more than 30 years, challenged all and was the victor of all storms. We all know that with this glorious corpse we lose the best guardian of public peace and the best defender of security and peace in Dominican homes... [*He aquí, señores, tronchado por el soplo de una ráfaga leve, el roble poderoso que durante más de 30 años desafió todos vencedor de todas las tempestades. Todos sabemos que con este muerto glorioso perdemos el mejor guardián de la paz pública y al mejor defensor de la seguridad y el reposo de los hogares dominicanos...*] [Lora 2002: para. 13].

Balaguer's words following Trujillo's death were highly guarded and just as ambiguous. The unassuming, diminutive president had never seemed a threat to anyone, which was probably why Trujillo trusted him to the degree that he did. Throughout the decades since the dictator's assassination, questions concerning Balaguer's possible role in his death have been raised more than once (including in Vargas Llosa's novel), though no final conclusions have ever been drawn. What is without question is that Balaguer was able to maintain his position as president after Trujillo's assassination and for some two months following the military uprising. At that time he found himself in a precarious situation. A 12-day general strike convinced Balaguer to ask the Congress to alter the Constitution by creating a seven-member *Consejo de Estado* (Council of State) to run the government while he remained as president. This move was meant to appease the different parties and unions forming as well as the Church by allowing them all representation.

The *Consejo de Estado* was short-lived. On January 16, 1962, Balaguer dissolved that body and replaced it with a five-man civilian-military junta. An even worse strike followed, and the junta was overthrown. At last, Balaguer abandoned the presidency and fled the country. Rafael F. Bonnelly was then chosen to head the *Consejo de Estado* that served as a transitional government until elections were held in December, 1962.

Elections, Civil War and U.S. Intervention

Juan Bosch, landslide winner of the 1962 elections, had returned to his homeland after more than 20 years of foreign exile. Unfortunately for the new president, the lengthy time he had spent abroad had put him out of touch with the present Dominican reality (Moya Pons 1995: 385). His enthusiastic liberal reform policies came across to many, Dominicans and foreigners alike, as communist. Bosch himself did very little to belie this image, for he tolerated the few Dominican communists in his desire to allow freedom of political parties in the aftermath of the Era of Trujillo.

After only seven months in office, Bosch, the first-ever democratically elected president in the Dominican Republic, was overthrown on September 25, 1963. The United States had seriously questioned Bosch's political ideology and gave its support to the triumvirate, headed by Donald Reid Cabral, that took over the rule of the country.

On September 26, 1963, the very day after the coup, Bosch issued his "Letter to the Dominican People following the Coup of 1963" [*Carta al pueblo dominicano después del gope de Estado de 1963*]. In this document, Bosch emphasized the civil liberties and freedom from the terror of dictatorship that had characterized his seven months as president of the Dominican Republic:

> Neither living nor dead, neither in power nor in the street will they succeed in making us change our conduct. We have opposed and we will always oppose privileges, stealing, persecution, and torture.
>
> We believe in liberty, in dignity and the right of the Dominican people to live and develop their democracy with human liberties but also with social justice.
>
> In seven months of government we have not spilled a drop of blood

nor have we ordered a torture nor have we accepted that a cent of the people end up in the hands of thieves.

We have permitted all types of liberties and we have tolerated all kinds of insults because democracy should be tolerant; but we have not tolerated persecutions or crimes or tortures or illegal strikes or robberies because democracy respects the human being and demands that public order be respected and demands honesty.

Men can fall, but not principles. We can fall, but the people should not permit that democratic dignity fall.

Democracy is a benefit of the people and it is up to them to defend it. Meanwhile, here we are, willing to follow the will of the people.

[*Ni vivos ni muertos, ni en el poder ni en la calle se logrará de nosotros que cambiemos nuestra conducta. Nos hemos opuesto y nos opondremos siempre a los privilegios, al robo, a la persecución, a la tortura.*

Creemos en la libertad, en la dignidad y en el derecho del pueblo dominicano a vivir y a desarrollar su democracia con libertades humanas pero también con justicia social.

En siete meses de gobierno no hemos derramado una gota de sangre ni hemos ordenado una tortura ni hemos aceptado que un centavo del pueblo fuera a parar a manos de ladrones.

Hemos permitido toda clase de libertades y hemos tolerado toda clase de insultos, porque la democracia debe ser tolerante; pero no hemos tolerado persecuciones ni crímenes ni torturas ni huelgas ilegales ni robos porque la democracia respeta al ser humano y exige que se respete el orden público y demanda honestidad.

Los hombres pueden caer, pero los principios no. Nosotros podemos caer, pero el pueblo no debe permitir que caiga la dignidad democrática.

La democracia es un bien del pueblo y a él le toca defenderla. Mientras tanto, aquí estamos, dispuestos a seguir la voluntad del pueblo].

[*Juan Bosch, Pilar de la historia dominicana* 2001]

Soon after Bosch's overthrow, many Dominicans who supported a democracy led by Bosch began to conspire with him from his exile in Puerto Rico. These individuals maintained that Bosch had been elected freely and constitutionally, and that he was the legal and rightful ruler of the Dominican Republic.

When elections were set for September 1965, Bosch and his party, the *Partido Revolucionario Social Cristiano*, also known as the Christian Democrats, called for a " 'return to constitutionality without elections' " (Moya Pons 1995: 387). In addition to Bosch's grievances at having been ousted after only seven months, he and his followers were certain that the upcoming elections would be fixed so Reid Cabral would become president.

Before Bosch could take action, his conspiracy was uncovered on April 24, 1965, and many Dominicans poured into the streets to support him. In the chaos, the military overthrew Reid Cabral and began talks with the Constitutionalists in an attempt to avoid armed conflict. No agreement was reached, and the following day, April 25, civil war erupted in the Dominican Republic.

Three days later the United States set into motion its second invasion of the Dominican Republic in order to prevent Bosch's return to power. The fear of communism was so prevalent at that time that the U.S. was concerned that Bosch would usher in another communist regime. The United States marines' mission, as summed up by President Lyndon B. Johnson, was to ensure that communism not be instituted in the Dominican Republic as it had been in Cuba (Moya Pons 1995: 388).

Despite the United States' military superiority, it was impossible for the marines to put down the Constitutionalists easily. For this reason, there were actually two governments in the Dominican Republic between May and September 1965. Negotiations between the two were interspersed with periodic fighting. At last, both governments agreed to resign and a provisional government was established with Héctor García Godoy as its head. This government organized elections for the upcoming year.

The two main candidates for these new elections were Joaquín Balaguer and Juan Bosch. Because of acts of violence against the Constitutionalists, Bosch was unable to leave his house to campaign effectively. Balaguer returned to the presidency with a convincing victory.

Thus, the U.S. invasion, "the result of an exaggerated fear regarding a potential second Cuba" (Hartlyn 1998: 89) prevented the return of the constitutionally elected Juan Bosch. Later, the truth revealed that there had really been no such threat whatsoever and that the OAS had not sanctioned the invasion. Nevertheless, steps taken within the OAS gave an appearance of legality to the United States' actions (Moya Pons 1995: 389).

Joaquín Balaguer and Neo-Trujilloism

Political fragmentation such as was common in the era of the great *caudillos* returned to the Dominican Republic between May 30, 1961, and Balaguer's ascension to the presidency five years later. During this time, "there were fourteen different governments in the country ... though six of them lasted sixteen days or less and two of them overlapped for four months under foreign military intervention" (Hartlyn 1998: 60).

The election of Joaquín Balaguer, Trujillo's last puppet president, brought a sense of stability back to the country. If nothing else, Balaguer's years as president (1960–1962, 1966–1978 and 1986–1996) contributed some continuity to Dominican life. Even his campaign slogans—such as "Balaguer is Peace" [*Balaguer es la paz*] and "A Path without Danger" [*Un camino sin peligro*]—were reminiscent of Trujillo's 1930 campaign reminder "There Is No Danger in Following Me" [*No hay peligro en seguirme*]. The words Balaguer had pronounced shortly after Trujillo's death seemed highly indicative of the path he would follow:

> Dear Chief: Farewell. Your spiritual children, veterans of the campaigns that you undertook during more than 30 years in order to exalt the Republic and stabilize the State, will look towards your tomb and we will not skip steps to impede that the flame you sparked in the altars of the Republic and in the souls of all Dominicans be extinguished... [*Querido Jefe: hasta luego. Tus hijos espirituales, veteranos de las campañas que libraste durante más de 30 años para engrandecer la República y estabilizar el Estado, miraremos hacia tu sepulcro y no omitiremos medios para impedir que se extinga la llama que tú encendiste en los altares de la República y en el alma de todos los dominicanos...*] [Lora 2002: para. 15].

The former president of the Dominican Republic (1960–1962, 1966–1978, 1986–1996), Dr. Joaquín Balaguer Ricardo, shown during a political meeting on February 20, 2000. One of Latin America's last great strongmen, Balaguer died in the early hours of July 13, 2002, in Santo Domingo. (Photograph/File: Miguel Gómez)

While Balaguer was in many aspects very much like his predecessor and continued many policies and practices that were very similar, he did not follow completely in Trujillo's footsteps.

As in the past, human-rights violations and lack of personal and civil liberties were common in the Dominican Republic. Just as Trujillo had done, Balaguer created and supported a paramilitary force known as "*La Banda Colorá*" (The Crimson Gang) to carry out acts of terror. Over 3000 Dominicans died in terrorist acts between 1966 and 1974. Balaguer claimed he had nothing to do with *La Banda* and that the government had attempted to control the group without success. Publicly, the president referred to *La Banda* as "'uncontrollable forces'" (Moya Pons 1995: 392) and insisted that "corruption stopped at his door" (Pearson 2002: B04). Nevertheless, Balaguer's 1988 autobiography, *Memorias de un cortesano de* la "*era de Trujillo*" (Memories of a Courtier of the "Era of Trujillo"), again raises the question of the extent of his involvement in *La Banda*'s activities. In his memoirs, Balaguer briefly mentions the unexplained disappearance and probable death of journalist Orlando Martínez Howley, who had written various articles in criticism of *La Banda* and the president. Balaguer leaves a blank page in his book that he claims will be filled after his death with the events surrounding the Martínez case:

> This page is inserted blank. It will remain silent for many years, but one day it will speak, so that its voice may be gathered by history. Silent, like a tomb whose accusing secret will be proclaimed when time permits that the tombstone beneath which the truth lies be raised.
>
> Its content is left in the hands of a friend who, for reasons of age, is supposed to outlive me and who has been charged by me to make it public some years after my death.
>
> [*Esta página se inserta en blanco. Durante muchos años permanecerá muda, pero un día hablará, para que su voz sea recogida por la historia. Callada, como una tumba cuyo secreto a voces se levantará, acusador, cuando el tiempo permita levantar la losa bajo la cual permanece yacente la verdad.*
>
> *Su contenido se deja en manos de una persona amiga que por razones de edad está supuesta a sobrevivirme y que ha sido encargada por mí de hacerlo público algunos años después de mi muerte*] [333].

The case of Orlando Martínez Howley is but one example of many. During Balaguer's first 12 years as President, "[t]housands of opponents, journalists, lawyers were assassinated by death squads that the president described as 'uncontrollable gangs'" [*[d]es milliers d'opposants, des journalistes, des avocats sont assassinés par des escadrons de la mort que le president qualifie de "bandes incontrôlables"*] (Caroit 2002: para. 3). By the end of Balaguer's 12-year rule, both national and international opinion ardently insisted that such sanctioned human-rights violations cease.

Although the protected yet unacknowledged acts of violence and terror were reminiscent of the Era of Trujillo, Balaguer never controlled the Dominican military as his own personal force the way his predecessor had. While Trujillo had been a military man through and through, Balaguer was certainly a civilian and he "never attempted or achieved the extent of control that Trujillo did. Rather, he assiduously practiced a policy of co-optation" (Hartlyn 1998: 100). A well-educated, bookish man, Balaguer had early adhered to the philosophy of Uruguayan José Enrique Rodó as explained in his 1900 essay *Ariel*. This view, also supported by Dominican scholar Pedro Henríquez Ureña, placed a greater emphasis on intellectual abilities than brute force. In this way, "[t]he attainment of wisdom ... would allow an enlightened leader ... to harness both intellect and force to serve his noble purposes" (Wucker 1999b: 174). Balaguer's intellectualism and ability to manipulate language allowed him to win support as well as "convert" many opponents with a handful of well-chosen words. His political opponents were often silenced in this way, as Balaguer could utterly humiliate and control them with a mere comment.

Like Trujillo, Balaguer's neopatrimonialism extended his rule in a way that was highly reflective of the *caudillo* mentality. Just as the great Dominican caciques of the nineteenth and early twentieth centuries had believed, Balaguer and many Dominicans were convinced that he was all that kept the nation from falling to foreigners. Balaguer desired to remain in power at all costs, and even after glaucoma claimed his eyesight in 1981, he did not retire from politics.

Balaguer's neo–Trujilloism also found him resorting to monetary and material gifts to win the favor of the masses. On presidential campaigns, envelopes filled with pesos were distributed. Bags of food and more packages of money were handed out to lines of people waiting outside Balaguer's home in Santiago and the National Palace in the capital (Wucker 1999b: 179–80). Personally, I remember a speech given by President Balaguer that I attended during my first trip to the Dominican Republic in 1993. The elderly president was helped to his seat by sunglasses-bedecked bodyguards. Following a rousing, nationalistic speech, the crowds cheered loudly, "*¡Viva Balaguer! ¡Viva Balaguer!*" (Long live Balaguer!) An announcement was then made that the president had a certain amount of stoves that he wished to give to the women, baskets prepared for soon-to-be mothers, bikes for the little boys, and dolls for the girls. After such a generous proclamation, the ecstatic crowd again began to cheer. This instance was by no means unique, as Balaguer commonly traveled into the nation's towns and cities, doling out money, toys and other gifts (Pearson 2002: B04; Caroit 2002: para. 4). In many ways, little had changed with Trujillo's death.

Balaguer continued to adhere to the long-held vision of a Hispanic, Catholic Dominican identity, and he also kept up the tradition of attributing all national ills to the proximity of Haiti or the presence of large numbers of Haitian immigrants within the borders of the Dominican Republic. As Dominican sociologist Rubén Silié notes, "'Balaguer allowed to awaken anew among "the good Dominicans" the idea that just as under Trujillo, they were protected by Balaguer against the new Haitian attempts at domination'" (Wucker 1999b: 135). Additionally, Balaguer's use of repressive tactics, his personalism, and the rampant corruption prevalent in his administration "brought back the worst vices of nineteenth-century Dominican politics" (Torres-Saillant and Hernández 1998: 7).

One of the areas in which Balaguer distinguished himself from his predecessor was in the realm of economics. In contrast to Trujilloist protectionism and policies to make the state his own personal enterprise, Balaguer's economic plans worked to develop and expand independent, private industries. Foreign aid was a crucial element in these projects. The United States in particular poured large amounts of economic assistance into the country. For example, in 1966, the Dominican Republic received more U.S. aid per capita than any other Latin American country; worldwide, only Vietnam was given more (Georges 1990: 30). Furthermore, foreign investors were eager to take advantage of available land, workers, and consumers in the Dominican Republic, and they located and invested money there. Simultaneously, "the nascent native bourgeoisie's commitment to furthering its wealth in the country created the necessary conditions to facilitate foreign capitalist accumulation" in the country (Torres-Saillant and Hernández 1998: 38–9).

Balaguer's projects expanded industry and commerce by a continuous increase of technology at the expense of manual labor (*ibid.*, 46). The resulting fall in the number of available urban jobs coincided with an increase in internal migration as numerous peasants moved to the cities. These new arrivals to the urban areas were unable to be absorbed, plunging them into ever-deeper poverty and thus widening the gap between the masses and the urban bourgeoisie that had benefited from Balaguer's import-substitution policies (Gramsuck and Pessar 1991: 38).

In 1969, the first of numerous Free Trade Zones (FTZs) that would be located in the Dominican Republic was opened in La Romana. Although the FTZs created jobs that were desperately needed, they played an extremely insignificant role in Dominican industrial development. The FTZs did not fall under protective labor legislation, and conditions within them were often difficult for the workers, the majority of which were women (Georges 1990: 30–1; Torres-Saillant and Hernández 198: 52). The harsh working conditions and long hours forced women to find alternative means to care for their children, and this added stress caused many to suffer nervous breakdowns.

Balaguer's economic policies and projects created a severe lack of jobs for both new and old urban dwellers. The internal goal of development and modernization through technological improvement, coupled with the effects of foreign companies' investment in and relocation to the island, produced a set of circumstances that encouraged mass out-migration, a theme which will be discussed in greater detail in Chapter 9.

PRD* Rule (1978–1986)

By the time of the May 16, 1978, elections, Dominicans had grown weary of the human rights and political abuses committed by or with the knowledge of the country's leaders. The people demonstrated their desire for change by voting for Balaguer's opponent, Antonio Guzmán of the Dominican Revolutionary Party or PRD (Partido Revolucionario Dominicano). Nevertheless, the president was not to be ousted so easily. While the Dominicans watched the *Junta Central Electoral* (The Central Electoral Committee) count the votes on national television, it became obvious that Guzmán had been the winner. Suddenly, soldiers entered and suspended the count. Ballots were destroyed and many individuals beaten. The public reacted with indignant yet peaceful resistance (Moya Pons 1995: 403).

The United States and several other OAS countries refused to acknowledge Balaguer's "victory," and at last, the president was forced to accept that he had lost. Balaguer did not turn the government over to Guzmán without some concessions. He forced the new president to agree to falsified election results that allowed Balaguer's party a majority in the Senate and more members in the Chamber of Deputies. This infamous resolution, supported by the pro–Balaguer *Junta Central Electoral*, has come to be known as the *fallo histórico*, an interesting name since "*fallo*" signifies both "ruling" and "error."

Guzmán took the first steps in tearing apart the Trujilloist machinery that both the dictator and Balaguer had used to run the country for decades. However, he seriously distanced many supporters by making the Dominican government his own personal government through appointments of numerous friends and family members. New jobs and titles were created to accommodate these individuals which consumed more and more government funds. Guzmán also attempted to co-opt opponents within his own political party by paying them off with government funds. So few monies were left thereafter that public works projects had to be suspended.

In addition to the uncontrolled government spending, the Guzmán administration coincided with a severe economic crisis that had actually begun under Balaguer's term. Agriculture and industry were unable to meet national demands. As the government printed money and inflation rose, Guzmán's popularity among the Dominican people rapidly declined.

With the 1982 elections approaching, Guzmán realized that he would not be nominated by his party, and he ardently supported his vice-president,

*The PRD (Partido Revolucionario Dominicano) was founded by Juan Bosch during his exile and returned with him to the Dominican Republic after the death of Trujillo.

Jacobo Majluta. Nevertheless, another candidate, Salvador Jorge Blanco won the nomination, and eventually the elections. Humiliated, Guzmán committed suicide weeks before his term ended.

Economic conditions under Jorge Blanco worsened just as he took office. Foreign creditors were hesitant to loan money to struggling Latin American countries due to the recent halt on repayments made by Mexico. An agreement made with the IMF in January 1983 did little to alleviate the country's economic woes, and disenchantment with the government grew. A subsequent agreement with the IMF in 1985 eased economic tensions and the peso began to appreciate in 1985 and 1986.

What might have been remembered as Jorge Blanco's greatest political achievement was his military reform. Jorge Blanco ardently worked to remove all Trujilloist officers from the armed forces, replacing them instead with young, upcoming officers. However, his zeal for professionalism in the military soon overtook him, as officers were hired and fired as if on a whim. The public began to fear that Jorge Blanco was reverting to the days of the great *caudillos* by creating a personal military force, and his popularity and support declined.

Throughout these eight years, Joaquín Balaguer managed not only to remain influential in Dominican politics but to strengthen his mythical image as the protector of the Dominican nation as well. The former president spent many of these years editing and compiling his writings in the form of essays, speeches, poetry, and historical writings. Glaucoma claimed his sight in 1981, though he did not publicly acknowledge his blindness until 1988. At that time, this "secret"—a secret that the Dominican people had already known even though Balaguer himself had never admitted it—was proclaimed in his 1988 publication, *La venda transparente* (The Transparent Blindfold). This collection of poetry allowed Balaguer to convert "his weakness into a medium for public adulation" (Wucker 1999b: 182), thus increasing his already widespread popularity. In one of his bids for the presidency during that decade, Balaguer's political opponents tried to point to his lack of sight as a strike against him. Balaguer, ever the expert at the turn of a phrase, calmly responded, "'I will not be asked to thread needles when in office'" (Pearson 2002: B04).

It was during this time that Balaguer republished an earlier work under the new title *La isla al revés*.* This publication, which was cited extensively in Chapter 2 of this book, heaped the blame for all of the nation's ills upon the Haitian presence in the Dominican Republic. Balaguer also emphasized his role as protector of the Dominican national identity by

---

*This work was originally published as a form of propaganda soon after the 1937 Haitian massacre under the title *La realidad dominicana*.

reminding readers of the overarching importance of purity within borders, even at the expense of liberty:

> Making a people free is less important than regenerating it; giving independence to a country is a feat that is incomparable to bequeathing it a national consciousness; to constitute a homeland has less merit than to make of it a clean and powerfully integrated nation [*Hacer a un pueblo libre es menos importante que regenerarlo; darle independencia a un país, no es hazaña comparable con la de dotarlo de una conciencia nacional; constituir una patria, tiene menos méritos que hacer de ella una nación limpia y poderosamente integrada*] [Balaguer 1994: 99].

The republication of this work is not surprising, considering the increasingly influential role that José Francisco Peña Gómez had been playing in Dominican politics. On more than one occasion, Peña's political opponents had "accused" him of being of Haitian descent because of his dark complexion. Balaguer again pointed the collective national finger at Haitians in *La isla al revés* in order to remind Dominicans that Haitian immigrants were the cause of all Dominican economic and social woes.

During the eight years of PRD rule (1978–1986) Balaguer was slowly re-opening his path to the presidency. He reunited his *Reformista* party whose origins lay with former supporters of Trujillo and formed an alliance between it and the Social Christian party. The latter was affiliated with the international social Christian movement, and this union provided Balaguer's new *Partido Reformista Social Cristiano* (PRSC)—Social Christian Reform Party—with international ties. Through his writings and his alliances, Balaguer "was reshaping his personal mythology and waiting for his opponents to self-destruct" (Wucker 1999b: 182). And "self-destruct" they most certainly did. Guzmán's nepotism, Jorge Blanco's chaotic "reorganization" of the armed forces, and the economic situation turned public opinion decidedly against them.

Balaguer's Return

The 1986 elections saw Joaquín Balaguer and Juan Bosch running against each other again, both as opponents to the PRD's candidate, Jacobo Majluta. Balaguer won the elections by a questionably slim margin but still ascended to the presidency for his fifth term.

Once in power again, Balaguer began to reshape the government along its former lines. The military was reorganized and former officers from the old regimes were reappointed. This practice went openly against a law prohibiting that any military member who had previously been dismissed be reappointed (Maya Pons 1995: 424). Nevertheless, Balaguer's actions went unquestioned and unchallenged.

Of special concern to Balaguer at this time was the political threat posed by Salvador Jorge Blanco, a man whom the president considered his most formidable obstacle to remaining in power. As in the days of *caudillos* Báez and Santana, Balaguer began a defamatory campaign against Jorge Blanco who was accused of a number of different charges, including an embezzlement charge of some $60 million (Wucker 1999b: 183). During this process, Jorge Blanco suffered coronary spasms due to his high blood pressure and was hospitalized. His condition drastically worsened when he was denied political asylum by the Venezuelan embassy. Eventually, Balaguer was convinced, though not sympathetically moved, to allow Blanco to be rushed to the United States for care; but he required those representing Blanco to sign an agreement stating that he was actually a prisoner and would return to prison once his condition improved (Moya Pons 1995: 426).

In this way, Balaguer easily eliminated his primary competition for the upcoming 1990 elections. Although economic conditions had seriously worsened, the masses still supported Balaguer because he succeeded in lowering the price of food and the value of the Dominican peso was held steady (Wucker 1999b: 133). When he and Bosch faced off again on May 16, 1990, Balaguer won his way to a sixth presidential term.

Soon after Balaguer began his new term, the treatment of Haitian cane-cutters in the Dominican Republic fell under international scrutiny. Numerous international human-rights groups criticized the conditions in which the cutters worked, and the United States stated that it would enact economic sanctions against the Dominican Republic if steps were not taken to improve those conditions. In response, Balaguer decreed that contracts be drawn up for each individual worker and that the cutters be protected legally. Basic conditions of health, education and life were to be improved as well (Wucker 1999b: 131).

While these steps alleviated international pressure, scant little was done to actually change the Haitian immigrants' situation. Balaguer craftily managed to twist the truth in such a way as to divert public attention from the national economic crisis by accusing the Haitians of being its very cause.

This issue fueled the fires of Balaguer's reelection campaign in 1994. Conservatives continued to insist that opponent José Francisco Peña Gómez was Haitian and to condemn him for it. Even though Peña conducted research to prove that his family was Dominican, the old, traditional fears were so sparked by the accusations of his Haitianism that his chances of success dwindled rapidly.

On election day, fear and fraud kept an estimated 45,000 individuals from voting, many of whom had intended to cast their ballot for Peña. Internationally, the fraudulent election results were condemned as unacceptable. Nevertheless, the United States and OAS took advantage of the situation to arrange a trade-off with Balaguer. He would be tolerated as long as he did his part to help control the Haitians who were immigrating to the United States illegally via the Dominican Republic. The U.S. and Dominican governments, therefore, signed an accord agreeing to allow the United States to station troops along the border to control the flow of Haitians.

Under international pressure, Balaguer agreed to shorten his term to 18 months and to organize elections to determine his successor. Nevertheless, the Dominican Congress soon passed the *Pacto Dominicano* (Dominican Pact) which lengthened the term to two years. This decision was seen as placing Dominican wishes above those of the United States. Certainly, memories of the two previous U.S. occupations could not have been far from politicians' minds as "Reformista legislators, wrapped in giant Dominican flags, denounced international plots that they claimed would deny them sovereignty" (Wucker 1999b: 164). The United States had tolerated Balaguer, just as it had Trujillo, because he seemed a better alternative than a communist leader. But the focus had since shifted, and now the U.S. was more concerned with halting the masses of illegal Haitian immigrants that so desperately wanted inside U.S. borders (*ibid.*, 165). Just as U.S. sentiments had changed toward Trujillo, they had changed toward Balaguer; now, the United States wanted him out, too.

Throughout the 90s, Balaguer worked to solidify the image that he would leave behind. Trujillo had wanted to be known as the builder of the Dominican nation, and Balaguer desired to be remembered in much the same way. He continued numerous public works projects, schools, nursing homes, and especially, the Columbus Lighthouse, in hope that they would remain as a concrete legacy of his years in power. The speech I attended at the dedication of a nursing home in La Vega was during but one of the numerous trips Balaguer made throughout the country to inaugurate such projects during the last years of his presidency. These appearances caused many to question what the old President might be planning. Would he ever step down and allow someone else to rule? The headline of a newspaper article that ran the day following the speech I attended read "*JB reitera: no va en el 94*" (JB reiterates: He Won't Run in '94) (Jiménez 1993: 1). In spite of such a definitive headline, however, the article was as typically ambiguous as the president himself.

The PRSC (*Partido Reformista Social Cristiano*, Reformist Social Christian Party) whose headquarters is seen here in Santo Domingo, posed 93-year-old Joaquín Balaguer as its candidate in the 2000 elections.

The 1996 Elections

Balaguer was critically selective of the candidate to whom he would give his support in the 1996 elections. Balaguer's accusatory campaigns against José Francisco Peña Gómez made supporting him out of the question, and Balaguer was not enthusiastic about backing his own vice-president, Jacinto Peynado, since he had prematurely proclaimed himself to be Balaguer's successor from the start. Balaguer wanted someone to win who would be indebted to him for his support and who would allow his mythical image to remain and grow.

As the elections drew near, Balaguer divided his support, giving just enough to Peynado and to the Dominican Liberation Party's candidate, Leonel Fernández, to split the vote. Peña, in third place, was out of the battle after this first stage of the elections, and the competition was taken to a second round. Balaguer then united with Bosch in backing Fernández, who won the second round two months later.

Fernández, who had emphasized his youth and energy by running under his first name only, was chosen in clean and fair elections (Wucker 1999b: 187). A full 35 years after the assassination of Rafael Trujillo, it appeared as if a new generation of politicians was finally coming into its own. However, it soon became clear that Balaguer's influence, like the old man himself, had not yet died. During his four-year term, Fernández, who had no choice but to acknowledge Balaguer's key role in his election victory, made it a point to pay regular visits to the aging ex-president for advice.

Like Balaguer, Fernández instituted policies to improve the Dominican economy. At the conclusion of his term, statistics proved that his programs had been successful. Neverthtless, as anti–Fernández voters pointed out in the 2000 campaign, what his programs had actually achieved was the creation of a macro-economy that widened the already-large breach between the small upper class and the country's poor masses. While the capital and the second-largest city (Santiago) could boast numerous new overpasses, highways and roads, and foreign fast-food chains such as Burger King, McDonald's, Wendy's, Pizza Hut, and Baskin Robbins, the poor could barely afford the traditional staples of rice and beans.

Leonel Fernández (president 1996–2000) lost his bid for re-election with the PLD (*Partido de Liberación Dominicana*, Dominican Liberation Party) in the 2000 elections. (Photograph: Julie Sellers)

The headquarters of the PRD (*Partido Revolucionario Dominicano*, Domini-can Revolutionary Party) is active in the days preceding the inauguration of their presidential candidate and winner of the 2000 elections, Hipólito Mejía. (Photograph: Julie Sellers)

Other programs revealed a lack of insight into problems that have plagued the nation's poor for decades. For example, one of Fernández's policies had been the installation of at least one computer in each school in the Dominican Republic. His intentions were to make computers acces-sible to even the poorest child. Critics, however, were quick to point out that computers would do little good if there was no electricity to run them due to the country's notorious blackouts.

Dominican Politics in the New Millennium

The 2000 presidential elections found Balaguer, now in his nineties, running on the PRSC (*Partido Reformista Social Cristiano*) ticket against Fernández, the very individual he had supported four years previously. Another popular candidate was Hipólito Mejía of the *Partido Revolu-cionario Dominicano* (Dominican Revolutionary Party) who was depicted and spoken of as a man of the people, a common man who had worked the land as a boy. Mejía's supporters emphasized his rural upbringing and primary education in a small rural school as well as his studies of agronomy and agribusiness.

When the first round of votes produced no clear winner, Balaguer effectively chose Mejía as Fernandez's successor by refusing to take the elections to a second round. On August 16, 2000, Hipólito Mejía was inaugurated as president of the Dominican Republic. In the next few days, the serious blackouts that were so common across the country disappeared and when they returned, they were shorter for at least a time, as Mejía had promised. Balaguer's influence, however, had not yet ended. Like Leonel Fernández, Mejía would also pay his visits to Balaguer, just as he had done during the campaign itself.

On August 25, 2000, as I was walking down Santo Domingo's Máximo Gómez Street, I came across a throng of reporters and other people in front of Balaguer's home. Everyone present was waiting for Mejía to exit after paying his first visit to the old leader following inauguration. As the new president's SUV pulled slowly out of the drive surrounded by broad-shouldered guards and men in dark sunglasses, reporters fired questions at him concerning the blackouts and the possibility of raising the price of gas. In the background, a tall man in tattered clothes shouted, "Ah, Hipólito. When are you going to visit your little friend again? Are you going to the beach together next time? I hope you have a lot of fun playing with your little friend. Who rules here, Hipólito? Who?"

That was the question on many Dominicans' minds. Just as the influence and memory of Trujillo had not yet been erased from the nation, Balaguer's power and influence were still felt even without him in office.

The years following the 2000 elections saw the end of an era in Dominican politics. Two years before those elections, José Francisco Peña Gómez, who had long been active in Dominican politics, had died. With Peña gone from the political scene, attention shifted to Juan Bosch and Joaquín Balaguer. Many believed the long-time political rivals were eternal and might never die, while others were certain that both would die the same day, each one unable to live without the competition of the other. Yet Balaguer outlasted Bosch in life, as had always been the case in politics. On November 1, 2001, Juan Bosch, the first-ever democratically elected president of the Dominican Republic, passed away. Some eight months later on July 14, 2002, Joaquín Balaguer died of cardiac arrest at the age of 95.

Reactions throughout the Dominican Republic were eerily similar to what had taken place following Trujillo's assassination four decades before. Suddenly, Balaguer's fraudulent elections, crimes against civil liberties, co-option of opponents and general political maneuvering were forgotten or excused away as acts done on behalf of and for the good of the Dominican nation and people. Following a four-day wake and a 16-hour funeral, Balaguer was laid to rest, surrounded by the wails of mourning of his supporters. Just as in the case of Trujillo, masses of the rural and urban poor from around the country gathered during the wee hours of the morning at the headquarters of Balaguer's *Partido Reformista Social Cristiano* to pay homage.

Balaguer, the "last of the great Dominican *caudillos*" [*último de los grandes caudillos dominicanos*] (*Listín Diario* July 18, 2002) was criticized by some and praised by others. Former Dominican president Fernández commented that Balaguer's death "creates a void in leadership in the Dominican Republic" [*genera un vacío de liderazgo en República Dominicana*] (*Listían Diario* July 14, 2002). Current president Hipólito Mejía and national leaders "exalted ... the political figure of ex–President Joaquín Balaguer, at the same time that they expressed their sorrow and consternation for the death of the leader of the Partido Reformista Social Cristiano" [*exaltaron ... la figura política del ex presidente Joaquín Balaguer, a la vez que expresaron pesar y consternación por la muerte del líder del Partido Reformista Social Cristiano*] (*Listín Diario* July 15, 2002).

As Balaguer himself once noted in his *Memorias de un cortesano de la Era de Trujillo* (Memoirs of a Courtier of the Era of Trujillo), "Political animosities are always circumstancial.... Today's enemy can change into tomorrow's best collaborator" [*Las enemistades políticas son siempre circunstanciales ... El enemigo de hoy puede trocarse mañana en el mejor colaborador*] (*Listín Diario* July 16, 2002). It was a truth Balaguer had seen and made happen during his lifetime, and more than likely, it was a reality he expected after his death.

Hipólito Mejía assumed the Dominican presidency in August 2000 to become the nation's first president of the new millennium. Like other presidents before him, Mejía visited former president Joaquín Balaguer in his home for "advice" before Balaguer's death in 2002. (Photograph/ File: Miguel Gómez

Whether they praised or criticized him, those talking about Balaguer returned to the same question:

While his cadaver is still warm, discussions about what conditions made it possible for Doctor Joaquín Balaguer ... to survive politically for seventy-two years, give rise to debates. Those unanswered questions could be the subject of forums and seminars and of as much interest to those governing as to those who are governed [*Tibio aún su cadáver, las discusiones sobre cuáles fueron las condiciones que posibilitaron que el doctor Joaquín Balaguer ... sobreviviera políticamente durante setenta y dos años, suscitan debates. Las interrogantes podrían ser objeto de foros y seminarios y de interés tanto para los gobernantes como para los gobernados*] [Lora 2002: para. 1].

Balaguer's obituary appeared internationally, and even abroad the curiosity of his ability to maintain power and retain influence in Dominican politics for decades was a common theme. Jean-Michel Caroit, writing for Paris's *Le Monde*, also commented on the phenomenon of forgetfulness demonstrated by Dominicans:

...he will have finished by seducing the majority of his enemies, to the point of being recognized as the model of democracy in spite of the numerous unpunished crimes, the corruption and clienteleism [...*aura fini par séduire la plupart de ses ennemis, au point d'être reconnu comme le parangon de la démocratie malgré les nombreux crimes impunis, la corruption et le clientélisme*] [2002: para. 5].

The always-pervasive presence of Rafael Trujillo had never truly left the Dominican Republic, thanks largely to Joaquín Balaguer. Although there appears to be no one supporter of Balaguer to take his place, it is doubtful that his influence on Dominican life will disappear very quickly. His presence is concretely before the people in the numerous works and constructions he ordered; his presence is experienced daily by many through the policies enacted during his decades of rule and by other presidents at his command. The official state vilification of the Dominicans' neighbors to the west was nurtured under Balaguer during and after his terms. In fact, only nine days after Balaguer's death, Dominican president Hipólito Mejía, on a trip to Washington, spoke with U.S. president George W. Bush and other ranking officials about "the urgent necessity to come to the aid of Haiti" [*la urgente necesidad de que se recurra en auxilio de Haití*] and to "warn about the repercussion of that situation on the stability of the Dominican Republic" [*advertir sobre la repercusión de esa situación en la estabilidad de República Dominicana*] (Pérez 2002: para. 11).

The Dominican mind is both quick to remember and slow to forget, as Rafael Herrera pointed out: "You remember everything, but you are incapable of learning anything. So much blindness seems incredible [*Lo recuerdan todo, pero son incapaces de aprender nada. Tanta ceguera parece increíble]* (Lora 2002: para. 7). How Balaguer's reign is remembered is just as important as what is remembered about it.

The Blank Page

With the death of one of the last strongmen of Latin America, Dominican politics appear to be poised to enter a new era. The future, however, will forever bear the mark of the irreparable past. Without Balaguer, Dominican politics is no more of a true virgin page than the blank page the old *caudillo* left in his *Memorias,* on which the details of journalist Orlando Martínez Howley's murder were to be written after his death. Absence speaks as loudly as presence; that which is not said or done has as much impact as that which is.

Under the order of President Fernández, the Martínez Howley case was reopened in August 2000, over two decades after the journalist's death. Balaguer, who was 93 at the time, "refused to testify in the trial, citing poor health. This supposed condition did not prevent him from running for president in May" (Rodríguez 2000: para. 16). In an unprecedented verdict, four former members of the *Banda Colorá* death squad were found guilty and sentenced to 30 years in prison, the maximum penalty possible according to Dominican law. Retired general Antonio Pou Castro, Mariano Cabrero Durán (a former Air Force sergeant), Rafael Lluberes Ricart and Luis Emilio de la Rosa Beras were also required to pay $312,500 in damages. These four individuals, who claimed they had merely followed the orders of their superiors, were the perpetrators of the crime; the intellectual authors of the murder remain unknown.

This historical ruling was apparently "the first step forward in putting an end to the long-standing impunity enjoyed by Dominican Republic military elites" ("Court Overturns Conviction" 2002: para. 4). But the victory was short lived. In November 2002, the earlier decision was overturned because, according to the Second Criminal Chamber of the Santo Domingo Appeals Court, "errors had been committed during the judicial process" (*ibid.,* para. 1). But the case was not to be laid to rest; in May 2003 the decision was made to reopen it the following month.

Despite the tennis-match speed at which the decisions of guilt or innocence in the Martínez Howley case have been made and overturned, the fact remains that those who instigated the crime—the intellectual brain power behind the actual deed—may never be known or tried. In spite of the importance given to reopening this case for over a quarter century, such abuses continue. As Tomás Rodríguez notes, during "the first full year of Fernandez's government, there were more than 50 extra-judicial executions carried out by the National Police with none of the state killers ever punished" (2000: para. 26).

Almost one year after Joaquín Balaguer's death, no one has yet stepped forward with the text to fill the blank page. Perhaps, as retired general Enrique Pérez y Pérez maintains, "the blank page was but a marketing trick to help sell more" of Balaguer's memoirs. Or perhaps its blankness tells the story not only of Orlando Martínez Howley but of thousands of other Dominicans who were killed or disappeared without a trace during the twentieth century. One blank page—*this* blank page—seems to speak volumes.

8

Post-Trujillo Merengue:
Tradition, Innovative Freedom
and Ethnic Questioning

*"...as social systems change the unique ways in
which music is produced, distributed and consumed also change."*
—Campbell Robinson et al. 1991: 33

Throughout the post–Trujillo period, merengue responded to the
death of the man who had held it in his grasp for over 30 years. Trujillo
had lent a sense of stability and continuity to merengue through his control and manipulation of the genre, just as his authoritarianism had
brought those same characteristics to politics and much of Dominican
life. Following his death, however, *merengueros* began to experiment with
the possibilities in their newfound musical freedom.

Merengue's subversive nature, held so long in check during the Era
of Trujillo, returned immediately with the assassination of the dictator
in "*Mataron al Chivo*" ("They Killed the Goat"), the popular merengue,
performed by Angel Morel and his orchestra, that celebrated Trujillo's
death:

Mataron al chivo	They killed the goat
en la carretera. (2×)	on the highway. (2×)
¡Déjenmelo ver! (3×)	Let me see it! (3×)

136

Mataron al chivo	They killed the goat,
y no me lo dejaron ver.	and they won't let me see it.
El pueblo celebra	The people celebrate
con mucho entusiasmo	enthusiastically
la fiesta del chivo	the party of the goat
el treinta de mayo.	on May 30.
Vamos a reír,	We're going to laugh,
vamos a bailar,	we're going to dance,
vamos a gozar—	we're going to enjoy ourselves—
el 30 de mayo	May 30,
día de la libertad...	day of freedom...

Although this merengue clearly refers to Trujillo, commonly called "the goat" by 1J4 participants and other conspirators, its contents also depict a typical Dominican scene that reduces the former dictator to a more prosaic level through a grotesque parallel. Goats wander untethered along Dominican highways and roads and are often hit and killed by passing vehicles whose drivers might stop and place the animal in their trunks, carry the kill home, and use the meat in a *sancocho* stew. This animalization of the terrifying, powerful dictator—and indeed slaughtering "the goat" so the meat can be used in a stew—gave those performing, listening to and dancing to this merengue a sense of control over him and over themselves that they had not experienced for over three decades.

Merengue, which had served as an instrument of governmental control and indoctrination for years, did not perish with the "goat." Furthermore, the Dominican people did not link merengue exclusively with the Era of Trujillo. Despite the fact that Trujillo had intentionally chosen merengue to be the official national genre and used the music to repress and manipulate, Dominicans still held it as their national music (Duany 1994a: 75). It may seem paradoxical that Dominicans would continue to consider merengue an integral part of Dominican-ness when it was Trujillo's assertion of the genre that allowed it to gain that status across ethnic, class and gender lines. But as we have already seen, Trujillo made an astute decision when choosing to embrace the *merengue cibaeño* above other music forms, for it had a history in the nation that was older than Trujillo himself. The perceived antiquity and pureness of merengue as a Dominican expression lent itself to the dance's continued acceptance after the Era of Trujillo came to an end. Popular music, though, must "be, above all else, *relevant* to the immediate social situation of the people" (Fiske 1989: 25), and so merengue had to adapt to the new contexts of the post–Trujillo Republic. Rather than reject merengue, whose roots went far deeper than the Era of Trujillo, the Dominican people embraced it as a tool for expressing their freedom from the dictatorship. New merengues were written that portrayed this liberty and by 1962, pro–Trujillo merengues had been outlawed. (Austerlitz 1997: 83).

Post-Trujillo Innovation and Change

The end to isolation brought Dominican composers and musicians into contact with the outside world. These influences were absorbed, bringing new dimensions to merengue.

A key innovation to merengue performance was an alteration in the structure of the groups that played the music. The Puerto Rican band *Cortijo y su Combo* experimented with a new type of organization, the *conjunto* or *combo*, which featured fewer musicians, an alteration that proved highly successful. Primitivo Santos was the first to adapt the *combo* structure to merengue, and soon, the old merengue ensembles of some 20 musicians began to be replaced by *combos* of eight or 10 musicians. Instrumentation was adapted to this new form, with piano, saxophone, trombone, trumpet and electrical instruments joining the *tambora*, drum and the *güira* as the mainstay instruments of the new *conjuntos* (Austerlitz 1997: 84).

Lyrics became more concerned with daily life. Merengue now had not one face, the face of Trujillo, but many faces as it represented the reality of the Dominican people.

The use of double entendre that was such an integral part of the music's lyrics before it was softened to make the genre more palatable to the elite returned with a vengeance upon the dictator's death. Themes and topics that would not have been treated during his era were re-introduced. For example, "*La agarradera*" ("The handle") is filled with sexual connotations:

Oye, este merenge es de la agarradera [repite].	Listen, this merengue is about the handle [repeat].
Lo baila las niñas y también	Little girls dance it, and so do older
las viejas [repite].	women [repeat].
La agarradera no la bailo yo [repite];	I don't dance the handle [repeat];
La bailó una vieja y del tiro	An old lady danced it, and she died
se murió [repite].	of the shot [repeat].
Ya, mi compadre y la vecina de al lao [repite]	Now, my buddy and his [female] neighbor [repeat]
La agarradera segurito que han bailado [repite].	Have certainly danced the handle [repeat].

| Oigan mujeres cuando vayan a festejar [repite], La agarradera es lo que deben bailar [repite]. | Listen, women, when you go to a party [repeat], The handle is what you should dance [repeat]. |

[Austerlitz 1997: 86, his translation]

In this selection, "the handle" can be interpreted as a phallic symbol, and dancing it as the sex act. Women young and old alike dance it, and one even died of the "shot." The singing voice is suspicious of his *compadre* and female neighbor, as they "have certainly danced the handle." Nevertheless, all women are encouraged to "dance the handle" when they go to parties.

These lyrics present a seeming double standard: the singing voice claims "I don't dance the handle" and makes somewhat critical remarks concerning his *compadre* and female neighbor yet encourages, "Listen, women, when you go to a party/The handle is what you should dance." Though the lyrics might well seem paradoxical, they represent two centuries-old views of women that are prevalent in Latin America: the pure mother-figure and the fallen woman. As in this merengue, the social ideal is the former while the object of men's desire is the latter.

"*La agarradera*," the most popular merengue of 1962, was performed by Luis Pérez and his *conjunto*, with Johnny Ventura as lead singer. This new style of merengue, so different from what was written for and performed in the ballrooms, was a music for the masses, and thus is considered "pop merengue" (Austerlitz 1997: 86). This nomenclature easily distinguishes this style of merengue as music with mass appeal in contrast to the old orchestra music of the elite and to the *merengue típico*.

The new merengue was best represented by Johnny Ventura, whose own style reflected the changes taking place in the Dominican Republic. As Batista Matos points out, "Johnny Ventura was the exorcist that stripped merengue of the ghosts of Trujillo" [*Johnny Ventura era el exorcista que despojaba al merengue de los fantasmas de Trujillo*] (1999: 72). The old merengue was associated with totalitarianism, and for this reason, the new merengue exhibited "greater liberality and a questioning of traditional values" (del Castillo and García Arévalo 1989: 87). This music, loosed from the repressive grip of the state, was more liberated, cheerful and bright.

Ventura took advantage of the end of isolationism to incorporate foreign elements into the national music. Specifically, he mixed rock-and-roll and the twist with traditional merengue in order to attract the young people of the new era. These innovations resulted in a faster merengue, which in turn brought about changes in the choreography (del Castillo and García Arévalo 1989: 87).

With the increasingly key role that television was playing in daily life, a new importance was also placed on the appearance of *merengueros*. Costumes, choreography and stage presence all came under close scrutiny, as did the music itself, and performers and managers worked to create a complete package that would appeal to a wider audience. Just as "[r]adio was vital to the massification of the merengue ... the marketing of records and the TV were the most effective complements in the consolidation of the rhythm's popularity, individuality and identity in that epoch of bloody social and political instability in the Dominican Republic" [*[l]a radio era vital para la masificación del merengue ... mercadeo del disco y la TV eran los complementos más efectivos para consolidar la popularidad, la individualidad e identidad del ritmo en esa época de cruenta inestabilidad social y política en la República Dominicana*] (Batista Matos 1999: 76).

Johnny Ventura in concert in March 2002. Ventura, who entered prominently into the merengue scene in the early '60s and continues to produce and perform merengue, is currently mayor of the Dominican capital city of Santo Domingo. (Photograph: Roosvert Pérez)

This new emphasis on the visual is most clearly reflected in Johnny Ventura's band, formed in 1964 as *Johnny Ventura y su Combo Show*. As the band's name suggests, the focus is on the innovations of the time, most specifically the smaller band or *combo* and the visual element, as reflected by the use of the word "Show." Ventura, who somewhat resembled Elvis in appearance and performance, associated merengue with hit music to make it a truly mass art form. Ventura's band was clearly the most popular of the 1960s (Austerlitz 1997: 87), and as Batista Matos notes, "Johnny Ventura and the Combo Show converted the merengue into a spectacle" [*Johnny Ventura y el Combo Show convertían el merengue en espectáculo*] (1999: 69).

Other top combos of the time were *Los Magos del Ritmo*, founded by Félix del Rosario in 1964, and Rafael Solano's *conjunto*. Del Rosario also experimented with new sounds: the alto sax, trumpet, and trombone were eliminated (Austerlitz 1997: 87). In contrast to Ventura's *conjunto*, *Los Magos del Ritmo* was less a band of the masses than one of the middle class. Pianist Rafael Solano's combo was a mix of the traditional and the popular, and although he had adopted the innovation of the combo organization, his music was as sophisticated as the merengue of the '50s (*ibid.*, 88).

The 1965 civil war and the subsequent U.S. invasion exploded into the midst of the new pop merengue. As in the past, merengue was put to political uses during this conflict. Johnny Ventura and other musicians sided with the Constitutionalists and directed their music towards them as a means of support. Ironically, Ventura's merengue, so heavily influenced by North American music, was again used as a sign of cultural resistance against the United States. In fact, the very presence of North American musical tendencies used with the Dominican national music lent a sense of control of the great power to the North (Austerlitz 1997: 88).

The Sonic Struggle

Following Balaguer's 1966 presidential victory, other dance music began to gain a following in the Dominican Republic. Intense jockeying for popularity among these styles reflected similar struggles in other aspects of Dominican reality. The different music appealed to and "represented the interests and values of distinct social and economic groups" (Pacini Hernández 1995: 103). For this reason, Dominican musician Luis Dias has labeled Balaguer's first 12 years as president (1966–1978) "'*la lucha sonora*'—" '*the sonic struggle*'" (*ibid.*)

The most heated battle of this "sonic struggle" was between salsa and merengue. Salsa, a dance music whose name refers to its mixture of musical influences, originated in New York City. In addition to its spicy rhythms, salsa's lyrics reflected the challenges of life in the urban centers. For this reason, it appealed to many Dominicans who at that time were migrating to cities and adjusting themselves to similar challenges both at home and abroad (Pacini-Hernández 1995: 108). In contrast to salsa's growing popularity in the Dominican Republic were those who still supported merengue as their preferred dance music, in part because it was "the" national music. Throughout the 1970s, merengue continued to become more and more creative at the same time that salsa fell into less innovative patterns. This helped merengue become recognized as the hottest Latin dance music at home and abroad (*ibid.*).

In addition to the economics involved in this battle, the *lucha sonora* was also a struggle over national identity (Pacini-Hernández 1995: 108). The fact that some Dominicans identified first with the urban and Pan-Latin lyrics of salsa rather than aligning themselves with the national music illustrates the difficulties of adapting to life in the cities that many faced.

The new openness felt at the end of the isolationist Trujillo regime is also reflected. Instead of emphasizing an urban identity, those who backed merengue in the "sonic struggle" identified themselves first on the national level by supporting the national music as opposed to what they considered a foreign invader. Supporting *lo dominicano* served as a form of resistance to the "Coca-Colonization" of Dominican culture (Manuel 1995: 105).

Nueva Canción: Questioning the Origins of Merengue

With merengue out from under Trujillo's thumb, the music's roots began to be called into question in the 1970s with the rise of the *nueva canción* (New Song) movement in the Dominican Republic. Originating in Chile in the 1960s, *nueva canción* had "a dual project of roots recovery and social criticism" (Mattern 1998: 39). This movement with its emphasis on traditional and local forms grew in popularity across Latin America quickly. *Nueva canción* musicians sought to create ties to the past by using older musical traditions to compose new creations. In much the same way that repeatedly listening to the same merengues lends a sense of community, this method contributed to the creation of such feelings that stretched back into the past, joining all members of a nation across time. Likewise, the use of rural folk forms and styles sought to unite the *campo* (country) with the city. *Nueva canción* musicians also stretched class boundaries as they appropriated the music of the lower class (*ibid.*, 40–42).

The *nueva canción* movement became a strong element of the Cuban Revolution. In the years that followed, *nueva canción* musicians and their songs would serve as the prototype for other Latin Americans who used it as a means to consider and perhaps alter their nations' own particular traditions through social, political and cultural commentary. *Nueva canción* music was far more than mere entertainment; it "had a clear sense of mission and purpose" (Pacini-Hernández 1995: 120).

Nueva canción manifested itself in the Dominican Republic in the form of a group of musicians and sociologists known as "*Convite.*" As in other Latin American nations, this *nueva canción* group was politically active. An international *nueva canción* festival known as *Siete Días con el Pueblo* (Seven Days with the People) was held in Santo Domingo in 1974. This event openly challenged the continued repressiveness of eight years of Balaguer's rule. It was the largest concert of its kind ever held.

Convite was specifically opposed to commercial merengue, believing that traditional merengue had been distorted by the innovations made to convert it into a pop music. *Convite* performed investigative fieldwork to seek out the roots of traditional Dominican music and then use those traditions to construct new creations. In this way, *Convite* aspired to educate the Dominican people about their cultural roots.

This approach inevitably led the investigators to consider the very origins of merengue. In contrast to the official view of the music so long supported by the Era of Trujillo, *Convite* openly recognized and emphasized the African influences evident in the national music. This position created a polemic that reached far into the depths of Dominican identity, for admitting a strong African musical contribution to the national music was also an admission of a strong presence of African blood in Dominican ethnicity. Many conservative and upper-class Dominicans flatly denied the validity of *Convite*'s position. These individuals reverted to the official identity imposed upon and accepted by them for decades and, as had been done for years, "cloaked their deeply ingrained racist attitudes in the guise of nationalism, defending the fatherland from the threat of Haitian invasion" (Pacini-Hernández 1995: 131).

An ongoing cultural debate concerning merengue's roots eventually resulted in two conferences held in the Dominican Republic in the late 1970s. The aim of the first, "Origin and Evolution of the Merengue" (1976), was to clarify and explain certain elements in the history of merengue. By the time of the 1978 conference, "Encounter with the Merengue," questions of race and ethnicity were at the heart of the discussion (Pacini-Hernández 1995: 132)

At the same time that Dominican *nueva canción* questioned issues of Dominican ethnic identity, the movement debated the national history as the country began to reconstruct itself after 31 years of Trujilloism. By defining certain cultural elements as authentic and traditional, they could be relegated to the history of the country as it strove to shake off all ties that bound it to the recent past. In this question, as in that of ethnicity, there were two opposing viewpoints. Some held that the nation should rebuild its future upon the past, upon *todo lo dominicano* (all things Dominican) while others desired to take advantage of the end to isolationism to incorporate the international and modern into Dominican life and culture. In summary, the "desire to assume the trappings of progress and modernity conflicted with a deep concern for preserving the authenticity of its national cultural identity" (Pacini-Hernández 133).

The tensions arising from changes to traditional merengue reveal popular music's role in both reflecting and creating social change. When what is considered a traditional and true representation of a people is changed, "community members are challenged to view their lives in new ways" (Mattern 1998: 22). For this reason, "even incremental musical change may spark fears that group identity is being jeopardized. The result is tension between tradition and innovation" (Morris 1999: 195). The issues being questioned in the Dominican musical world were essentially the same as those being posed in political, social and cultural realms.

Those who adhered to a traditionalist, conservative view of merengue reacted to innovation by coining neologisms for the new sounds finding their way into the national music. In this way, they hoped to preserve the purity of the merengue in the face of foreign cultural invaders. Nevertheless, marketers and promoters rarely employed these new names, for the terms were not as readily recognizable as "merengue." The Dominican audience did not want to hear what they felt to be their national music branded with another title, a stance that demonstrates the link between musical genre and meaning (Austerlitz 1997: 104).

Merengue of the '70s and '80s

Outside influences continued to shape merengue. In the 1970s and 1980s, disco began to leave its mark on merengue, just as rock-and-roll had previously. The Dominican music was well suited to these influences, since its steady, pronounced beat was kept on the *tambora* drum and disco's strong beat was kept with a bass drum. In this way, innovation was blended with tradition, a process that, as Morris notes, "contributes to the continuity of musical forms even as they change" (1999: 195). Given the popularity of disco, the bass drum took on an important role in merengue of the era, drawing the younger generations to the national dance. The bass drum and the steady disco beat were quickly adapted by other pop *merengueros*, too.

Transnational influences also entered merengue by way of compositions known as *fusilamientos* (shootings). These songs were merengue versions of other hits, most commonly *baladas*, romantic ballads. By appropriating the lyrics of an already popular song, *balada-merengues* all but guaranteed themselves a hit as well. Since *baladas* are generally not typical to one specific country or locale—their lyrics speak of love and love lost—they had long enjoyed Pan-Latin and international popularity. Likewise, the success of *balada-merengues* stretched across borders because their themes were more universal than many typical merengues (Austerlitz 1997: 93).

Innovations to merengue did not come solely from foreign sources, as the development of a new rhythm known as the *maco* (the toad) illustrates. The exact origins of this rhythm are unknown, although several musicians claim to be its creator. In the 1960s, the *maco* was not considered a typical merengue beat; rather, it was viewed as a completely different rhythm. The *maco*, which emphasizes a strong one-two rhythm, was used more and more throughout the '70s and '80s by popular groups such as Fernando Villalona's *Los Hijos del Rey*. By the 1990s, the *maco* was more common in merengue than the traditional four-beat *cibaeño* rhythm. Because it was reminiscent of disco music, the *maco* rhythm also affected how merengue was danced, as many couples broke away from the ballroom couples position to dance separately (Austerlitz 1997: 94–5).

With the new alterations came a new king of merengue. Fernando Villalona's innovative interpretations of merengue as well as "an electrifying charisma" [*un carisma electrizante*] made him the popular teen idol of the seventies (Batista Matos 1999: 117–118). Villalona's instrumental experimentation resulted in a slightly melancholic yet still melodic tone. Villalona's merengues highlighted both melody and harmony to a greater extent than previously had been known and were performed at a pace situated half-way between the slower merengue of the past and the current accelerated craze (*ibid.*, 121). In addition to his rich voice, Villalona appealed to his audience on a number of levels:

> Fernando was the incarnation of a gamut of human and artistic elements never before seen in another performer of the genre: seductive physical attributes, an exceptionally beautiful voice, originality of style, high quality of orchestration and a parcel of behavioral conflicts [*Fernando era la encarnación de una gama de elementos humanos y artísticos, jamás vistos en otro intérprete del género: seductores atributos físicos, voz de excepcional belleza, originalidad en el estilo, alta calidad orquestal, y un fardo de conflictos de conducta*] [*ibid.*, 120].

Fernando Villalona, merengue heartthrob of the 1970s, continues to enjoy popularity as a merengue favorite. (Photograph: Miguel Gómez)

Los Hermanos Rosario have also laid claim to the origins of the *maco* rhythm (Batista Matos 1999: 242). Comprised of a group of brothers, the band met with

instantaneous success when it debuted in 1978. Although the band's original style was popular throughout the nation, it fell under the attack of a
number of critics who proclaimed its lack of seriousness and quality.

When Pepe Rosario, who had been director of the band and filled a
number of other key roles, was brutally murdered by a crazed fan in 1983,
Los Hermanos Rosario ceased to perform or record. After a time of grieving, the band released an album with the single "*Las locas*" which would
firmly establish its popularity among the masses in the years to come.
Their place among the most influential *merengueros* of the late twentieth
century was set in 1985 with their merengue "*Borrón y cuenta nueva*" which
combined rich melodic, lyrical and harmonic elements (Batista Matos
1999: 242–3). The quality of this and subsequent releases established the
band's musical abilities, thus silencing its former critics. Although the
group has undergone a number of changes—the band presently consists
of Rafa, Luis and Tony del Rosario—*Los Hermanos Rosario* remains a
favorite merengue band among Dominicans.

In the '70s and '80s, *Wilfrido Vargas y sus Beduinos* also rose in popularity. Vargas's merengues were performed at an accelerated pace faster than
those of the '60s. Technological advances of the time opened a new realm of
possibility for instrumentation, as electronic instruments were incorporated
into the *conjuntos*. These instruments, capable of producing numerous sounds,
enriched merengue, for now the same small number of musicians could produce infinitely more sounds (del Castillo and García Arévalo 1989: 89).

Wilfrido Vargas's style catapulted him and his band to transnational
stardom. In addition to the breakneck speed of his compositions, unexpected changes of key and rhythms within a single merengue appealed to
both a national and an international audience. Of Vargas's numerous hits,
one of the most popular was "*La Abusadora*" ("The (female) Abuser"), a
merengue whose furious pace made it absolutely contagious for many and
whose lyrics made it just as repulsive for women of the feminist movement (del Castillo and García Arévalo 1989: 89). The male voice addresses
himself to his former girlfriend, the "abuser," accusing her of feeling no
emotion when she leaves him. Nevertheless, he takes satisfaction in knowing that now that he is with another woman, the first feels badly and wishes
she could return to him.

During these years, Johnny Ventura once again experimented with
his style to keep pace with the ever-changing genre. As Ventura explained
in an interview with Carlos Batista Matos, "'I was convinced that if it didn't
evolve, the merengue was going to disappear and along with it, those of
us who made our living from this music'" [*estaba convencido de que si no
evolucionaba, el merengue iba a desaparecer, y, con él, también los que
vivíamos de esta música*] (1999: 100).

The various transformations that merengue underwent in the decades following the death of Trujillo did nothing to distance the music from its place at the heart of Dominican national identity. In fact, the music was so closely linked to Dominican-ness that marketers and advertisers began to take advantage of that connection in their campaigns to boost sales of products considered typically Dominican, such as tobacco and rum. Dominican rum companies Barceló, Bermúdez and Brugal have all made use of the national music in their ads. For example,

> The Brugal company's ads suggested that music is inextricable from national identity. A television shot shows a decanter of vodka, while an announcer explains that "this bottle contains the essence of the Russian people." The top of the bottle comes off, and Russian-sounding music plays. The scene shifts to a bottle of Brugal rum. The announcer continues: "In the same way, Brugal rum represents the essence of the Dominican people." Merengue plays when the Brugal bottle top comes off [Austerlitz 1997: 102].

Additionally, Dominican tourism ads in the United States featuring Dominican baseball star Sammy Sosa include shots of *merengueros* as well. Ads such as these make proficient use of what Dominicans already believe—that merengue is in their blood–and the connection with a nationalistic identification is instantly made.

Because of its international association with Dominican-ness, merengue itself is a product for tourist consumption. As former hotel manager Apolinar Pérez explained to me, tourists come to the country expecting and wanting to hear merengue, and hotel clubs and discos play it almost exclusively. "The only American music you might hear is a bad imitation of Frank Sinatra," Pérez concluded (2000). Foreign tourists' expectations, then, also help to solidify merengue as a marker of Dominican identity.

The Merengueras

The migration of large numbers from the countryside to the cities, especially to the capital, brought about an increase in the number of women in the workforce. As has been noted, women were the primary workers in the FTZs (Free Trade Zones). The economic crisis that grew during the terms of Guzmán and Blanco made it impossible for many families to sustain themselves on one income, and women were left little choice but to move into the workforce (Pacini-Hernández 1995: 155–6). The necessity for women to leave the home and enter the public, working

Fefita la Grande, the queen of *merengue típico*, and Héctor Acosta, well-known Dominican *merenguero* of the *Los Toros Band*. Since forming her own *merengue típico* band in 1964 at age 18, Fefita la Grande has been an influential model for other *merengueras* by proving wrong the long-held *machista* belief that performing merengue is unsuitable for women. (Photograph: Miguel Gómez)

world made them "literally ... *mujeres de la calle* as they enjoyed increased access to ... public spaces" (Aparicio 1998: 128). This alteration in the traditional Dominican family structure also affected marriage patterns. Working women saw that, should the need arise, they were financially capable of taking care of themselves and their children, and for this reason, consensual marriages came to be more and more the norm (*ibid.*, 156).

Merengueras began to gain a foothold in the music industry as well. The merengue, as has been noted, is essentially a *machista* dance. When danced in the traditional, ballroom style, the man leads and determines the turns and direction in which the couple moves. The option that couples have of dancing the merengue *pegados*—stuck together "close enough to grind grain" (Cocks 1986: 91)—allows for socially acceptable close physical contact between the sexes (Austerlitz 1997:114). Merengue lyrics, with their often overt double entendres, emphasize the commonly misogynist character of a *machista* society's attitudes towards sexuality.

In much the same way that men control the dance, they have controlled the production of merengue. For generations, women were denied the access to the streets and the informal musical training that their male counterparts were given in that public realm (Aparicio 1998: 173). Furthermore, it was believed that women were incapable of playing the typical merengue instruments and that such a profession was totally unsuitable for them.

Eighteen-year-old Manuela Josefa Cabrera Taveras proved that idea wrong. In 1964, she formed a *merengue típico* band that would pave her way to stardom. This artist, known at different points in her career as La Vieja Fefa, La Mayima and currently Fefita la Grande, began playing the accordion at age seven. The people of the rural community where Fefita's family lived were amazed at her natural talent, as well as the fact that a young girl would dare to play merengue on the accordion ("*Fefita la Grande*" para. 1). The popularity of Fefita's music grew throughout the following decades because of her musical originality and her electrifying and energetic stage presence. Although Fefita performs accelerated merengue, her music's roots are never far from the *perico ripiao* she first embraced. Considered the queen of *merengue típico*, Fefita la Grande has been an influential model for other *merengueras*.

By the mid–1980s, a handful of female merengue groups had made their way onto the merengue scene to disprove the commonly-held *machista* beliefs about their ability to perform. In 1984, Belkis Concepción formed the first of such bands, and was followed by other *merengueras* such as *Las Chicas del Can, Milly, Jocelyn y los Vecinos*, Sonia López, and Mayra.

The introduction of these *merengueras* to center stage did not, by any means, represent a feminist movement, even though their music offered a feminine point of view and at times contained feminist themes. The most polemic element of the *merengueras'* music is the occasional appropriation of typical tropes used by male performers to objectify woman or place them in a dominated position within the music. For example, the lyrics of "*Menéalo*" ("Shake It" or "Move it"), a house merengue by Puerto Rican Fransheska, represent "a woman's contestatory response to objectifications of the female body" (Aparicio 1998: 149). The female singing voice in this merengue is strong and self-assured as she proclaims that her song and her movements are intended to catch the reporters' attention so they will write about her. By proudly noting that all men who see her shaking it go blind in one eye, she affirms her sexuality and acknowledges the strength and power it gives her over men.

It has been difficult for *merengueras* to completely assert feminist views and themes since the majority of female merengue bands were begun by male *merengueros* who already enjoyed success in the business; this tendency led to a general consideration of female bands to them as the "'property' of the male businessmen" (Austerlitz 1997: 117). Furthermore, the suggestive outfits worn by these female musicians insinuate that a great part of their popularity lies in their sex appeal rather than their music. Nevertheless, the *merengueras'* use of their own appearance to help sell their music can also be interpreted as a re-appropriation of their own bodies (Aparicio 1998: 151). In other words, while some social pressures might insist that women not play merengue nor dress suggestively, women performers' use of such clothing shows that they control their own bodies.

Juan Luis Guerra and Merengue Dual

Since the 1980s, one of the *merengueros* most influential in the treatment of social themes has been Juan Luis Guerra. Guerra, who had been involved in the Dominican *nueva canción* movement, studied at the Berklee College of Music in Boston. While his first compositions reflect a strong influence of Manhattan Transfer, Guerra eventually returned to his Dominican roots and blended these with other influences. In contrast to most popular merengues whose lyrics were often "'pedestrian and nonsensical'" (Rodríguez Demorizi, cited in Duany 1994a: 76), Guerra's poetic merengues demonstrate the influence of such poetic greats as Pablo Neruda and Federico García Lorca.

Guerra often bases his compositions in Dominican folklore. For example, "*Guavaberry*" deals with the customs of *cocolos*, English-speaking Caribbean black immigrants to the Dominican Republic. Specifically, this merengue highlights the *cocolo* tradition of drinking *guavaberry* on Christmas Eve. By focusing on this marginalized, non–Hispanic group, "*Guavaberry*" points to the "truly Caribbean, versus solely Hispanic, nature of Dominicanness" (Austerlitz 1997: 110).

"*La bilirrubina*" is another example of Guerra's use of an element of Dominican folklore. This 1990 composition deals with the traditional belief in a substance known as "*bilirrubina*" that is found in the human body. According to the song, the protagonist's *bilirrubina* is on the rise because he is suffering from heartache and he accuses the woman of being the cause of his malacly and subsequent need to seek medical attention. His is an illness that cannot be cured by Western Medicine but rather with kisses. After injections, x-rays and surgery fail to remedy the case, the protagonist appeals directly to the object of his affection, pleading with her for love in the form of shots and vitamins.

Soon after "*La bilirrubina*" was released, Guerra received numerous letters from doctors, medical personnel and even other Dominicans, suggesting that he had made an error in terminology and that to be medically correct, he should consider using "adrenaline" instead of "*bilirrubina*." Guerra had not intended to be completely medically correct, and left the song as was.

Guerra's music is not limited to Dominican traditions and folk customs. As the 1998 release "*Mi PC*" ("My PC") illustrates, other themes deal very specifically with the technological, political and social concerns of the late twentieth century. This merengue lightly plays with tradition and the international language of the computer and the Internet. As in the tradition of Spanish Golden Age poetry, woman is objectified by focusing on the individual parts of her body. In contrast to literary tradition, these elements are compared not to rubies, pearls, and gold, but to computer components. In the line of merengue tradition, *Mi PC* contains a humorously sexual double entendre as the male voice asks the woman to open her e-mail and states that he plans to send her a disk containing some of his love.

Despite his use of the traditional and folkloric, Guerra's songs often contain a clear message—social, political and even cultural. Although Guerra aims for his music to be enjoyable dance music, he also intends it to make people think. As Batista Matos states, "Juan Luis offered a merengue for the head and for the feet" [*ofertaba un merengue para la cabeza y para los pies*] (1999: 153–4). For this reason, Guerra himself has called his particular type of merengue *el merengue dual* (Austerlitz 1997: 107). For example, "*Mi PC*," with its playful double entendres, also carries strong political and social criticisms of President Leonel Fernández's policy of providing a minimum of one computer to each Dominican school, despite the common blackouts that make it impossible to operate them. The chorus of the merengue, in which the singer denies that he needs Pizza Hut, Burger King, Hugo Boss fashions, Shaq and other foreign trappings brought on by the new macro-economy, is a criticism of Fernández's economic programs that widened the gap between rich and poor and also contributed to a growing Dominican taste for imports.

Another clear example of the type of statement Guerra's music makes is found in his 1989 "*Ojalá que llueva café*" ("Let's Hope it Rains Coffee"). These were times of economic hardship and crisis in the Dominican Republic, and this merengue focuses on the plight of the *campesino* and the strains felt in the rural areas due to poor soil and bad weather. The image of raining coffee implies an abundance of a common crop and

signifies hope in the face of current despair. References to typical Dominican foods such as yucca, *queso blanco, mapuey* and *batata* as well as col-
loquialisms such as "jarina (a light rain) and piti salé (a Haitianism)"
(Duany 1994a: 78) (the latter being a type of salted meat), make the lyrics
easily accessible for Dominicans of all social strata. The traditional call-
and-response format and versification fit neatly into the established structure already known. Nevertheless, this merengue reflects the increasingly
complex instrumentation and polyrhythms of the late 1980s (*ibid.*).

Most importantly, the lyrics of "*Ojalá que llueva café*" go much farther than a commentary on *lo típico*; rather, they are a social criticism of
the conditions endured by rural Dominicans. As was noted in the previous chapter, Balaguer temporarily purchased the loyalty of the *campesinos*
rather than providing them with any sort of infrastructure by which they
could improve their own conditions. "*Ojalá que llueva café*" expresses the
hope that not only the weather and soil fertility in the rural areas will
improve but that the overall situation of these areas will be bettered as
well. The inclusion of a chorus of children towards the end of the piece
emphasizes this hope for the future.

A similar composition by Guerra, "*El costo de la vida*" ("The Cost of
Living"), also expresses a strong social commentary. This 1992 merengue,
which criticizes rising inflation, the increasingly influential foreign involvement in the Dominican economy, and political corruption, also contains
timely comments about the 500th anniversary of Columbus's "discovery"
of the Americas by questioning exactly who was discovered by whom. The
lyrics contrast the relative smallness of the island in terms of the immen-
sity of the sea with the key role that Hispaniola played in the history of
the Americas by emphasizing the 500th anniversary of the Encounter. The
melding of the three different worlds is highlighted in the merengue's
description of Dominicans as a colorful people comprised of European,
African and indigneous groups.

A 1998 merenrap, Juan Luis Guerra's "*El Niagara en bicicleta*" ("Niagara Falls on a Bicycle") contains similar economic and social criticisms.
The song takes its name from a common Dominican refrain, "crossing
Niagara Falls on a bicycle," which means that one is suffering economic
misery. In the composition, the singer-protagonist describes a literal
attempt to cross Niagara Falls on a bike and the pitiful public health conditions that await him in a Dominican hospital afterwards. In addition to
emphasizing that not all Dominicans enjoy the improved economy of the
Fernández term, the merengue also highlights the discrepancy in quality
between private health care and the free public health care that the masses
must use through the disbelief of the protagonist as he finds that there are
no supplies or medicines available for his care. Additionally, the national

problem of the common blackouts is present in the words of the nurse attending the protagonist who states that they cannot perform an EKG because there is no electricity.

In addition to such social and political criticisms, Guerra's compositions have acknowledged the inherent African influence in the national music. For example, "*A pedir su mano*" ("To Ask for Her Hand"), off the 1990 album *Bachata Rosa*, was inspired by a Central African melody. The song begins with a heavily African-influenced chant before switching to a bright merengue. Especially innovative for the time was the incorporation of shots of *cocolos* (English-speaking black immigrants) drumming in the song's video. Although Guerra's inclusion of and emphasis on Afro-Dominican elements sparked the use of these components by other composers, these compositions have done little to bring any drastic alterations in the strongly rooted beliefs about Dominican ethnicity and the ethnic influences present in merengue (Austerlitz 1997: 111).

Given Guerra's record of politically, culturally and socially relevant merengue themes, it is certain that his poetic and lively merengues will continue to mirror as well as shape Dominican reality as events unfold in the twenty-first century.

Merengue of the '90s and of the New Millennium

In addition to the music of Juan Luis Guerra, merengue at the end of the twentieth century encompassed a wide variety of themes, expressing a panorama of realities experienced by Dominicans at home and abroad. Merengue is produced by Dominicans and musicians of other nationalities as well, and represents a wide variety of themes. *Merengueros* who are new to the business as well as those with years of experience— many of the most popular musicians of the era had their start in the 1980s—continue to write, perform and produce compositions that are both a reaction to and an influence on the world around them.

Although decades have passed since his death, Trujillo continues to reappear in the world of merengue. In contrast to the over 300 merengues written in praise of the dictator during his regime, Wilfrido Vargas's 2000 merengue entitled "Trujillo" condemns the brutalities of the dictator. The lyrics describe the heartless dictator and his complete control over the country while reminding listeners of the number of Dominicans killed during the regime. Trujillo's crimes against the people, including his lust for women and his control of the *campesinos'* land, are included as well. The action on the highway between the dictator and the *ajusticiadores* (executioners) during the ambush is relayed play by play, and the lyrics note that the violent Trujillo ends up in the trunk of a car. The song goes on to praise the bravery of the conspirators who assassinated him by listing off each of their names as heroes and comments on the magnitude of their sacrifice.

Despite its continued popularity and its position as the Dominican national music, some merengue has come under harsh criticism from middle- and upper-class Dominicans who feel that the lyrics of certain compositions denigrate the genre. In spite of the overwhelming national and international popularity of some of these merengues, they are often attacked by those Dominicans who consider the double entendres in them too risqué and blatant or feel that the compositions lack musical and lyrical quality. Often, critics claim that the compositions in question are not "true" merengues at all.

One such merengue that has come under heavy fire is "*La vaca*" ("The Cow"), an international favorite with long-lasting popularity. Performed at an almost undanceable speed by the artist Mala Fe, "*La vaca*"* appeals to many while its lyrics appall others. Regardless of the "moo" repeated in the call-and-response series throughout the merengue, it is clear that the *vaca*, the cow, is a woman who is objectified and under the control of the male voice which proclaims:

...*Tengo una vaca lechera*	...I have a milk cow,
Una vaca de verdad. (2×)	a real cow. (2×)
No la vendo ni la cambio	I won't sell her or trade her
Si te la quieres comprar (2×)...	if you want to buy her (2×)...

The male voice also comments that his cow causes him a lot of problems in the *barrio*, since "This cow's milk is really pure" [*La leche que es de esta vaca es bien pura de verdad*]. Other men therefore pose a threat: "All the shady characters/hoodlums on the corner want to milk her for me" [*todos los tígueres de la esquina me la quieren ordeñar*" and his neighbor—a bull—is falling in love with his cow [*el toro de mi vecino se enamora de mi vaca*].

The music of Tulile (José Manuel Rivera) has also been harshly criticized as merengue that lacks quality and substance, despite his indisputable popularity with the masses. The artist's 2000 release "*La cuca*," with its contagious combination of accelerated merengue and swing, was an enormous hit despite critics' claims that it was merely a street merengue with no literary quality. Tulile, who also catches the public's attention because of his controversial form of dress and general daring, rejects these

---

*Lyrics by J. Gutiérrez, courtesy of J&N Publishing.

criticisms by emphasizing the great mass popularity of his music, which without a doubt is what matters most to the people.

Dominican political parties clearly support Tulile's point of view above those who cry for a purer, more musical and literary merengue. During the May 2002 elections, the PLD sponsored a show featuring Tulile and other renowned musicians—*Los Hermanos Rosario* performed in a similar concert for the PRD. Dominican politicians of the new millennium clearly have not forgotten the lessons of the old: that merengue is "an effective competitive weapon among candidates and political parties" [*un arma efectiva de competencia entre candidatos y agrupaciones políticas*] ("Tulile y Los Rosario": para. 1). Popularity sells albums and popularity wins elections, and often substance is of little importance to the public in either case.

The reception or rejection of merengues according to these criteria of musical and literary quality is a new theme in the long tradition of questioning which aspects of the genre are appropriate and which are not. Just as some denounced the merengue in the nineteenth century for steps that seemed too lascivious, some merengues—compositions with double entendres within a genre of double entendres—are currently being denounced for lyrics that are not sufficiently "cultured." Only time will tell how soon these songs will be accepted and what the next topic of criticism will be.

Bachata: Growing Popularity on the Global and National Scenes

Prominent musical stars' performance of *bachata* has greatly altered this other genre of Dominican music. Originally known as *canciones de amargue* (songs of bitterness), *bachata* is a guitar-based romantic form that was traditionally a music of the lower classes of the *campo* and later, the urban barrios. Like merengue, *bachata* lyrics contain numerous double entendres often considered vulgar and uses everyday language and street slang. Extremely popular among members of the huge Dominican lower class, *bachata* was shunned for years by the smaller middle and upper classes. Artists were not allowed airplay on radio or television, and recordings were cheaply done and sold only by vendors on the streets.

In the 1990s, however, musical stars such as Wilfrido Vargas and Juan Luis Guerra began to perform versions of *bachata*. For example, Guerra won a Grammy with an album entitled *"Bachata Rosa."* International exposure and popularity thus helped lead to *bachata*'s "'validation through visibility'" (Slobin, cited in Averill 1994: 168).

Bachata's acceptance was not immediate, however. While the *bachatas* performed by established musicians were hits and given considerable airtime, those by musicians known only to *bachata* enthusiasts were still mainly songs of the small neighborhood bars and the streets. But by the mid–1990s, however, *bachata* recordings could be found for sale in middle-class stores and featured in *discotecas* (Austerlitz 1997: 114). Today, *bachata* is a transnationally recognized genre, and recordings can be purchased over the Internet.

I am personally able to attest to this rapid transition. During my first visit to the Dominican Republic in 1993, *bachata* was not mentioned save as the title of Guerra's award-winning album. By 2000, however, the genre had become so popular that Dominican friends were insisting that I learn its steps so that my Dominican musical repertoire would be complete. In much the same way that merengue's inherent importance to Dominicanness had been explained to me before, one 26-year-old friend remarked, "Every Dominican knows how to dance *bachata*." In contrast, middle-aged Dominicans from the middle-and upper-classes commented with a scoff and a shrug, "*Bachata*? I don't know anything about that. Let's just dance merengue." Taken together, these two points of view emphasize the relatively recent popularity of the genre. And although *bachata* has come to be considered the favorite romantic music of the Dominican Republic, merengue holds firm to its place as the national music and the preferred dance music in the nation (Manuel 1995: 115).

El festival del merengue

Soon after the fall of Trujillo, the secretary of tourism, Angel Miolán, began work on a project that would take merengue to the world by encouraging the world to come to merengue. The *Festival del merengue* (Merengue Festival), held annually around July 25 in Santo Domingo, showcases not only the dance but other traditional cultural elements, such as crafts, food, and arts.

The 10-day festival is truly popular in nature, with the activities taking place along Malecón Avenue, which runs along the Caribbean Sea. Hotels, restaurants and other businesses organize as many related events as possible to entertain Dominicans and the thousands of foreigners in attendance. The merengue as it is believed to have been danced at the time of its origin is performed in costume, as are other dances considered folkloric. Additionally, live bands entertain the crowds, and people dance in the streets, in the parks, on the beach—anywhere there is space.

The *Festival del Merengue* provides an example of a practice being validated through exposure to an outside world that accepts and expects that practice as traditional of a certain group. In this case, a strategy originally undertaken to develop the tourist industry through a popular annual festival has reiterated the connection between the merengue and Dominican-ness. The process is circular, as what is considered Dominican within the Dominican Republic is presented for foreign visitors who in turn accept the merengue as Dominican and expect to see more of it. Both through the large-scale visibility to Dominicans and the expectations of foreign tourists, the *Festival del Merengue* strengthens the bond between merengue and Dominican identity.

Post-Trujillo Merengue in Summary

The death of Rafael Leonidas Trujillo Molina and subsequently the end of the Era of Trujillo brought profound social, political and cultural changes in the Dominican Republic. It is not surprising that the national music, so long an instrument of control and repression, evolved as well, for "as social systems change the unique ways in which music is produced, distributed and consumed also change." (Campbell Robinson et al. 1991: 33). Even as President Joaquín Balaguer's neo–Trujilloism lent a sense of continuity and tradition to Dominican politics, other aspects of society and politics were decidedly different. Likewise, Dominican merengue adapted international elements and incorporated novel innovations even as the national music remained founded in tradition.

Ironically, the size of the post–Trujillo Dominican recording industry does not directly correspond to the merengue's international popularity. The "*cuna del merengue*" (birthplace of the merengue) lacks a strong recording infrastructure because of the expense of producing compact disks (Batista Matos 1999: 176). This weak link in musical production is the result of "the meager record market, which is explained in well-defined economic and social factors" [*la estrechez del mercado del disco, cosa que se explica en factores económicos y sociales bien definidos*] (*ibid.*). Much Dominican merengue, then, must be produced elsewhere and reintroduced into the nation.

The end of Trujilloist isolationism opened the nation to the outside world. International influences flowed freely into the country, and Dominicans poured out into the transnational community as restrictions to emigration were relaxed. Dominicans on the island and those in the Diaspora were joined by merengues produced both at home and abroad.

9

Merengue and Transnational Identities

*"Nací en Nueva York pero no me digas gringo." [I
was born in New York, but don't call me a gringo.]*
—Proyecto Uno's "Está pega'o"

Following the death of Rafael Trujillo, increasing numbers of Dominicans spread out into the world. These emigrants carried with them their
language, a taste for certain foods, the Catholic religion, and their national
music. These traditions, however, did not remain static in the Dominicans' new homes. The cross-cultural experiences of these emigrants
affected both host and home countries, resulting in a two-way flow of
ideas and products. Merengue continues to serve as a representation of
Dominican identity that unifies and defines Dominicans as a people,
despite geographical location.

Dominican Emigration Trends

During his 31-year rule, Trujillo had kept a tight hold on emigration,
encouraging population growth to simultaneously strengthen his power
and provide workers for his industries and crops. For this reason, most
emigrants at that time were from elite families who had connections or
enough money to buy their way out of the country. Others leaving the

Dominican Republic during the Era of Trujillo were political exiles, such as Juan Bosch. Still, in the decade from 1950 to 1960, 9,800 Dominicans immigrated to the United States (Georges 1990: 37).

The United States' immigration restrictions were significantly altered and relaxed following the 1965 Marine invasion. Numerous Dominicans took advantage of the new regulations to leave the chaos of their home country in hope of finding a more stable life and income elsewhere. While Trujillo had merely eliminated any opponents that might threaten his position, Balaguer incorporated emigration into his pacification policies. Those who could not or would not be converted to his way of thinking were often "encouraged" to leave the country. The number of Dominicans in the United States exploded between 1960 and 1970, and in New York City the total "increased by over four hundred percent" (Graham 1998: 45).

The increasingly poor Dominican economy encouraged more and more Dominicans to leave the country during the 1970s. Although New York City itself was suffering difficult economic times, it continued to be the primary destination for Dominican emigrants (Gramsuck and Pessar 1991: 197). During this period blue-collar employees constituted 25 percent of all Dominican immigrants to the United States (Torres-Saillant and Hernández 1998: 64).

The continually worsening economic conditions in the Dominican Republic of the 1980s brought about a shift in the type of Dominicans moving to the United States. At this time, there was "an increase in the number of professional and technical workers who emigrated because of the decline of public services, the drastic fall in the Dominican peso, and the loss of stable and well-paid jobs" (Torres-Saillant and Hernández 1998: 59).

While the majority of emigrants made the United States their destination, Puerto Rico was the second most common site. Of those Dominicans immigrating to the United States, the 1990 census showed that 65 percent of them lived in the state of New York (Torres-Saillant and Hernández 1998: 61). At that same time, the number of Dominican-born individuals living in the United States equaled approximately 24 percent of the population of the capital of the Dominican Republic, Santo Domingo. Given that the population of the second-largest city in the Dominican Republic, Santiago, was about 279,000 at that time, New York was probably the city with the second-largest Dominican population (Graham 1998: 45). The six years between 1990 and 1996 showed that more than 300,000 Dominican legal residents entered the United States (*ibid.*, 44).

As this process of mass out-migration continues, the country is losing many of its most skilled individuals, for despite the large numbers of unemployed in the Dominican Republic it is not these people that migrate.

Rather, it is those workers with at least some amount of education "whose wages and security are threatened indirectly by the existence of a large reserve labor" (Gramsuck and Pessar 1991: 95). Additionally, the largest number of Dominican immigrants to the United States are women who work in the manufacturing or service sector in the major cities of the Northeast (Georges 1990: 9). The backgrounds of those who leave the Dominican Republic are diverse, but nevertheless, their destiny tends to be the working class (*ibid.*, 46).

"Here" and "There"

The Dominican immigrants in the United States constitute a transnational community, that is, a community "characterized by a constant flow of people in both directions, a dual sense of identity, ambivalent attachments to two nations, and a far-flung network of kinship and friendship ties across state frontiers" (Duany 1994b: 2). Immigrants belong not only to their host community but to their home as well, and as a result of these associations, they develop extremely fluid identities. These new identities are neither based entirely on the home identity nor on that of the host; rather, they are a blend of the two.

In the case of Dominican immigrants, the trend has been to place the greatest emphasis on the home nation as opposed to the host. The focus of the majority of these people remains on the island, and most emphasize that they plan to make their stay in the United States a temporary one. They carefully save up their money for return trips back to their nation of origin, especially at Christmas, and keep up to date with events in the Dominican Republic.

In an investigation among New York Dominicans, Jorge Duany found that the majority of those he interviewed—31 of 37—"felt Dominican, not American and not even Dominican-American" (1994b: 33). There is a constant psychological and verbal distinction between the immigrants' new residence and their home country, "emphasized ... [by] the possessive adjective (*mi*) when referring to the Dominican Republic but not to the United States, which they usually called *este país* ('this country'). This semantic distance denoted an emotional distance and a critical attitude toward the host society" (*ibid.*, 34). The separation between the host and home nations was also emphasized by immigrants' use of "*aquí*" and "*allá*" ("here" and "there") when contrasting the United States with the Dominican Republic (*ibid.*, 40). This practice is not surprising, given that "[d]iasporas always leave a trail of collective memory about another place and time and create new maps of desire and attachment" (Malkki 1996: 448).

Therefore, the distance between *allá* (there) and their current location within the United States reinvents a vision of "homeland" and "Dominican" for Dominicans of the Diaspora.

In an attempt to make *este país* (this country) as much like their own nation as they can, Dominicans replicate many aspects of their culture. This is facilitated in New York City by the fact that Dominican immigrants have tended to cluster in specific neighborhoods. The largest concentration of Dominicans in New York is found in Washington Heights; Hamilton Heights and Inwood are also common Dominican barrios. In these areas, *bodegas* (typical small grocery stores) and other common Dominican businesses line the streets. Small religious shrines and Dominican-style decorations adorn the homes. Dominican newspapers are sold, restaurants serve typical foods, men play dominoes and shout *piropos* (flirtatious comments) at the women passersby, and merengue is heard, though it is not always a product of Dominican musicians in the home country.

Links to the Dominican Republic are commonly maintained through family ties. Many immigrants return a monthly portion of their paycheck to relatives on the island, and on trips back to the Dominican Republic they fill suitcases with North American goods to take home as gifts. The impact of these funds should not be underestimated, for "[b]y 1996 they [the immigrants] would be wiring a billion dollars back to their country each year" (Wucker 1999b: 203). The high rates of Dominican migration have also affected the country socially, for it "has permitted thousands to acquire the sociocultural trappings of upward mobility without the wrenching transformations that such mobility would have required if it had been generated locally" (Gramsuck and Pessar 1991: 95).

Nevertheless, many Dominican immigrants have not enjoyed a greatly improved economic situation in the United States. There are many who are still below the poverty line and who suffer the related social consequences. Still, Dominicans continue to leave their homeland for the North for various reasons. Some were "invited" by the government to emigrate during the Balaguer years. Land concentration has forced many dispossessed *campesinos* out of the Dominican Republic, and still others are merely "*loco para irse*—'obsessed with leaving'—motivated by consumerism" (Manuel 1995: 107) and adventure.

Among the problems that have become prevalent among Dominican immigrants are those of crime and drug trafficking. Because of the violence and bloodshed associated with narcotics, the Dominican group as a whole has been branded with an unwanted identity as drug dealers or *Dominican Yorks*. Those involved in this illegal trade are but a small percentage of Dominicans in the United States and are commonly Dominican youth who are unable to find jobs. (Torres-Saillant and Hernández

1998: 93–5).* Despite several prominent cases exploited by the media, it is inaccurate and unjust to label all Dominican immigrants as drug traffickers. As Silvio Torres-Saillant aptly notes, "[d]efamatory portrayals of Dominicans in the press have serious detrimental effects on the community.... Dominicans in the United States have lost the privilege of individuality—that is, the ability of a person of Dominican descent to commit a crime or an act of charity and be judged individually" (1998b: 142–43).

"[U]mbilicalism"—the Dominicans immigrants' continuous ties to the home nation (Graham 1998: 47)—successfully discouraged many of them from becoming involved in politics in the United States. The strong and ongoing focus on the island, as well as the dream of many Dominicans to return home after accumulating sufficient wealth, has resulted in extremely low rates of citizenship among them. Because most have not yet become citizens (Duany 1994b: 5), they have not been sufficiently represented politically on local, state and national levels.

At first, the focus on "*alla*"—on the home country and events there—prevented Dominicans from taking an avid interest in the politics of their host nation. Many of the immigrants were politically oriented towards the Dominican Republic, and political groups that Dominicans did form in their new home were generally focused on happenings on the island. In much the same way, only small numbers of Dominican immigrants in Puerto Rico have become citizens of the United States (Duany 1998: para. 49). This common decision demonstrates that "state and territory are not sufficient to make a nation, and ... citizenship does not amount to a true nativeness" (Malkki 1996: 446). Diasporas such as this, then, show us that nation and nationality "[have] powerful associations with particular localities and territories ... [and are] a supralocal, transnational cultural form" (*ibid.*, 447).

A shift in attitudes towards American citizenship began in the late 1980s when a generation of Dominicans who had spent most of their lives in the United States reached the age at which they could begin to participate in their host nation's politics. These young men and women, educated in North American schools, were able to make contacts and ties with other Dominicans and Latin Americans. The cultural identification with the Dominican Republic then served to unite Dominican-Americans behind their own political candidates in the United States.

In 1991, Dominicans made their first inroads into New York City politics when Guillermo Linares was elected to the New York city council. Five

---

*A song performed by Sandy Reeves emphasizes the difficult situation of Dominican immigrants that has driven some to embrace crime and drugs: "'Here your life isn't worth a rotten guava; if the hoodlums don't kill you, the factory will'" [*Aquí la vida no vale una guayaba podrida; si un tíguere no te mata, te mata la factoría*] (Manuel 1995: 107; translation in Notes, 260).

years later, Adriano Espaillat was elected to the New York State Legislature, making him "the highest level elected official of Dominican origin in the United States" (Graham 1998: 40). The outlook for Dominican participation in host country politics continues to improve, thanks in part to a 1996 amendment to the Dominican Constitution that allows all Dominicans born in the Republic to retain citizenship even if they became citizens of another nation.

Immigration forces a reconsideration of individual and collective identity. This process results in "narcissistic injuries through loss of status and the loss of such self-objects as familiar surroundings and the persons or customs upon which much of a sense of self is based" (Torres-Saillant and Hernández 1998: 91). The term by which those in the Republic refer to emigrants, *los dominicanos ausentes* (the absent Dominicans), not only emphasizes a geographical distance from "home" but a psychological one as well (Austerlitz 1997: 131). As newcomers, Dominicans must rethink numerous elements of their individual and national identities. For them, the most disconcerting of these adjustments has been the need to reconsider questions of ethnicity and race in the United States and Puerto Rico.

Immigration and Notions of Race

Race is rigidly binary in the United States, defined as either black or white. Whereas a person of mixed race would not even be termed a *mulato* in the Dominican Republic, that individual would immediately be labeled as black in the U.S. Dominicans who are considered and identify themselves as white in their home nation suddenly find themselves face to face with racial discrimination when they immigrate to the United States. The majority of Dominicans in the U.S. does not associate culturally with African Americans, and in fact, Dominicans strive to create a distinction between themselves and that group "by speaking Spanish, dancing the merengue, rejecting black hairstyles and speech patterns, and associating themselves primarily with other Latinos" (Duany 1998: para. 41). Furthermore, the Dominican immigrants attach themselves to Dominican national symbols, such as merengue and typical Dominican foods, to carve out their own niche within the Latino group. Some Dominicans, however, do identify themselves as black when in the United States, though they define themselves as *indio* or white when in their home nation (*ibid.*, 50). In this way, they are capable of creating for themselves an identity that fits more comfortably in each of the racial paradigms within which they must operate.

Dominican immigrants to Puerto Rico, too, have found themselves to be on the receiving end of racial discrimination. In contrast to the situation in the United States, Puerto Ricans consider mulattos of light complexion white, just as in the Dominican Republic. Puerto Ricans tend to see *mulatos* as a distinct group and acknowledge them as part of their multiracial heritage (Duany 1998: para. 20). The brunt of anti–Dominican discrimination in Puerto Rico comes not from racial questions of black or white but rather from questions of nationality. Just "[l]ike Haitians in the Dominican Republic, Dominicans in Puerto Rico are becoming scapegoats for underlying racial tensions" (*ibid.*, para. 48). These tensions have contributed heavily to the lack of Dominican assimilation into Puerto Rican culture.

Merengue in and of the Diaspora

In the United States, Puerto Rico and elsewhere, Dominicans have continued to embrace symbols of their identity as a means of dealing with the stresses of immigrant life. One of the most common elements in this process has been the national dance. Dominican migrants carry their music with them, and that music responds in turn to their new situations. Not only do Dominican immigrants compose music about their situation away from home in a foreign land; Dominicans on the island also include themes by and about the *dominicanos ausentes* in their repertoire.

Juan Luis Guerra, in his 1990 merengue "*Visa para un sueño*" ("Visa for a Dream"), captured the essence of what had become a common experience for many Dominicans of diverse backgrounds: waiting in line to apply for a visa to leave their home country for another. The lyrics reveal the dishonesty often used as the hopefuls resort to any means to acquire the piece of paper that will allow them to leave. Periodic references to the time of day mark its slow passage and the desperation that mounts with each hour.

This merengue also deals with those Dominicans who, unable to obtain that particular "visa for a dream," try to immigrate illegally to Puerto Rico by boat (Duany 1994a: 77). Towards the end of the song, the sound of a helicopter is heard, alluding to the United States immigration officials who search out and deport illegal immigrants. The merengue's impact is strengthened by reminding listeners of those individuals whose efforts to emigrate to Puerto Rico by boat are thwarted when their tiny vessels capsize and they become "*carne de la mar*"—fishbait (*ibid.*).

Dominicans from home often travel to visit relatives and friends who have immigrated to the United States. Likewise, those still living on the island eagerly await holidays and other opportunities for the immigrants to return to visit them in the Dominican Republic. The things that link the two worlds take on a magnified importance for both groups. Among these ties, one of the most commonly recognized was Flight 587, the most popular flight of the day between New York and Santo Domingo, especially during the Christmas holiday season.

In 1996, Kinito Méndez composed a merengue about the flight entitled "*El vuelo 587*" ("Flight 587"). Performed and recorded with Johnny Ventura, the lively and happy merengue highlighted that symbol joining the two worlds of "here" and "there." Although this merengue was recorded five years before, the song was revisited when that very flight, American Airlines Flight 587, crashed in New York in 2001. Additionally, Méndez's 2002 album *Sigo siendo el Hombre Merengue* (I'm Still the Merengue Man) included a new composition dealing specifically with the tragedy of the crash of Flight 587, entitled "*¿Qué pasó ahí?*" ("What Happened There?"). The song's lyrics captured the anticipation of those who took the flight and emphasized the sense of collective loss on the part of the Dominican people. The merengue served as a common bond and a common language to join grieving Dominicans worldwide and called on Dominicans to honor those lost in the crash by being hardworking and humble representatives of their country so that they could say "'I'm Dominican/but with dignity" ("*soy dominicano/pero con dignidad*").

> *Son las siete de la mañana*
> *de un día de noviembre.*
> *Los pasajeros se preparan para abordar*
> *con sus maletas cargados de sueños,*
> *regalos y esperanzas para la isla.*
> *Una mañana, mes de noviembre,*
> *arranca el vuelo lleno de gloria*
> *y va cargando de gente buena,*
> *de gente humilde y trabajadora*
> *con la esperanza de ver su gente,*
> *ver su familia y llevar felicidad.*
> *Y el destino le cambió total*
> *su vida de manera brutal.*
> *Tres minutos el vuelo que duró*
> *ese viaje que finalizó*
> *con la vida de mi gente*
> *que quisieron estar presente pa'*
> *pasar una feliz Navidad*
> *lleno de felicidad...*
> *...El 587,*
> *el vuelo de la mañana,*

iban llenos de esperanza
*mi gente dominicana...**
It's seven in the morning
on a November day.
The passengers prepare to board
with their suitcases full of dreams,
gifts and hopes for the island.
One morning in the month of November,
the flight takes off, full of glory
and carrying good people,
humble and hardworking people,
with the hope of seeing their people,
seeing their family and carrying happiness.
And destiny changed their lives completely
in a brutal way.
The flight lasted three minutes,
that flight that ended
the life of my people
who wanted to be present
to have a Merry Christmas
full of happiness...
...Five eighty-seven,
the morning flight,
they went, full of hope,
my Dominican people...

In the same way that radio forms a sense of simultaneity and community by allowing individuals in diverse locations to listen to the same songs, Dominican immigrants to the United States, Puerto Rico and other nations listen to recordings of merengues to psychologically strengthen their ties to their nation of origin. In situations in which they feel their identity to be threatened—such as racial discrimination in the United States and anti–Dominicanism in Puerto Rico—the music serves to unify them as a collectivity and to separate them from other groups. This need for a sense of unity with Dominicans in the homeland aptly illustrates the duality of Diasporic identities: "on the one hand, we have global identities because we have a stake in something global and, on the other hand, we can only know ourselves because we are part of some face-to-face communities" (Hall 1996: 343).

In its new settings, merengue has become a popular dance music among Latinos and non–Latinos alike. For this reason, Delfín Pérez has commented that "'[m]erengue has taken over just the way the aggressive,

---

*Lyrics by J. del Carmen Ramírez, courtesy of J & N Publishing.

hard-working Dominicans have taken over entire neighborhoods of New York'" (in Manuel 1995: 109). As the Dominican communities grew in the United States and Puerto Rico, merengue groups began to organize. Unlike the so-called "transplant" musics that have no ties with their home countries, merengue is a transnational music precisely because of the strong links that unite immigrants with the Republic (Austerlitz 1997: 124). Merengue flows in both directions and remains popular in each place.

In Puerto Rico, merengue had a following for quite some time because the country is a Spanish-speaking nation with a Caribbean culture that shares similarities with Dominican culture (Austerlitz 1997: 128). Dominican immigrants to Puerto Rico began to form their own merengue bands, and these rapidly became successful. The first of such groups to make strong inroads to popularity in Puerto Rico was *Conjunto Quisqueya* in 1974 (Batista Matos 1999: 181). Soon, merengue had become so common in Puerto Rico that many *puertorriqueños* began to accept it as their own music (*ibid.*).

Although merengue appealed to the Puerto Rican masses, it did not appeal to the Institute of Puerto Rican Culture (ICP). This state body determines the official cultural identity of the Puerto Rican people, an image that has many similarities to that of the rustic *campesino cibaeño* (peasant from the Cibao region) of the Dominican Republic. Any ICP-sponsored cultural event, therefore, contains what are officially deemed traditional music and dance. The New York–born Latino hybrid, salsa, is excluded from ICP programs, as is merengue, "which is criticized for being an 'inferior rhythm' and an example of *chabacanería* (what is cheap and inferior)" (Davila 1997: 195).

This vision of merengue is linked to the racism and discrimination that Dominicans have endured as immigrants to Puerto Rico. The association between merengue and Dominican-ness is so strong that the ICP refuses to include the music in its events lest they "'turn the festival into a Dominican rather than a Puerto Rican cultural festival'" (Davila 1997: 195). Nevertheless, this identification has only served to strengthen Dominican pride in the national music, for "[a]s a defensive strategy, many immigrants are reasserting their own cultural background" (Duany 1998: para. 48). Dominican immigrants play their merengue, display their national flag and follow their customs in an aggressive stance that Duany has defined as "an oppositional or reactive identity" (*ibid.*).

Despite the tendency of the ICP and the elite to shun merengue, the same companies and corporations that sponsor official cultural programs in Puerto Rico also help fund local events that feature the music. These events are not considered "cultural" because they contain foreign elements (Davila 1997: 201). Regardless, these programs and dances continue to appeal to the masses.

Batista Matos attributes the growing acceptance of merengue in Puerto Rico to the music of such merengue greats as Johnny Ventura and Wilfrido Vargas (1999: 187). He also points to a boycott of Dominican merengue orchestras imposed by the Federation of Puerto Rican Musicians, which served to inspire Puerto Ricans to create their own merengue groups (*ibid.*, 188).

The 1990s marked merengue's solidification of popularity in Puerto Rico (Batista Matos 1999: 181). It is important to note that this phenomenon is not one of "rhythmical symbiosis or social syncretism ... but rather the supplanting of one musical culture by another distinct one" [*la simbiosis rítmica o ... [el] sincretismo social ... sino ... la suplantación de una cultura musical por otra distinta*] (*ibid.*, 186). In other words, Puerto Ricans have not borrowed from merengue or combined it with what they or the ICP consider "traditional" Puerto Rican rhythms; rather, they have embraced merengue as a whole and perform it in the same way as Dominicans. The uniformity of Dominican and Puerto Rican merengue is primarily the result of uniform record-production practices. Because Santo Domingo's recording studios are better, merengueros from both islands record in those studios (*ibid.*, 192).

The degree of the Puerto Rican fever for merengue has resulted in a strange situation: by 1995, "Puerto Rico would not only have more merengue orchestras than salsa but also, more orchestras than the Dominican Republic" [*Puerto Rico no sólo tendría más orquestas de merengue que de salsa, sino también, más orquestas que la República Dominicana*] (Batista Matos 1999: 189). By 1999, Puerto Rico could boast three times the number of merengue orchestras as the Dominican Republic (*ibid.*, 193)

Several Puerto Rican *merengueros* have achieved transnational acclaim. For example, Elvis Crespo held a prominent place on the international merengue stage with his 1998 release *Suavemente* (Softly). Crespo's slower-paced merengue has proven quite popular; in fact, *Suavemente* sold over 600,000 copies. Two of Crespo's subsequent releases—*Píntame* (1999) and *Urbano* (2002)—have been very successful as well. Despite short passages that include other styles, and a handful of pop ballads, Crespo's music has retained a danceable merengue base.

Crespo emphasizes that his merengue is structurally the same as Dominican merengue, and he reiterates the link that identifies merengue with the Dominican Republic. Crespo notes that Puerto Rican and Dominican merengue are uniform: "'[I]t's the same. The same merengue with the same meaning, a merengue with quality. It is the merengue that we Puerto Ricans interpret, because the merengue as such is Dominican'" (Alas n.d.: para. 8).

Likewise, Puerto Rican *merenguera* Olga Tañón, whose first record was released in 1992, has enjoyed great popularity in the global arena. In fact, Tañón has been so successful that she has been labeled the *"Reina del Merengue"*—the Queen of Merengue. Tañón's nationality does nothing to dissuade Dominicans from being fans of her music, and it is popular among Dominicans around the world.

Merengue's acceptance in the North American market occurred later than in Puerto Rico, no doubt because of the language difference. The first inroads made into the United States were in 1967 when Primitivo Santos, Joseíto Mateo and Alberto Beltrán performed merengue at Madison Square Garden. This concert marked the arrival of merengue on the transnational stage (Austerlitz 1997: 127).

In the 1970s, merengue continued its climb. Toward the end of the decade, salsa degenerated into a less exciting and more predictable music at the same time that merengue's popularity and degree of innovation continued to rise. An easier dance for non–Latinos to learn, the merengue surpassed salsa as the most popular Latin dance music in the United States in the 1980s.

Puerto Rican *merenguero* Elvis Crespo became internationally recognized with his 1998 *"Suavemente."* Merengue has exploded in popularity in Puerto Rico, despite the Institute of Puerto Rican Culture's refusal to include it in official cultural events. (Photograph: Gina Aversano, Elvis Crespo World Fan Club)

Merengue's rise to stardom was accelerated by the growing popularity of the poetic lyrics of Juan Luis Guerra. The artist's achievement of a Grammy for Best Latin Tropical Album in 1991 catapulted the Dominican music into the global spotlight. Not only was merengue popular in the Dominican Republic, Puerto Rico, and the United States, it became a hit in Europe and Asia as well.

As the Dominican community grew in the United States, various merengue bands formed there. Some of the first of such groups were *Milly, Jocelyn y los Vecinos, La Gran Manzana* and the New York Band. Of these, the most popular both in the host and the home countries was *Milly, Jocelyn y los Vecinos,* a group comprised of two sisters as vocalists and their brothers as musicians. This band, which was discussed in conjunction with the role of *merengueras* in Chapter 8, also produced merengues whose themes dealt with "the tensions and transformations emanating from the experience of migration" (Torres-Saillant and Hernández 1998: 136). In an interview with Paul Austerlitz, lead singer Milly Quezada commented that her band had been organized "'out of a need ... to kind of stay in tune with what was happening with our music and with our cultural background in general'" (Austerlitz 1997: 126). This illustrates the concrete link to *allá* that merengue provides for Dominican immigrants.

New York has long been an important site in the merengue recording industry. Thanks both to Dominican artists and Dominican immigrant groups, "New York City has recently become the commercial capital of the Dominican music industry" (Duany 1994b: 7, footnote). Merengue's New York base has also facilitated the music's dispersal and acceptance on the global stage. Now, the music flows simultaneously between the island and the States, and outward to points around the globe.

Generation Ñ and "Crossover" Music

At the beginning of the twenty-first century, Dominican-Americans are in a prime position to make a mark on North American culture. These Dominican immigrants are Latinos, the fastest growing minority in the United States. The 2000 census revealed that Latinos "have become the largest minority group in the U.S., surpassing African Americans at least six years sooner than expected" (Tumulty 2001: 74). The influence of Hispanic youth, a full 13.6 percent of U.S. adolescents in 1999, has already begun to make its impact on North American culture and retail trends (Stapinski 1999: para. 13).

The younger Dominicans who are becoming politically active—those who have spent all or the better part of their life in the United States—are part of a group that Bill Teck has named "Generation Ñ." With this term, Teck refers to younger Hispanics who do not quite fit the depiction of American "Gen-Xers." These are individuals who are "truly bicultural Latinos, coming into their 20s and 30s with demographic clout, education skills and cultural juice their parents never imagined" (Figueroa et al. 1999: 53). Their identity is a mix of their two heritages and they must "[live] in two worlds at once without losing anything in the translation" (*ibid.*). For the most part, they are bilingual, though their primary language is often English.

The members of Generation Ñ are distinguished from their parents' generation in that they are not aiming for assimilation. While surveys found that most Latinos 35 and older identified themselves as Americans, most of those under that age consider themselves Hispanic. This marks a notable change from previous generations of Latino immigrants.

According to Stapinski, music is the first ingredient in most "cultural waves" to impact mainstream society (1999: para. 12), and Latino "crossover" artists have already made an impression.* Singers with Hispanic backgrounds such as Gloria Estéfan, Jon Secada and Selena were some of the biggest names of the 1990s. As Aparicio points out, we must

> think of crossover music in terms of audience configurations, needs and reception practices associated with cross-cultural dynamics.... [C]rossing over has been made possible by a new emerging Hispanic audience "increasingly imbued with Anglo culture and energized by its very own political and economic aspirations" rather than "from an appeal to some new, largely Anglo audience" [1995: 111].

Given the growing self-awareness among members of Generation Ñ, it is not surprising that the most significant surge in Latino crossover began in May 1999 with Puerto Rican singer Ricky Martin's explosion onto the North American music scene with his hit "Livin' La Vida Loca." This song, which featured Latin sounds and rock mixed with Martin's Elvis-like stage presence and appearance, was a tremendous success not only among Hispanic-Americans but also in the rest of the American and international public. Martin, whose Spanish-language albums (as well as recordings in French, German and Portuguese) had already enjoyed international popularity—four of his solo albums were gold or platinum worldwide—was suddenly vaulted onto center stage of the American pop music scene. His concerts were sold out and throngs waited for hours to see him perform. Martin's first English-language album was released on May 11, 1999, and by the end of that month his popularity had ballooned to such an extent that he was featured on the cover of *Time*.

Ricky Martin was but the first of several Latin artists who began making their way onto the North American stage at that point. Soon, Spaniard Enrique Iglesias soared up the charts with "*Bailamos*" ("Tonight We Dance"), and salsa sensation Marc Anthony's first English-language release came not long after. Colombian rock musician Shakira, who was awarded a World Music Award in 1998 for "best-selling female Latin artist" for her 1996 *Pies Descalzos*, has risen to rapid popularity with her English-language album *Laundry Service*. The Latin rock band Maná is also reported to be considering doing some songs in English.

---

*Although "crossover" is the predominant terminology used to describe these artists, its appropriateness is questionable, as we shall see in the following pages.

This recent surge in Latino "crossover" has brought with it several polemic issues concerning authenticity "and to what extent it can be compromised in an effort to reach a wider audience" (Gardner 1999: para. 10). While the inclusion of certain instruments and rhythms mixed with a phrase or two in Spanish and some fancy footwork is capable of giving a music "Latin flavor" (*ibid.*), does it really make that music "Latin?"

At the same time, the question is posed: who qualifies as a "crossover" artist? Are Ricky Martin, Jon Secada and Gloia Estéfan "crossover musicians" merely because they were born in Latin American countries? If this is the case, then where does one situate two-time Grammy winner Marc Anthony, the popular *salsero* who was born to Puerto Rican parents in New York City? Does the term "crossover" apply in both directions so that included within this rubric are North American boy-bands like 98°, whose song "Give Me Just One Night" ("Una Noche") incorporates Spanish and a stereotypical Latin beat?

Often, "crossover artists" are defined as those who were successful in the Spanish-language market before recording in English. If this is the case, then one must ask how to consider musicians such as model-actress-turned-singer Jennifer Lopez (another New Yorker of Puerto Rican parents) and Christina Aguilera. As J.D. Considine reminds us, "[m]erely having a Hispanic surname does not make a singer a Latin super star. Jennifer Lopez might have played Latin phenom Selena in the movie, but with her own album ... Lopez comes across as the New York born pop/soul singer she is in real life. Nor is there anything particularly Latin about the sound of Christina Aguilera's self-titled debut" (1999: para. 6).

Issues of authenticity remind us that these Latin musical forms themselves often bear North American influence. As in the case of merengue, rock and disco heavily influenced the Dominican national music. Other North American musics such as jazz, blues, soul, rap, house and hip-hop have left and are leaving their mark on numerous forms of *música latina*; this in turn influences North American music. As we consider the impact of the mix of Latin and North American musical styles and forms, it is necessary to keep in mind that "[a] group adopts or adapts certain musical styles for reasons that go far beyond the simple compatibility of styles" (Seeger 1992: 459).

As the current North American pop-music taste for things Latin continues, it is best not to apply the label of "Latin music" loosely. As Considine so aptly insists, "[w]hat makes it [the music] Latin is language" (1999: para. 9). According to this definition the music that has become so enticing in today's U.S. pop music charts cannot truly be considered "Latin." Rather it is a blend, a mix of cultures—just like the fusion of identities lived daily by Hispanic Americans of Generation Ñ. If Latin music is music in the languages of Latin America, a Latin "crossover artist" could most aptly be defined as one "who previously has appealed only to Spanish-speaking music fans" and who "ends up with an equally large audience of English-speakers" (*ibid.*, para. 9)

In studying the Latin "crossover" artists who have enjoyed the greatest success, it is absolutely necessary to consider questions of race. Those that have truly "made it" in the North American pop music industry so far have been, by and large, "white, middle- and upper-class, educated musicians" (Aparicio 1998: 108). Gloria Estéfan, Rubén Blades, Juan Luis Guerra, and more recently, Ricky Martin, Enrique Iglesias and Shakira— all fit neatly into this paradigm. As in the Dominican Republic where merengue was popularized by the elite only after certain stylistic alterations were undertaken to better mask the African influence, in the United States Latin "'black musics were accepted only in a white disguise'" (Willie Colón, cited in Aparicio 1998: 115).

The word "crossover" implies a certain binary parallelism between cultures and musical styles. In this paradigm, one cultural form, Latin music, has merely changed lanes to enter into the North American mainstream at full speed. This image largely ignores that "crossing over has been made possible by a new emerging Hispanic audience ... rather than 'from an appeal to some new, largely Anglo audience'" (Aparicio 1995: 111).

At the same time, the term "crossover" carries with it a certain sense of hierarchy. Despite the fact that Northern musics have already had impact on many of the styles and forms that are now shaping U.S. pop music, this term implies a one-way direction of influence. This system leaves little room for question. Latino artists are seen as not only moving over but moving up as well. Global interest in and acceptance of Latin and Latin-based music, therefore, has resulted in the music's "'validation through visibility'" (Averill 1994: 168), a visibility made possible by its English lyrics.

Rather than a binary model, it is more accurate to consider Latin music's entrance onto the North American pop scene as a process of filtering. Merengue's history provides a clear example of this phenomenon. From its heavily Afro-Caribbean roots (not excluding Haiti), merengue was systematically whitened across the decades and centuries to make it more appealing to groups that saw themselves as white. First masked under the guise of *danzas típicas* in the early 1900s, merengue was altered to such an extent under Trujillo that it became appealing to the elite. The result was a decisive split between the *típico* and *orquesta* styles of the genre. Post-Trujillo merengue incorporated enough foreign (and specifically, North American) influences that the resulting product was yet another style, pop merengue. As the music passed through Puerto Rico, it was at first scorned because of its association with Dominicans; later, merengue became acceptable there when Puerto Ricans claimed it to be their own. Finally, merengue has gained transnational popularity in large part due to artists such as Juan Luis Guerra and Puerto Rican Elvis Crespo, artists, as we have already noted, who are "white, middle- and upper-class, educated musicians" (Aparicio 1998: 108).

This process of filtration accurately illustrates how music responds not only to national stimuli but to international stimuli as well. Such alterations demonstrate the effect of neo-colonial attitudes on Latin music. What neo-colonial powers expect of and will accept in Latin forms directly affects how those styles will be altered and commercialized to win international acceptance and appeal.

In addition to the softening or outright extraction of more pronounced African elements, the Latino music that is gaining a strong following in the United States has undergone one final step to make it acceptable to North American audiences: its language has been "whitened" as well.

"Crossover," therefore, seems an inaccurate term for this style. Given the filtration this music has undergone to finally "make it" in the North American pop music arena, it seems more appropriate to give this innovative blend a name that better distinguishes it as a genre, such as "New Hispanic."

Within this current craze for things Latino in the United States, who are the Dominicans and Dominican-Americans who are playing a role? In the world of literature, Dominican-American writers such as Julia Álvarez and Junot Díaz have had widespread success with their novels and stories in English about the Dominican immigrant's experience in the United States.* Likewise, Dominican fashion designer Óscar de la Renta has won international acclaim, as have Sammy Sosa and numerous other Dominican baseball players.

But what about Dominican "crossover" musicians? In his 1991 article about Juan Luis Guerra, Tim Padgett commented that "U.S. music watches warn that without a couple of English tunes, the gringos may step out to dance to Guerra on Friday night but will never keep him on their car stereo on Monday morning" (75). Although Guerra and other merengueros have gained a following in the tropical dance clubs, none has yet achieved the popularity of artists such as Ricky Martin, Gloria

---

*Julia Alvarez has also written two historical novels about well-known figures of Dominican history: the Mirabal sisters in *In the Time of the Butterflies* (1994) and nineteenth-century poet Salomé Ureña Henríquez in *In the Name of Salomé* (2000).

Estéfan and Marc Anthony, whose bilingual (or at times, purely English) music represents a mix of Latin sounds with North American styles.

Is merengue, which has served as a type of language to communicate Dominican identity for over 150 years, capable of "crossing over?" Or, is merengue in English truly still merengue? Given the traditionally polemic nature of determining what is appropriate or inappropriate, what is or is not truly merengue, an attempt to term any English-language merengue as merengue is likely to meet with heated resistance by Dominicans both at home and abroad.

Proyecto Uno

As was noted earlier, musical forms resulting from alterations to merengue have tended to be labeled with different names, though at times

Proyecto Uno, the creators of merengue hip-hop. Nelson Zapata, founder of the band, began working with merengue at age 22, combining it with other musical genres such as techno, house, rap and hip-hop to produce a new creation that "reflected how ... [his] life was, a mixture of both worlds" (Zapata 2002). (Photograph courtesy of **Proyecto Uno**)

Proyecto Uno (**Photograph courtesy of** *Proyecto Uno*)

these very similar rhythms—such as the *maco*—were still identified as merengue by many Dominicans. *Proyecto Uno*, a band whose music exemplifies the duality of being Dominican-American, has created a highly original hybrid musical form that blends the Dominican national music with various North American styles. Known as "merengue hip-hop," this music combines merengue and the Spanish language with rap, hip-hop, reggae and English. Dominican-American Nelson Zapata, who created this genre in 1988, admitted in a personal interview that he was not a huge fan of the Dominican national music before he immigrated to the United States with his parents at age 14. In fact, Zapata notes, he was far more "in touch" with music in English than in Spanish before leaving his home country.

It was the alienating experience of being an immigrant that led Zapata to the music of his homeland. "When I moved to New York, I missed my home country; then I started getting more familiar with merengue music to the point I got to love it" (Zapata 2002). "Homesick, he and his Dominican friends used to sit in the Seward Park High School cafeteria drumming tambora and guira rhythms on the tabletops.... Eventually, he ended up playing guira and singing in a merengue band" (Valdes 1996: para. 20).

At the age of 22, Zapata began working with merengue innovatively, blending in techno, house, rap and hip-hop in his desire to create something that "reflected how ... [his] life was, a mixture of both worlds" (Zapata 2002). *Proyecto Uno*'s first release, "*Todo el Mundo,*" was a hit throughout the Americas. Merengue hip-hop was born. The band's success in Latin America was tremendous, and even in the United States club-goers were dancing to the English-language version of their hit "*El Tiburón.*"

Merengue hip-hop is a new language to communicate the Latino immigrant's experience in the United States: "'Our sound doesn't need translations. It is only rhythm and dance'" [*Nuestro sonido no necesita traducciones. Es tan solo ritmo y baile*] (Nelson Zapata, quoted in www.proyecto-uno.com). It is the innovative nature of the style that makes "hard, acid or heavy merengue the freshest creation, which exhibits the common street slang of Upper Manhattan" [*[e]l merengue duro, ácido o heavy, es el invento más fresco, que expone la jerga vulgar callejera del Alto Manhattan*] (Batista Matos 1999: 175).

In addition to being a mix of languages, traditions, rhythms and musical styles, merengue hip-hop represents a fusion of two identities. *Proyeto Uno*'s innovative sound "is full of the New York Dominican and Puerto Rican flavor. It is the sound of the Latinos in New York that celebrate their native heritage while they include the sound of their new land" [*se llena del sabor neoyorquino dominicano y puertorriqueño. Es el sonido de los latinos en Nueva York que celebran su herencia nativa mientras incluyen el sonido de su nueva tierra*] (www.proyecto-uno.com).

It is precisely the Dominican-Americans' dual identity that band members point to as the reason for their success: "'We are what we do.... It's all 100 percent real with us'" (Valdes 1996: para. 17); "'[i]t's very true that we're the first group to capture this market ... the reason being that we've lived everything that we're doing'" (*ibid.*, para. 35). The music represents the diverse influences to which they have been exposed—the Spanish television that their parents and grandparents watched and the MTV that the younger generations preferred (Zapata 2002). It is a concrete representation of the two identities of many Dominican-Americans. Therefore, it is accurate to say that the genre's creator, Nelson Zapata, "a product of the Dominican migration, collaborated only with the two sides of himself" (Valdes 1996: para. 39) in the creation of this unique musical form.

This dual identity lends itself perfectly to hip-hop, a musical form that mixes numerous stylistic elements. For example, a traditional Spanish children's song used to learn to add numbers appears in the heart of *Proyecto Uno*'s "*Está pega'o*":*

Dos y dos son cuatro,	Two and two are four,
y cuatro y dos son seis.	and four and two are six.
Seis y dos son ocho	Six and two are eight
y ocho deiciseis.	and eight are sixteen.
Let's go!	Let's go!

Like much merengue and rap, *Proyecto Uno*'s merengue hip-hop at times exemplifies a pronounced sense of machismo. Double entendres reminiscent of merengue abound, and the masculinity of the singing voice is glorified: "*Soy macho, macho, macho*" [I'm macho, macho, macho] (from "*Brinca*"†). Following the aforementioned children's song in "*Está pega'o*," the male voice includes a tally of the number of different women he has been with in a single week, emphasizing the international nature of the immigrant's situation:

Diferentes chicas en una semana:	Different girls in a week:
siete dominicanas, cuatro cubanas,	seven Dominicans, four Cubans,
un par de peruanas	a pair of Peruvians,
y una panameña,	and a Panamanian,
otra puertorriqueña	another Puerto Rican,
y una de Pennsylvania.	and one from Pennsylvania.

Likewise, in "*El Tiburón*" ("The Shark")‡ the male protagonist enters a *discoteca* in search of "*una fresca*" (a fresh woman). First, he has some rum, identifying himself with the national Dominican drink by saying, "where I'm from sometimes you need some." He sees a woman that interests him—"*una princesa*," "*una muñequita*" [a princess, a little doll]. Before

*Lyrics by J. Wilson, N. Zapata, and P. DeJesús, courtesy of J&N Publishing.
†Lyrics by J. Wilson, N. Zapata, and P. DeJesús, courtesy of J&N Publishing.
‡Lyrics by J. Wilson, N. Zapata, and P. DeJesús, courtesy of J&N Publishing.

he gets much farther another man, the infamous *Tiburón* (Shark), takes her from him. Spying another woman, he tries again, this time slipping off his wedding ring and hiding it in his pocket as he hits on her. Once again his amorous efforts are thwarted by the Shark. This song reflects some of the themes found in traditional merengue: male virility and objectification of the female as illustrated by the repeated phrase *"se la llevó el Tiburón"* [the shark took her away for himself]. The repetition of *"el Tiburón"* in the background is sung onomatopoetically to mimic the sound of something being devoured.

In addition to the fast-paced, light-hearted merengue hip-hops already mentioned, other *Proyecto Uno* songs exhibit a deeply romantic side. In contrast to the man who goes out to the bar in search of a good time, devotion is central to the composition *"25 horas"*:

> *Veinticinco horas al día,*
> *Vida mía.*
> *Ocho días a la semana*
> *Si te da la gana. (2×)*
> *Ya no sé cómo decírtelo, Querida.*
> *Pa' que sepas que eres la única en mi vida.*
> *Sé que el amor te ha fallado en el pasado*
> *Pero te asegruo que ahora es de verdad.*
> *Dame la oportunidad de quererte una vez más.*
> *Déjame enseñarte como se conjuga el verbo amar.*
> *Eres todo para mí y no te quiero perder*
> *¿Es que tú no ves? Me vas a enloquecer...**
> Twenty-five hours a day,
> My love.
> Eight days a week,
> If you want. (2×)
> I don't know how to tell you, Honey.
> So that you know that you're the only one in my life.
> I know love has let you down in the past
> But I assure you this time it's real.
> Give me the chance to love you again.
> Let me show you how to conjugate the verb love.
> You're everything to me and I don't want to lose you.
> Can't you see? You're going to drive me crazy...

The Dominican-American immigrant perception of "here" and "there" is also present in *Proyecto Uno*'s romantic songs, as most clearly exemplified by *"Al otro lado del mar"* ("On the Other Side of the Sea"):

---

*Lyrics by N. Zapata, R. Tavar and J. Cedeno, courtesy of Jelly's Jams.

Qué tal mi amor
Ves como pasa el tiempo
Hace tanto que ya no te veo
Pienso en ti en cada momento
Yo por aquí, tú por allá
Dime si eso no es tormento
Y yo deseando tenerte a mi lado
No puedo aguantármelo más.
Al otro lado del mar
Es allá donde te he de encontrar
No sé como ni cuando baby
Pero te voy a buscar
Al otro lado del mar
Es allá donde te he de encontrar
Sólo quiero llegar
Allá dónde tu estás
*Para poderte amar.**
How are you, my love?
See how time passes?
It's been so long since I've seen you.
I think about you every moment.
Me here, you there.
Tell me if this isn't torture.
And me wishing I had you by my side.
I can't stand it any more.
On the other side of the sea
Is where I'll find you.
I don't know how nor when, Baby,
But I'm going to come for you.
On the other side of the sea
Is where I'll find you.
I just want to get there
Where you are
To love you.

Originally performed with a merengue beat, the band released a *bachata* re-mix of "*Al otro lado del mar*" on their 2002 album, *Pura Gozadera* (Pure Fun), thus emphasizing the growing popularity of this other Dominican musical form.

Despite its innovations to the national music and its incorporation of African American and North American music, *Proyecto Uno* continues to hold tightly to a Dominican identity, as illustrated in the following excerpt from their merengue hip-hop "*Está pega'o:*"

*Lyrics by N. Zapata, courtesy of Jelly's Jams.

En mi país	In my country
¿Qué país?	Which country?
Santo Domingo tan lindo.	Beautiful Santo Domingo.
Nací en Nueva York	I was born in New York,
pero no me digas gringo.	but don't call me a gringo.
Yo siento el calor de mi gente.	I feel the warmth of my people.
No necesito Tito para cruzar	I don't need Tito to cross the
el puente;	bridge;
No necesito Julio para ir a la iglesia	I don't need Julio to go to church.

The final two lines of this excerpt are a cunningly crafted play on words, as the surnames of Tito Puente and Julio Iglesias are taken for their literal meanings, "bridge" and "churches," respectively. This denial of the group's need for these icons of Latin music, along with constant repetition of the band's and its members' individual names, emphasizes independence from established musical styles. Nevertheless, they still feel the "warmth of [their] people" (as opposed to the coldness of North Americans). The lyrics indicate that band members feel closely tied to their homeland, and present the belief in an inherent cultural identity that is free from the influence of outside elements and not determined solely by place.

Another *Proyecto Uno* hit, "*Latinos*,"* also reiterates the immigrant's self-identification as Latino, regardless of actual or current citizenship and his or her pride in this identity:

España, Puerto Rico, Venezuela, Santo Domingo,
Honduras, Guatemala, México y Nicaragua,
Chile, Ecuador,
Panamá, el Salvador,
Perú y Cuba,
Uruguay, Paraguay, Colombia,
Costa Rica, Argentina, Bolivia
I am feeling you
mi gente está caliente
latinos hasta la muerte
Spain, Puerto Rico, Venezuela, Santo Domingo,
Honduras, Guatemala, Mexico and Nicaragua,
Chile, Ecuador, Panama, El Salvador,
Peru and Cuba,
Uruguay, Paraguay, Colombia,
Costa Rica, Argentina, Bolivia
I am feeling you
My people are hot
Latinos till death

*Lyrics by M. Quashie and J. Wilson, courtesy of Jelly's Jams.

This expression of a Pan-Latin and Pan-American identity reminds us that claims of national identities are not necessarily determined by geographical boundaries or borders. The contrast of the intensity and warmth of Latinos with the typical Latino view of North Americans as cold, distant and reserved is an important distinguishing factor.

The question of authenticity—who is and who is not Latino, as well as what can truly be considered merengue hip-hop—is present in "*Latinos*" as well:

> ...*Mi gente*
> *Fotocopia, no invente*
> *Estoy harto de la Macarena*
> *Y el chupacabra* y merengue house discos*
> *Que no dicen nada...*
> ...My people
> Not a photocopy
> I'm sick of the Macarena
> And the Chupacabra and merengue house albums
> That don't say anything...

In *Pura Gozadera* (2002), *Proyecto Uno* continues to explore the blending of genres and languages. For example, "*Holla*" is a mixture of reggae and rap, while other songs on the album speak to the world of the twenty-first century. "I Want You to Be My Baby"† specifically deals with love via e-mail and chat rooms:

> *I want you to be my baby...*
> *My super-sonic lover,*
> *I want you like no other.*
> *Le pedí amores a través de la computadora.*
> *Me haces enloquecer,*
> *Te quiero conocer.*
> *Nos vamos a encontrar en horas del atardecer.*
> *Una fotografía me envió.*
> *Qué bonita cara...*
> *Se parece a Sofía Vergara.*
> *Todo listo para la ocasión.*
> *I want her just for me...*
> *La quiero para mí...*
> *[...]*

---

*The *chupacabra* is a mythical creature that reappears throughout Latin America. It is believed to suck the blood from goats (*cabras*) and other animals, but is never spotted in the act.
†Lyrics by N. Zapata, courtesy of Hogland Records.

E-mail a toda hora,
Me dice que me adora.
Tengo una cita con la chica que a mí me devora.
I'll meet you by the mall,
No tardes por favor.
Cita a ciegas, primera vez...
¡Y la última tal vez!
Dime qué hago se ella me mintió
Y qué voy a hacer,
Si esa foto no es de esa mujer.
Todo listo para la ocasión
I want her just for me...
La quiero para mí...
I want you to be my baby...
My super-sonic lover,
I want you like no other.
I asked for love on the computer.
You drive me crazy,
I want to meet you.
We get together at dusk.
She sent me a picture.
What a pretty face...
She looks like Sofía Vergara.
Everything's ready for the occasion.
I want her just for me...
I want her for me...
[...]
E-mail at all hours.
She says she adores me.
I have a date with the girl who devours me.
I'll meet you by the mall,
Please don't be late.
Blind date, first time...
And maybe the last!
Tell me what I should do if she lied to me
And what am I going to do
If that picture
Isn't of that woman?
Everything's ready for the occasion.
I want her just for me...
I want her for me...

Proyecto Uno incorporates another Dominican musical practice for the first time in *Pura Gozadera*. This percussive form, called "*palos*" or "*atabales*," was traditionally performed during religious festivals and wakes (Alas 2002: para. 1).

In *Proyecto Uno*'s *"Bajando,"** however, the *atabales* are mixed with merengue, rap and the affirmation that *Proyecto Uno* was the first merengue hip-hop band:

> *Cinco, cuatro, tres, dos, uno...*
> *¡Es Proyecto! Como ninugno,*
> *Número uno.*
> *Somos los originales...*
> *[...]*
> *...Este es un rítmo de palo con un flow para quemar...*†
> Five, four, three, two, one...
> It's *Proyecto*! Like no other,
> Number one.
> We're the originals...
> [...]
> This is a *palo* rhythm with a flow that burns...

Like merengue, merengue hip-hop is malleable, innovative and constantly being reinvented. Nelson Zapata, founder of *Proyecto Uno*, sees a bright future for the style he originated and remains passionately dedicated to it: "I'm not gonna let it die.... As long as there's music ... and love for it ... while I still have love for it I'm gonna keep doin it" (Zapata 2002).

A Look Forward

Singer Milly Quezada believes that Dominicans in the Diaspora will eventually go through a questioning of their identity, just as have other Latinos with longer histories in the United States. Nevertheless, she sees her band as part of a preservation process to "'keep what we have, because to lose your identity is kind of rough'" (Austerlitz 1997: 130).

Torres-Saillant and Hernández also predict that the "trend of the Dominicans of the next generation will probably not continue to be that of replicating the established forms from the home country. Rather, it will be the creation of alternative forms, combining the rhythms of the native land with those found in the host county" (1998: 137). Proyecto Uno has already paved the way for this type of musical experimentation and inno-

---

*The title of this song carries with it several different interpretations, as explained in the vocabulary list accompanying the CD: "Of course it means to get off, as in to descend. It also applies to downing drinks, getting down dancing in the disco, and other things." [*Claro que significa bajar, de descender. También se aplica de bajar tragos, bajar bailando en la discotecas [sic], y otras cosas más.*]
†Lyrics by N. Zapata, J. Medina, W. DeJesús, J. Salgado and C.S. Jurry, courtesy of Hogland Records.

vation, and other groups—such as Ilegales and Sandy y Papo—have followed suit.

Similarly, the group known as Fulanito has continued the pattern of mixing traditional forms with hip-hop and rap. In this case, Dominican-American rapper Rafael Vargas's combination of these forms with *merengue típico* or *perico ripiao* was hugely successful. In 1997, Fulanito vaulted to international stardom; his album *El hombre más famoso de la tierra* (The Most Famous Man on Earth) sold 500,000 copies.

It is likely that this trend among Dominican Americans of creating innovative "alternative forms" (Torres-Saillant and Hernández 1998: 137) of music will continue; after all, merengue has proven itself to be malleable enough to incorporate the identity of all Dominicans, regardless of race, background, and now, geographical location and cultural situation. Nevertheless, the function of merengue as a means of communicating a sense of *dominicanidad* to Dominicans across the decades and across geographical borders links it even more tightly to language itself. As was the case in the past, it is quite possible that the products of these new musical innovations will wear a different label than that of the national music, as in the case of merengue hip-hop, merenhouse and merenrap.

Dominicans on the island have not experienced the situations that those in the Diaspora have, and pop music must be "above all, *relevant* to the immediate social situation of the people" (Fiske 1989: 25). For this reason, it is likely that Spanish-language merengue, while it will continue to evolve, will do so based more in the merengue's musical tradition than the hybrid musics that will be created in the Diaspora. Each musical style, nevertheless, will continue to serve as a marker of identity, be it Dominican or Dominican-American.

10

Caribbean Comparisons

*"Caribbean musics have evolved in a complex
process of creolization, in which Caribbean peoples
have fashioned new, distinctly local genres out of
elements taken from disparate traditions....
Caribbean musics are thus the products of the
dialectic interaction of distinct ethnic groups and
social classes, and they often combine elements of
cultural resistance as well as dominant ideology
and of local traditions as well as those borrowed
from international styles."*
— Manuel 1995: 2

Merengue's role in the formation and solidification of Dominican identity is similar to musical identity processes in other Caribbean nations. Commonalities and differences in colonial histories, racial and ethnic composition and definition, musical influences, political tendencies and diasporic movements have contributed to the development of specific identities. The rich variety of musical forms and identity processes and activities in the Caribbean offers a number of paths for future consideration. This chapter will provide a glimpse into those possibilities by briefly considering the ways in which music has been used as a marker and a maker of identity in Haiti, Cuba and Puerto Rico.

Haiti

Music has been viewed in a strikingly different light in the Dominican Republic's closest neighbor. Haitian attitudes towards their highly creolized musical forms have tended to place a high value on their African elements. In the twentieth century this has resulted in several roots-music movements. Of these, the most influential has been the *mizik rasin* (roots music) movement of the late twentieth century.

As in the Dominican Republic, slave labor was a common element of Haitian colonial life, as was racial mixing. By the end of the eighteenth century, the black population of French Saint-Domingue outnumbered the white inhabitants 10 to one. *Afranchi* (the offspring of French colonists and the female slaves that bore them children) as well as slaves and *mawon* (runaway slaves) began to agitate for freedom from the white colonists in power. In August 1791, Boukman Dutty, a slave and voodoo priest of Jamaican origin, led a group of Haitian slaves against their masters. These rebels burned plantations and killed numerous whites before Dutty was captured and executed. Thus began the Haitian Revolution, a bloody power struggle that would last over a decade.

When the fighting at last ended, the Republic of Haiti became the first independent black republic and the second independent constitutional republic in the world. But although the slaves now had freedom, they still did not hold power. Instead, the *afranchi* had risen to replace the white colonists and to control the nation. Split into two groups, the *milat* (mulatto) and *nwa* (dark-complected), the *afranchi* continue to constitute the Haitian elite yet today.

Despite the emphasis placed on liberation from the French colonial power, the fledgling republic's ruler, Jean-Jacques Dessalines, oriented the new nation towards the Western world. Rather than base his government on the more traditional Haitian *lakou* system, Dessalines followed the course of events in Europe by naming himself Emperor Jaques I in October 1804.*

Likewise, the official language of the Republic of Haiti remained cemented in its colonial legacy. *Krèyol ayisyen* (Haitian Krèyol) was not recognized as the national language until the 1980s, and French continues to be the official language of Haiti. This linguistic division follows class lines, as only the elite are able to afford an education in French (Manuel 1995: 121).

---

*Lakou refers to a traditional system that the Maroons and Africans established in Haiti and that was prominent in the Haitian countryside. Various homes were built around a single courtyard, emphasizing the sense of community. "'The land is for the community, for the spirit'" (Lolo Beaubrun, cited in Heilig 1999: 44).

As in the Dominican Republic, racial classification in Haiti has been and continues to be highly stratified. The Haitian constitution of 1804 "asserted that all Haitians were henceforth to be considered *nèg*" (Averill 1997: 5). This classification created a plurality of meanings for the word since *nèg* could represent "person," "Haitian" or its original "black." By the same token, *blan* signifies either "white" or "foreigner" (*ibid.*). However, this practice did not entirely eliminate racial classification in Haiti. Wucker notes that in the 1970s there existed "twenty-two racial categories and ninety-eight subcategories (for varying hair types, facial structures, color and other distinguishing factors)" (1999b: 34). Racial discrimination in Haiti, as in its neighbor to the east, also follows class lines: the *afranchi milat* and *afranchi nwa* make up the upper class while blacks constitute the enormous lower class. A Haitian proverb is telling in its revelation that "'*Nèg rich se milat, milat pòv se nèg*'" [A rich black is a mulatto, a poor mulatto is a black] (Averill 1997: 5).

As in the Dominican Republic, there were numerous dances and musical forms as well as regional variations of those forms in Haiti. Among the highly-creolized dances, the *mereng* (a Hatian version of the merengue) was a popular style. The debate over the origin of *mereng*/merengue exists in Haiti, and it is every bit as heated as in the Dominican Republic. The Haitian *mereng*, on the other hand, did not experience the animosity in the 1800s that its Dominican cousin did. In fact, "[i]n nineteenth-century Haiti, the ability to dance the *mereng* ... was considered a sign of good breeding" (Manuel 1995: 131). The dance was not linked solely to the lower class but instead "was claimed by both elite and proletarian Haitian audiences as a representative expression of Haitian cultural values" (*ibid.*). Two forms of the dance developed along class lines, just as had been the case in the Dominican Republic. While the lower class favored the style of *mereng* performed for Carnival, the Haitian elite preferred the *méringue lente* or salon *mereng*.

Another form of Haitian music of long-standing tradition is *rara*. This refers to a "seasonal festival related to Vodou belief that takes place all over Haiti during Lent, when *rara* groups take to the streets for days of exhausting processions" (Averill 1997: 243). *Rara* groups and their music are not limited to Lent, and groups form at other times to celebrate special occasions, political happenings, or spontaneously to sing and play (*ibid.*).

Twentieth-century Haitian history had much in common with the Dominican Republic. In 1915, the United States occupied Haiti, just as it would the Dominican Republic the following year. One of the ways in which the Haitian elite protested the nearly two decades of U.S. occupation was through cultural practices, just as the Dominican upper class of the Cibao would do to the east. The view of the United States as "Other" during the occupation pushed Haitians to reconsider what they believed about their cultural forms and to celebrate them as a form of resistance.

Haiti's proximity to the Dominican Republic allowed for the easy entrance of the increasingly popular merengue in the 1950s. In fact, Dominican merengue began to influence Haitian *mereng*, and in 1955 the band *Ensemble aux Calebasses* altered the beat of the dance to produce a new form, *konpa dirèk*.

Soon thereafter, Haiti was to enter a period of dictatorial rule that would equal that suffered by the Dominicans to the east. In 1957, François Duvalier won the presidency on a noirist platform, though he never instituted the *négritude* policies under which he had campaigned. In 1964, Duvalier proclaimed himself president for life. Terror spread throughout Haiti by means of the secret police—the V.S.N. (Volunteers of National Security)—and a band of thugs known as the *tontons makouts*, named after "Uncle Strawbag ... the bogeyman of Haitian folklore, who would take small children and sweep them up in his bag" (Manuel 1995: 135).

The regime of "Papa Doc," as François Duvalier would be known, was as graft-ridden as that of Trujillo. One of the dictator's greatest sources of income was the selling of Haitian *braceros* (laborers) to sugar companies in the Dominican Republic to cut the cane. The inhumane contract between the Haitian and Dominican governments would endure long after the deaths of both Papa Doc and Balaguer.

When Papa Doc died in 1971, his 19-year-old son, Jean-Claude ("Baby Doc"), ascended to the presidency thanks to an alteration Papa Doc had made to the constitution. Less apt at ruling than his father, Baby Doc soon alienated the military. His 1980 marriage to divorcée Michèle Bennett further distanced him from his supporters. The couple—and especially the First Lady—spent money lavishly while lower-class Haitians were starving or selling themselves as cane cutters.

During this time, a young priest of the Salesian order, Jean-Bertrand Aristide, had been openly criticizing the abuses and excesses of the government. So controversial were Aristide's diatribes that he was sent out of the country for "'pastoral reorientation'" (Wucker 1999b: 118). By the time he returned in 1985, the internal opposition to Baby Doc had mounted. Haitians were repeating what the Pope had told them in their native tongue during his 1983 visit: "*Fok sa chanje*"—things must change.

Throughout the Duvalier period of power, masses of Haitians fled the country. At first, these exiles, known as "Boeing People," were primarily "middle-class professionals and intellectuals who could afford airplane tickets and qualify for U.S. visas" (Wucker 1999b: 98). By 1980, a new word, "*botpippel*" (boat people), had been added to Krèyol to signify the thousands of Haitian refugees desperately seeking to escape the country by boat (*ibid.*, 153–4).

It was during the Haitian Diaspora that the first songs appeared to protest the years of Duvalier rule. Baby Doc's marriage to Michèle Bennett brought an increase in the number of these *mini-djaz* compositions. Eventually, opposition to Baby Doc arose within the military, and the forces rose up against the dictator. On February 7, 1986, the Duvaliers fled the country and a military government was established.

A period of *dechoukaj* (uprooting) followed the overthrow, in which Haitians attempted to remove all aspects associated with the dictatorship. Now, the *tonton makouts* were searched out and killed, just as they had done to others before.

Dechoukaj was not a complete break with the tyranny of the past. The November 29 elections were canceled since the majority of Haitians refrained from voting after word spread of killings at one of the balloting centers. Leslie Manigat, winner of later mock elections, was soon overthrown by the military. His successor, General Namphy, also remained in power but a short while before Prospère Avril wrested control from his hands.

Aristide's denunciations continued throughout this time. With each new coup came the old abuses, but the priest refused to be silenced. At last, he was expelled from the order; yet even without a parish, Aristide spoke out against the government and promoted his *teyoloji liberayson* (liberation theology).

Another voice of opposition arose at this time in the form of *mizik rasin*. By around 1990, this roots-music movement had made its way into Haiti's musical spotlight. Averill believes that "[t]he heightened interest in roots ... emerged out of the crisis in national identity linked to the fall of Duvalier. Meanwhile, the temporal and political connections between Duvalierism and *konpa* led many to call for a musical *dechoukaj* of *konpa*" (1997: 177). According to *mizik rasin* musician Lolo Beaubrun, the Haitian youth needed a music to express what they were feeling and experiencing following the end of almost 30 years of dictatorship and the subsequent coups (*ibid.*, 178).

As a movement, *mizik rasin* looks for "a more 'authentically Haitian' musical experience" (Averill 1994: 164). Traditional elements taken from voodoo ceremonies, such as drumming and dance, are mixed with electric instruments to create a neo-traditional sound and style.

Like Dominican *nueva canción*, *mizik rasin* is primarily a middle-class movement that aims to create unity among Haitians. These musicians also believe that their work "[supports] the aspirations of the *piti pèp-la* (literally, the small people)" (Averill 1994: 173). The movement focuses on the experience of the Haitian and

> works to create a historical counternarrative; this narrative creates a history not of dates and Haitian presidents but of slavery and oppression and of a struggle for cultural survival. The songs of *mizik rasin* work to make slavery a contemporary concern, relating it to neo-colonial patterns, international relations, and current Haitian politics [*ibid.*, 167].

Rather than the Western orientation favored by Dessalines, *mizik rasin* is a call to remember the people who suffered as slaves in the Colonial period. That experience is seen to be the unifier between the slavery of the past and the slave-like conditions of the present.

Nouvel jenerayson (New Generation), a bourgeois musical style that came into being in the 1980s and continued to grow in popularity during *dechoukaj*, differs from *mizik rasin* in that it is more of a pop music. Roots musicians criticize it as an "'opportunistic music'" (Averill 1994: 173) because of its attempts to copy traditional *rara* following the fall of the Duvaliers. In spite of these efforts, the style is still "linked to liberal, technocratic political initiatives" (*ibid.*, 178). Internationally, *nouvel jenerayson* as well as *konpa dirèk* have been rejected by audiences "for not sounding 'Haitian enough'" (*ibid.*, 169). For this reason, the neo-traditional *mizik rasin* has gained a stronger global following than either.

Of the various *mizik rasin* bands, one of the most popular and influential has been *Boukman Eksperyans* (Boukman Experience). This group, named for Boukman Dutty, the priest who launched the Haitian Revolution, was formed in 1978, a time when roots music was not popular among the middle class. The band's goal, as stated by its leader, Lolo Beaubrun, was "'to help the people retain their culture ... to make the people come back and be proud of their heritage'" (Booth 1996: para. 17). The band sings in Krèyol and emphasizes Haiti's African roots and the suffering and misery of slavery.

Boukman Eksperyans maintains that spirituality has been and remains the focal point of their music (Heilig 1999: 42; Provencher 1995: para. 13). Nevertheless, the group's lyrics took on an increasingly political edge as governmental abuses continued unchecked following the fall of the Duvaliers. Songs such as "*Pran Chenn, Wet chenn*" ("Get Angry, Remove the Chains") encouraged Haitians to bring about change:

> *Pran chenn, wet chenn*
> *Wa kase chenn-nan ki fè n paka ini nou*
> *Pou n ka sekle lakou-n*
> *Woy woy woy woy woy, o!*
> *Depi Lafrik nap soufri*
> *Nan bo isit se pi rèd*
> *Sa fè rèd, o wayo*

> Get angry, remove the chains
> Break the chains that keep us from uniting
> So that we can weed out our homes
> Woy woy woy woy woy, oh!
> Ever since Africa, we've been suffering
> It's so much harder here
> It's really difficult, o wayo.
>
> [Averill 1994: 167–8; his translation]

This song, winner of the 1989 *3ème Konkou Mizik* (3rd Music Contest), brought *mizik rasin* to a new plateau. *Boukman Eksperyans* became not only the "most popular" but the "most controversial" band in Haiti (Averill 1997: 179).

Carnival 1990, only the second Carnival held in Haiti since 1985, found *Boukman Eksperyans* performing another controversial song, "*Kè m pa sote*" ("My Heart Doesn't Leap, I'm Not Afraid"). This composition made use of several traditional techniques of Haitian music, including the *pwen*, or the point. Typically, *pwen* songs aim to make their point without ever stating it directly. The indirect signification in the composition made the government extremely nervous, though it was never directly mentioned:

> *Sanba sa fè mal o*
> *Gade sa nèg yo fè mwen*
> *Sanba san m ap koule*
> *Yo ban m chay la pote*
> *M pa sa pote l*
> Samba,* this hurts, oh
> Look what those guys do to me
> My blood is running samba
> They give me a burden to carry
> I'm not going to carry it
>
> [Averill 1997: 181; his translation]

This song was quickly picked up and adapted by street and rural bands throughout Haiti, thus spreading the message across the nation. When the military shot a young girl several days later, "*Kè m pa sote*" became the adopted song of the national strike that followed as a protest (*ibid.*, 182). Soon thereafter, Avril was no longer able to retain his hold on the nation, and he resigned.

Campaigning for new elections began under the supervision of the Haitian Supreme Court president. Roger Lafontant, former leader of the

---

*Traditional rural singer associated with *rara* bands (Averill 1997: 243)

tonton makouts, and Marc Bazin posed their candidacies. A new party, the National Front for Change and Democracy, chose as its candidate Father Jean-Bertrand Aristide.

Music played a crucial role for all parties throughout the campaign. Given Haiti's high rate of illiteracy, songs were the most effective way to campaign, and each candidate had his own repertoire. The great majority of these songs were *mizik rasin* compositions, which illustrates that the language of the people—the black roots—had become the common musical language of the nation (Averill 1997: 184). Specifically, Aristide's campaign made numerous intertextual references to popular neo-*rara* songs, and he employed various musical metaphors in his speeches.

When the tally was finally counted, Arisitde won the election with 67 percent of the popular vote. He was the nation's first democratically elected president. *Boukman Eksperyans* which had used its music against the previous dictatorial governments, was "largely credited with helping remove … Avril" (Booth 1996: para. 3). They were chosen to play at Aristide's inauguration.

Though freely elected, Aristide retained his power for only a few months before he was overthrown by a military coup and exiled to the United States. For three years, *Boukman Eksperyans* continued to openly criticize the military government, a dangerous practice that brought them into disfavor with the rulers and cost one of their musicians his life. Bassist and percussionist Michel-Melthon Lynch suffered from meningitis and took medication for it. Although the OAS/U.S. embargo and sanctions against Haiti had been established to protest the coup, medicine was still allowed to enter the country. Somehow, a supply of Lynch's medication was "lost" after it had been shipped, and he died as a result.

Abuses and repression of all Haitians who dressed in the "neo-peasant and African identity garb" (Averill 1994: 166) were common under the military rule. *Boukman Eksperyans* band members received numerous threats, though no outright violence was used against them due to their international renown. It would not do for the government to eliminate the band that had been the first from Haiti to receive a Grammy nomination. Songs such as *"Nwèl Inosan"* ("Innocent Christmas") and *"Kalfou danjere"* ("Dangerous Crossroads") brought new threats to band members, but nothing more. The latter song, "perhaps the most-quoted Haitian song of the decade," held *Billboard's* world-music number one spot for eighteen weeks (Averill 1997: 198). The song was banned from Carnival because its *pwen* was considerably more direct:

> *Ou manti, ou chaje ak pwoblèm*
> *Nan kalfou, kalfou nèg Kongo*

O wou o, Kalfou nèg Kongo
Touye, nou pap touye
Jwe, nou pap jwe la ...
Liars, you'll be in deep trouble
At the crossroads of the Congo people
O wou o, the crossroads of the Congo people
We're not doing any killing
We're not going to play that game ...

[Averill 1997: 1999; his translation]

Although fans were often tear-gassed and shot at during *Boukman Eksperyans* concerts, the band's popularity continued to grow. As Peter Manuel notes, music in Haiti has been an important tool of expression in a land where other freedoms have been silenced. For this reason, "Haitian music continues to be a vital outlet in the continued political struggle of Haitians" (1995: 139–40).

The voice of *Boukman Eksperyans,* as well as those of the Haitian people, was eventually heard. In September 1993, an agreement was finally reached between the military government and the United States, which had threatened to invade Haiti if Aristide were not allowed to resume the presidency. One month later, Aristide returned to power.

Haitian *mizik rasin* aptly illustrates another example of the fluidity of identities in the Caribbean. In contrast to the Dominican Republic which has emphasized European (white) elements above indigenous and African influences in merengue, Haitian roots music prioritizes the latter. The call to return to "traditional" *rara*-voodoo sounds that have a continued association with the Colonial situation of slavery is a cry to remember Haiti's place in history as the first black republic.

Rather than a "whitening" of Haitian music, the opposite has occurred. While *nouvel jenerayson* tends more toward European pop influences, *mizik rasin* claims a return to Haitian (i.e., black) roots. Indeed, the music's name itself is essentialist in nature: the movement seeks to go back to the roots, the origin, the essence of what it means to be Haitian.

International reactions to Haitian music have contributed to the form it has taken. Styles such as *nouvel jenerayson* and *konpa dirèk* have not been as popular on the global stage because they do not seem "Haitian enough." These attitudes demonstrate once again the role of outside opinion and reception in validating a music's popularity and acceptance within a nation.

Mizik rasin as a symbol of Haitian identity has been solidified in contrast to an internal "Other"—the ruling elite. Bourgeois *mizik rasin* musicians seek to connect with the *piti pèp-la* and thus cross class lines and unite Haitians as one.

Cuba

Cuba, like Haiti, has embraced an Afro-Caribbean identity. Since the mid–1800s, the proportions of blacks, whites and mulattos have been fairly equal in Cuba. There, it was somewhat easier for slaves to purchase their freedom, so that by the early 1700s, there were sizeable communities of free blacks throughout the nation.

Organizations known as *cabildos* or *cofradías* (brotherhoods) united free blacks as well as slaves of the "same ethnic community or 'nation'" (Victoria Eli Rodríguez 1994: 93). In this way, the freemen and slaves were able to retain many elements of their African background while blending them with aspects of Caribbean culture. Afro-Cuban music and *santería*, a Creole religion composed of Yoruba and Catholic practices, continue to shape life on the island as well as in the Cuban Diaspora.

Cuba experienced an earlier consolidation of nationalism than the Dominican Republic. By as soon as "the second half of the eighteenth century ... Cuban nationality emerged as such" (Olavo Alén Rodríguez 1994: 110).

Unlike Dominicans, Cubans have long acknowledged Afro-Cuban cultural elements as part of their national identity. Several Cuban intellectuals and musicians figured prominently in the *negritud* movement of the early 1900s. In Cuba, the focus of this Caribbean movement (approximately 1925–1937) was "on rescuing the validity of the African cultural features present in Cuban culture" (Victoria Eli Rodríguez 1994: 110). The aim of this emphasis on blacks was "to find an intrinsically Cuban or national expression" (*ibid.,* 100). This attitude is in stark contrast to the importance given to the hierarchical categorization of ethnicities in the Dominican Republic that holds white above Taíno and black.

The Communist Revolution and rule of the latter half of the twentieth century and into the new millennium has strongly shaped the production and consumption of music in Cuba. In contrast to members of the capitalistic entertainment industry, Cuban musicians were state employees. Being a musician in Cuba earned an individual little fame or wealth. Both the U.S. embargo on Cuba and Castro's isolationism inhibited the commercial development of Cuban music by blocking the performance of Cuban bands in the United States.

The communist government has refrained from appropriating Cuban music to the extent that Trujillo did. For the most part, "musicians ... have not been pressured to politicize their art (though they would also be ill-advised to criticize the basic goals of the Revolution in public)" (Manuel 1995: 46). Self-censorship has served as the main form of control. Pop music was, nevertheless, suppressed for some 30 years as the Castro regime trained its most talented musicians in Soviet-style conservatories (Larmer 1997: para. 4; Gates 1998: para. 5). Musicians were state employees, as were all Cubans, and even the most gifted received little monetary reward.

The change to a communist government in Cuba brought with it the need to establish an identity that would follow along that same ideological path. Specifically, it was important to embrace an identity that would contrast with the economic and political structure of the United States. The new identity ought to encompass and unite black, white and mulatto Cubans as well as "support socialist ideology and egalitarian behavior" (Daniel 1995: 143). It was with these aims in mind that the Ministry of Culture appropriated the rumba.

The Creole dance music known as rumba appeared in Cuba in the latter part of the nineteenth century. It was a popular component of parties held in the lower-class black barrios (Manuel 1995: 24). As in the case of merengue, there were different variations of rumba, three of which exist yet today.

Before the Cuban Revolution, rumba was primarily a dance of the masses and shunned by the elite who associated the dance with the working class. It "was considered African, Afro-Cuban, *baja cultura* (low culture), obscene, or too sexual by some" (Daniel 1995:117). Nevertheless, the "need to reinforce the goals, objectives, and hopes of the Revolution prompted the government through its ministries to use all aspects of social expression and to embark on a selection process" (*ibid.*, 16). It was specifically because of rumba's association with the people and the workers that the government embraced the genre as a form of propaganda to "[educate] the public toward government objectives and as a means of indoctrinating new values" (*ibid.*, 143).

To accomplish this goal, the Castro government paid rumba musicians and dancers to perform for the entire Cuban population. In this way, the state won the support of the masses by embracing their music. Rumba schools and choreographed events such as Rumba Saturday have converted the music's spontaneous, people-initiated character into a carefully planned, state-initiated dance form (Daniel 1995: 118). The primary messages sent are those of anti-racism, egalitarianism and identification with the worker—all of which are at the heart of Cuban communist ideology.

The use of rumba to spread the communist political ideology mirrors Trujillo's appropriation of merengue to extend his control across class lines. In both cases dance and the momentary sense of freedom it brings served as a means for releasing pent-up tensions and frustrations. In this way, rumba, like merengue, encompasses contradictions within Cuban society: "spontaneity, freedom and, simultaneously, structured form and set order (Daniel 1995: 147).

With the fall of the Soviet Union, the Cuban music scene was suddenly altered. Left alone, Castro was forced to encourage tourism and to highlight those artistic forms internationally considered Cuban to attract visitors (Gates 1998: para. 1; Larmer 1997: para. 4). Although rumba remains under the government's thumb, Castro has allowed pop musicians more freedom since 1993. Now, they are able to negotiate contracts and hold on to some of their earnings (Larmer 1997: para. 4). Cuba's most popular musicians have suddenly found themselves to be part of "a rare breed in Cuba: wealthy capitalists" (*ibid.*, para. 5).

A new style of music, the *timba*, has also developed as the musical expression of post–Soviet Cuba. This genre, "a combination of jazz and rumba spiced with reggae, funk and hiphop ... is the modern mambo, a hard-edged cha-cha-cha" (Pasternostro 1999: para. 13). *Timba* is "the voice of the average Cubans, of those who allow their cubanía—the Cuban identity that combines a joy of life, a sensuousness, a macho attitude—to seep out" (*ibid.*, para. 14). *Timba* lyrics deal with daily life in post–Soviet Cuba and represent a return to traditional Cuban styles and forms. In this way, music is once again being altered to reflect changes in politics and society. *Timberos* (*timba* musicians) are forging a new music to represent a new reality and a new identity that is based in tradition.

Part of the government's more relaxed stance towards mass music during this time rests on music's power to act as a type of "social escape valve" (Larmer 1997: para. 6). This new degree of liberty is not without its limits, as the group *La Charanga Habanera* discovered after performing "*El mango.*" The song's double entendre likening the elderly Castro to a mango that refuses to fall from the tree despite being ripe was evident to listeners and Castro alike: "'Hey green mango, now that you're ripe, why have you still not fallen?'" (Larmer 1997: para. 7). The group was banned for six months because of the reference to the aged Castro in his army fatigues.

Castro's loosening hold on music in combination with the Cuban Democracy Act, passed in the United States in 1995, have made it possible for Cuban bands to venture onto U.S. soil for the first time in over three decades. This act "made it legal to exchange cultural information, including music, if it did not directly profit the Castro regime" (*ibid.*, para. 3). Hidden from the world's eyes for so long, Cuban dance music has swiftly become one of the spiciest sensations on the global music scene.

The recent international popularity of Cuban music also exemplifies what Slobin has defined as "'validity through visibility'" (Averill 1994: 168). The lack of exposure to these styles has made them appear pure to global eyes. Certainly, embargo and isolation have blocked many foreign influences, yet Cuban music has not remained stagnant, as the case of the rumba has shown us. Still, to international eyes, Cuba seems "'the last great reserve of music in the world'" (Larmer 1997: para. 2). Such views illustrate the essentialist theory of identity by portraying music as an inherent element of a people that remains more or less unaltered unless touched by outside influences.

Nevertheless, Cuban music has gone through processes of change. Cuban identities in the Diaspora, like those of Dominican and Haitian immigrants, have incorporated music as a marker of identity. Questions of music, politics and identity have become particularly heated in Miami where "Cuban American politicians ... have made sure that no singers or other musicians can perform" (Music 1994: 1). Since Castro would not allow dissident voices to play abroad, a 1996 ordinance was passed banning such performances in Miami. It was believed that allowing the concerts to take place in Miami would indicate "acceptance of the regime's repression of cultural dissidents" (*ibid.*, para. 6). Nevertheless, the same groups that are banned from performing live are not inaccessible to Miami's large Cuban population, since the albums are on sale in most of the city's music stores.

In contrast to a "whitening" process, we must understand the Creolization of Cuban music. Forms such as the rumba are Creole musical forms to begin with; nevertheless, the *afrocubanismo* movement stresses not only African culture but how aspects of it have interacted with other influences to form a truly hybrid and unique Afro-Cuban product.

Cuba's unique political situation also makes it necessary to consider the "equalizing" nature of musical development as music (such as the rumba) has been used to spread socialist ideals. State-sponsored rumba serves as a tool to celebrate the worker and communist ideology. Only time will tell of the effect that the *timba* might have on the political, economic and social situation in Cuba.

Insomuch as the Castro government strives to create a strict line between itself and non-communist countries, Cuban identity is constructed against capitalism and democracy as the "Other." Cuban music's complete lack of commercialism until the 1990s and its 30-year isolation contributed to the view of a pure, untouched music in the minds of nationals and internationals alike. In much the same way as the global music world has responded to *mizik rasin* as a more authentically Haitian music, the international reception of Cuban dance music has helped to solidify a Cuban identity.

Puerto Rico

Puerto Rico, like Cuba and Hispaniola, experienced the early extinction of its indigenous Taíno. The use of African slaves to compensate for the lack of labor was a common practice in Puerto Rico as well.

Like Cuba, Puerto Rico was a Spanish colony until 1898, at which time the island fell under U.S. control. Over the next 50 years, the North American presence in Puerto Rico would alter the island's "society beyond recognition" (Manuel 1995: 56). The best agricultural land fell under the control of North Americans. Consequently, "most *hacendados* were bankrupted and the *jíbaros* were dispossessed" (*ibid.*). The *jíbaros* (peasants from the inland mountains) began to migrate in a steady flow to the nation's cities, causing the rate of urbanization to surge upwards. For this reason, almost all elements of *jíbaro* culture have disappeared, just as was the case with the Taíno before them.

The continued U.S. presence in Puerto Rico has had a profound impact on Puerto Rican identity processes. Although an ethnic triad is acknowledged, each of those ethnicities is placed in a hierarchy. As in the Dominican Republic, the ethnic element that is believed to have contributed the most to Puerto Rican culture is the Spanish. The Taíno, despite their swift extinction, rank immediately behind the European heritage and "add temporal depth to the national myth by representing the nation's roots in the past while supplying continuity with the present that is essential for establishing the legitimacy of a nationalist ideology" (Davila 1997: 70). Puerto Rico's African heritage, called *la tercera raíz* (the third root), is believed to have added the least to the island's culture and ethnicity (*ibid.*). The lyrics of a 2003 song performed by Puerto Rican star Ricky Martin, "*Raza de mil colores*" ("Race of a Thousand Colors"), provide a telling glimpse into this line of thought by emphasizing each of the three ethnicities present in Puerto Rican culture and identity. Each of these three groups is in turn linked to a specific human element.

In these lyrics, the most essential element, the soul, is the heritage of the Europeans; a noble character is an inheritance of the Taíno, while the African influence is the "flavor" added to spice up an existing composite. This system of racial hierarchy with its emphasis on European and indigenous contributions allows Puerto Ricans to embrace an identity that is neither that of the white master (i.e., the United States) nor that of the African slave and at the same time reiterates the enduring notion of the *buen salvaje* (noble savage) of the nineteenth century. This identity hearkens back to a proud epoch of independence and freedom while at the same time avoiding complete identification with the colonial and neocolonial powers.

Puerto Rican musical forms and their acceptance have mirrored the importance attributed to each of the three ethnic elements. No pure indigenous forms remain, though commonly used instruments such as the *güiro* and *maraca* are claimed to be of Taíno origin. The *seis*, "one of

Puerto Rico's most popular, and most Spanish song types" (Duany 1992: 74), was the music of the *jíbaro* peasants who inhabited the highlands. Numerous variations of the *seis* have developed, but the music itself "remains closely attached to its Spanish colonial models" (*ibid.*, 75). The *bomba*, in contrast, has its roots in African musics that were brought to the Americas by slaves from differing regions of Africa. African-influenced music developed along the coastal areas of the island where larger numbers of slaves were concentrated on sugar plantations. Yet another dance, the *plena*, is a syncretic blend of elements. According to island tradition, the *plena* was a product of Ponce, Puerto Rico's second largest city. As the center of the sugar and rum industries, Ponce was home to a large number of slaves, though it also retained many Spanish cultural practices. Although there is no concrete proof that the *plena* originated in Ponce, many Puerto Ricans uphold the legend that "*en Ponce nació la plena*" [The *plena* was born in Ponce]* (*ibid.*, 77).

The Institute of Puerto Rican Culture (ICP) determines and propagates the official Puerto Rican cultural identity. In the realm of music, *jíbaro* styles that are considered folkloric, such as the *seis* and *aguinaldo*, are held up as the music of the nation. This is the music that the ICP supports in state-sponsored cultural functions. *Bomba* and *plena* are also performed, though not to the extent of the peasant music. Often, the *bombas* and *plenas* presented at ICP-sponsored events are "whitened" versions performed by peasant groups rather than by actual *bomba* and *plena* musicians (Davila 1997: 78).

The ICP's stance towards each of these musical forms brings to light interesting questions concerning the propagation of a specific identity. As Davila points out, the *jíbaro* and his music are always portrayed as white "with a tinge of Indian heritage" (*ibid.*, 71–2). The Institute tends to "[veil] the fact, documented by Puerto Rican ethnomusicologists, that 'jíbaro' music and culture never developed independently of African influences" (*ibid.*, 72). The ICP's acceptance and inclusion of the peasant's music as folkloric, as well as the inclusion of "whitened" versions of *bomba* and *plena*, allow the Institute to control or silence identities that might go against the official national identity.

Salsa, on the other hand, is not considered "cultural" by the Institute because of its *Newyorican* origins. For this reason, salsa is not allowed to be part of state-sponsored programs and activities, though both it and merengue are popular and common features of local, non-state functions.

As in the case of the Dominican Republic, Puerto Rican identity can-

---

*This was a line from a well-known *plena* by César Concepción (Duany 1992: 77).

not be considered without figuring into the schema the enormous Diasporic community. Puerto Rico's status as a U.S. Commonwealth makes immigration to the United States easier for them than for groups such as Haitians. Like Dominicans, the majority of Puerto Rican migrants make New York City their destination on the mainland.

Puerto Rican immigrants to the United States have experienced many of the same psychological stresses as Dominicans. The search for jobs, the adaptation to North American systems of racial classifications, lack of political representation and separation from family and loved ones on the island have all contributed to these tensions. Puerto Ricans also face an additional identity stressor for "[t]he migration experience has heightened the long-standing identity problem felt by some Puerto Ricans, already self-conscious of their status as perpetual colonial subjects" (Manuel 1995: 67).

As in the case of Dominicans, there is a continuous flow of people and information between Puerto Rico, so that the mainland and emigrants' "ties with the homeland are never totally severed" (Duany 1992: 80). Nevertheless, the attitudes of some Puerto Ricans towards emigrants (particularly those living in New York City) is markedly different. *Newyoricans* have tended to create for themselves "a new cultural identity that at once embraces island tradition and engages actively with mainstream society" (Manuel 1995: 70). *Newyoricans* are sometimes viewed as "decultured half-breeds" by the islanders who, in turn, are considered "provincial" by the mainlanders (*ibid.*).

Puerto Ricans in New York have commonly settled in barrios in an area that became known as Spanish Harlem. Like Dominicans, Puerto Rican immigrants have tried to familiarize their new surroundings by integrating elements of island culture into them. In this process, music has exercised an important role as "a source of solace and recreation" (Manuel 1995: 66).

Unlike Dominican immigrants and their merengue, Puerto Ricans in the U.S. did not embrace a "national" music. Long experts at borrowing Cuban musical genres and integrating them into their own music, Puerto Rican immigrants instead created a new sound based on the Cuban *son*. A polemic exists over whether salsa is a Puerto Rican or Cuban invention, and discussion of this topic abounds. As Jorge Duany reminds us, however, even the *son* (as other forms of Latin music) was a blend of various cultures, styles and sounds. Salsa is, therefore, "a mixture of mixtures" (1992: 72). While salsa is based on the *son*, there are marked differences in sound, instrumentation and most importantly, theme.

Whether these differences are great enough for us to consider salsa a new genre, or if it should be thought of as an extension of the *son*, can best be determined by the social and historical stimuli that brought about its birth. The 1960s found marginalized groups in the United States demanding to be treated fairly and to be allowed the basic social services. Taking as their model the Black Panthers, a group of *Newyoricans* formed as the Young Lords. These activists organized and mobilized their countrymen in New York to demand these same rights (Manuel 1995: 73). Music also entered into this campaign since "[t]he new social consciousness called for a new musical movement that could at once embrace Puerto Rican culture and capture the spirit of the barrio in all its alienated energy and heightened self-awareness" (*ibid.*). That new form was salsa. It comes as no surprise that the themes of the first salsas were "the alienation, violence, and lurking malevolence of barrio life" (*ibid.*, 76). Because this sense of alienation was so much a part of the reality of other Latino immigrants and Latinos who had migrated to the large urban centers within their own nations, salsa became a symbol of Pan-Latino identity.

Salsa's popularity across Latin America and among Latino immigrants was tied partly to the means by which it was produced. Following its inception, salsa's growth was intimately linked to Fania Records, founded in 1964. Since Fania Records invented the name for the genre to depict a spicy new style, many consider the term to be nothing more than a marketing strategy. Critics claim that salsa is nothing more than a rendition of the *son*. It is true that the basic structure of salsa is the same as that of mid-century Cuban dance styles. Nevertheless, a distinctive name for the music created among *Newyoricans* is justifiable because of the differences in sound, instrumentation, and most importantly "the way in which the music voiced the militant self-consciousness of the new generation of Latinos" (Manuel 1995: 75).

Despite its association with a new outlook, little in salsa has changed stylistically since its birth. Salsa reached its climax in the 1970s and though it has remained a favorite Pan-Latin music, many have turned to the more innovative merengue for their dance music. Acculturation has also resulted in the growing popularity of North American styles among Latino immigrants.

The most significant change in salsa has been in the area that most distinguished the genre before. Gone are the charged lyrics and confrontational attitude that differentiated salsa. *Salseros* now sing of the typical themes of love and love lost to better sell their wares in a "capitalist entertainment industry … [that] has generally tended … to co-opt and neutralize 'rebellious art forms'" (Manuel 1995: 91). The Latinos who would have suffered the greatest discrimination in the United States are not today's salsa stars; rather, salsa musicians are the typical "cuddly, predominantly white singers" that mainstream culture embraces (*ibid.*). Salsa, therefore, has been not only whitened but converted into "a more bland, depoliticized pop—ketchup rather than salsa" (*ibid.*).

Despite its less-political leanings, salsa continues to serve as a marker of Pan-Latino identity. As in the case of merengue, language differences and dancing ability set it apart from mainstream North American culture. As Manuel points out, salsa will no doubt remain a strong symbol of *Newyorican* and Puerto Rican identity because of the island's neocolonial status as Commonwealth.

Although it is a popular dance, salsa is not promulgated by the ICP as an official music of Puerto Rico. Instead, the government continues to hold up folkloric music as a more essential symbol of Puerto Rican identity.

The case of Puerto Rico offers an interesting study in the fluidity of identity and how identities can be symbolized by musical genres. As a Commonwealth of the United States, official discourses uphold an identity that is neither master nor slave. In this way, Puerto Ricans have chosen an ethnic identity that seems a middle ground. By promoting Creole musics such as the *seis*, this official view emphasizes the nation's boundaries and uniqueness within them. These genres also delineate the line between Puerto Rican culture and the system imposed by the U.S. "Other." Likewise, these musical genres contrast with the ever-growing popularity of Dominican merengue on the island. Official Puerto Rican identity is "whitened" as well as "creolized."

Puerto Rican identities in the Diaspora have followed a different pattern as immigrants forge new identities that are a bridge between the island and the mainland. In the same way, a new genre, salsa, emerged to represent the reality faced by those individuals and how they chose to respond to it.

The Singularity of Merengue

Although certain broad generalizations can be made about the role of music in Caribbean identity processes, no musical genre has been as central to those processes as merengue has to Dominican identity. Despite continued popularity of certain musical forms in Haiti, Cuba and Puerto Rico, no single style has enjoyed the all-encompassing status of "national music" that merengue has, nor has any genre had its staying power. Furthermore, none of the styles that have been embraced as symbols of identity in the other Caribbean countries discussed have served as such a unifying force; nor have they served as a language to communicate a national identity both at home and in the Diaspora.

Merengue offers us a unique study of how music aids in the solidification of national identities. This case also demonstrates how an "essential" element—one that already existed among the people—can be manipulated to assist in the creation and maintenance of national over-arching identities. The adaptation of merengue to differing circumstances across history illustrates that musical forms considered "essential" are not stagnant but rather are capable of being altered to better fit those changes. Merengue has been part of a process of identity construction and solidification unlike any other music in the Caribbean Basin.

Conclusion

"¡Sólo se siente!"

*"El merengue, lindo tema. Pero no hay mucho que
decir. ¡Sólo se siente! Los dominicanos, sólo hay
escucharlo, empiezan a mover el esquelto" [The
merengue, lovely topic. But there's not much to say.
It's only felt! Dominicans only have to hear it and
they start moving their skeletons].*

—Ikeda 1999

Merengue poured out of both speakers of an enormous boom box,
filling the sweltering July night with its contagious rhythm.

"You must learn to dance the merengue," my Dominican friends had
said earlier that evening. "You can't live in the Dominican Republic for a
summer without learning our national dance."

Deciding there was no time like the present, we had piled into a tiny
car and headed off in search of batteries for the boom box. Half an hour
later, I was being instructed in the basics of merengue on a rooftop patio.
The shadows of the palm trees were perfectly immobile in the still night.
Above, the stars seemed to twinkle in time to the music; below, the lights
of Santiago burned intensely.

After an hour or so of practice, I felt no closer to being able to dance
the merengue than before my lessons. Drenched with sweat under the
oppressively humid Caribbean night, I begged for a short break. As I sat
fanning myself, my friend Víctor assured me that I had actually made some
progress and encouraged me to keep trying.

"Don't be discouraged," he told me. "Merengue is completely Domini-can. It's natural for us to dance—we are born with the rhythm inside us."

Years later, I would remember that comment when another Domini-can friend asked me, "Did you hear about the European who went to the Dominican Republic and found a Dominican who really didn't know how to dance the merengue? He looked at the Dominican and said, 'How can it be that you, a Dominican, don't know how to dance? I thought the merengue was in your blood.' And the Dominican answered him this way, saying: 'Oh, it's true, and I carry the rhythm in my blood, too. It's just that I have bad circulation, and it doesn't make it to my feet.'"

I wished I'd had that excuse several years before, when my friends were attempting to teach me their national dance. It seemed like an impos-sible enterprise, and I wondered how *I* was ever going to learn to dance the merengue if it was in *their* blood.

My friends' essentialist claim to their national music has some truth to it. Merengue was born as a creolized music form somewhere in the Caribbean, combining elements of the peoples of Europe, Africa and the Americas. Historical, social, and political events have affected the music, and actors have consciously manipulated it and constructed Dominican identity around it for specific goals.

The blend of cultures present in merengue has allowed certain ele-ments to be emphasized while others were de-emphasized. Traditionally, Dominican leaders have promulgated a Hispanic identity: the white, Span-ish-speaking Catholic. Taíno influences fall just slightly beneath the Euro-pean in this world view while black contributions receive little to no recognition at all. In this way, the diverse groups that constitute *domini-canidad* (Dominican-ness) are represented and encompassed, though the preferences given have little basis in the ethnic configuration of the nation.

This fluidity is also evident in identity processes at work in the Dominican Diaspora. Dominicans have continued to embrace their national music as a marker of identity in the psychologically traumatic experience of immigration. Their reality is different from that of their friends and families back home, and merengue has evolved to portray their concerns and situations. Other hybrid genres such as merenrap and merengue hip-hop reflect the rethinking of identities that has been a com-mon aspect of the Dominican immigration experience.

Merengue has become most firmly established as a symbol of Dominican identity on occasions when that identity faces real or perceived threats from outside the nation's borders. This process reinforces the notion of geographical boundaries and purity within them. Trujillo's iso-lationism only served to intensify this sense of musical purity within the nation's borders.

A variation of typical merengue or *perico ripiao* performed with a *güira* and two drums.

Traditionally, merengue has stood as a type of musical border between the Dominican Republic and the Haitian "Other." Dominican reaction to the 1916–24 U.S. occupation gives another example of how the music helped differentiate the Dominicans from their perceived oppressors. This tendency has repeated itself in the Diaspora, where merengue differentiates Dominicans from other Latino immigrants and North Americans.

Merengue's rise from a style scorned by the elite to its place as the national music goes hand in hand with the whitening of merengue. In a country where class and race run parallel to each other, early merengue was completely unacceptable to the elite. Filtered versions of the dance in the early 1900s were masked behind the name of "*danzas típicas*" (folk dances) to make the music more appropriate for orchestral settings. Merengue's temporary popularity among the predominantly white Cibao elite during the first United States occupation did not last long after the troops left, though this upper class association with the style made it acceptable at the time. Finally, the alterations made to *merengue típico* under Trujillo were so decisive that a new genre, *merengue de orquesta*, was born. It was this style that appealed to the elite, while the *merengue típico* remained most popular among the lower classes. As merengue has spread globally, the whitening process has continued. It is telling that most merengue that has thus far achieved global acclaim has been performed by white, middle- to upper-class musicians.

Musical forms, like identity in general, have their roots in a group of people. These bases are not divorced from historical, social and political events and participants, however. Influences flow both ways, as those events affect music and as music shapes them. It is impossible to view identity processes either as purely essentialist or as wholly constructed. Rather, it is most appropriate to consider the origins of an identity marker and how historical events and individuals have managed to manipulate the views of those origins to create, re-create or alter a desired identity.

Merengue is an unparalleled case. While the genre is a musical representation of the blend of the three cultures that constitute *dominicanidad*—Taíno, European and African—it is also a representation of the way in which individual actors have succeeded in ordering those elements, those three "bloods," to make one of them the most dominant, so dominant that it overshadows the others. Merengue truly is "in the blood" of the Dominicans—in the cultural and ethnic blend of three peoples, as well as in the constructed vision of the predominant component of that blend.

Merengue has served as a language specific to the Dominican Republic—a part of the culture that has continuity yet is ever-changing with the passage of time. Just as languages are not discarded when a new fad comes along, merengue has not been abandoned in the face of some other genre. Rather, merengue is a definitive element of *dominicanidad* that is elastic enough to adapt to the changing realities of Dominican life and continue to communicate those realities effectively.

Perhaps merengue seems so natural to Dominicans because of the intensity with which it is performed, played and danced throughout the nation. It surrounds them every day, practically 24 hours a day. As merengue pours from stores or street vendors' stands, those waiting on a nearby corner for public transportation begin to sway to it, shuffle their feet and move their hips, dance it in place right on the spot. People crowded on tiny buses cannot sit still. Walking along the street, others sing along with their favorites. Small children in pre-schools, whose music lesson or recess consists of dancing in the patio, are already experts. Though the national music no longer carries propaganda or the reminder of the total control of the state, it still fills Dominicans with a message of who they are with its very (omni)presence.

A close Dominican friend, upon learning of my work on this project, was quick to remind me of the inherent quality and naturalness of her national music. "*El merengue, lindo tema*" she wrote to me. "*Pero no hay mucho que decir ¡sólo se siente!*" [The merengue, lovely topic. But there's not much to say. It's only felt!] (Ikeda 1999).

Bibliography

Alas, Jessica (No date). "Elvis Crespo" Online. *lamusica.com*. Available: http://www.lamusica.com/elviseng.htm. (1999, October 30.)

_____ (2002). "*Proyecto Uno*: Merengue, hip hop, reggaetón y ahora palos." Online. *Netmío.com*. Available: http://www.netmio.com. (2003, March 20.)

Anderson, Benedict (1991). *Imagined Communities*. New York: Verson.

Aparicio, Frances R. (1998). *Listening to Salsa: Gender, Latin Popular Music, and Puerto Rican Cultures*. Hanover, NH: Wesleyan University Press.

Aquino, Miguel (1997). *Holocaust in the Caribbean: The Slaughter of 25,000 Haitians by Trujillo in One Week*. Waterbury, CT: Emancipation.

Austerlitz, Paul (1997). *Merengue: Dominican Music and Dominican Identity*. Philadelphia: Temple University Press.

Averill, Gage (1997). *A Day for the Hunter, A Day for the Prey: Popular Music and Power in Haiti*. Chicago: University of Chicago Press.

_____ (1994). "'*Se Kreyòl Nou Ye*'/'We're Creole': Musical Discourse on Haitian Identities." In Gerard Béhague (ed.), *Music and Black Ethnicity in the Caribbean and South America* (pp. 157–185). New Brunswick, NJ: Transaction.

"Background Notes: Dominican Republic, March 1998." (1998). Online *DOSFAN*. Available: http://www.background_notes/dominican_repub_0398_bgn.html 1999, January 25.

Balaguer, Joaquín (1994). *La isla al revés*. Santo Domingo: Corripio.

_____ (1988). *Memorias de un cortesano de la "era de Trujillo."* Santo Domingo: Corripio.

"Balaguer murió esta madrugada" (2002, 14 July). Online. *Listín Diario*. Available: www.listindiario.com.do. (18 July, 2002.)

Balibar, Etienne (1992). "The Nation Form: History and Ideology." In Geoff Eley and Ronald Grigor Suny (eds.), *Becoming National* (pp.132–149). New York: Oxford University Press.

Batista Matos, Carlos (1999). *Historia y evolución del merengue.* Sto. Domingo: Editora Cañabrava.

Bergman, Billy (1985). *Hot Sauces: Latin and Caribbean Pop.* New York: Quill.

Bosch, Juan (No date). "Carta al pueblo dominicano después del Golpe de Estado de 1963." Online. *Juan Bosch, pilar de la historia dominicana.* Available: www.chasque.net/ps/Juan%20Bosch.htm. (2002, July 27.)

Booth, Philip (1996, September 6). "Freedom Fighters." *The Tampa Tribune,* p. 20. Online. Available: Lexis-Nexis Academic Universe (1999, November 8).

Broughton, Simon, Mark Ellingham, David Muddyman and Richard Trillo (eds.). (1994). "Merengue." In *World Music: The Rough Guide.* London: Penguin.

Burr, Ramiro (1997, May 4). "*Proyecto Uno* Embraces Adventure." *The Houston Chronicle, 2 STAR Edition Online,* p.18 ZEST Section (571 words). Available: Lexis-Nexis Adademic Universe (1999, November 5).

Campbell Robinson, Deanna, Elizabeth B. Buck, and Marlene Cuthbert (eds). (1991). *Music at the Margins: Popular Music and Global Cultural Diversity.* Newbury Park, CA: Sage.

Caroit, Jean-Michel (2002, July 15). "Décès de Joaquin Balaguer, l'un des derniers caudillos latino-américains." Online. *Le Monde.* n.p. Available: www.lemonde.fr (2002, July 28).

Chang-Rodríguez, Raquel, and Malva E. Filer (eds.). (1988). *Voces de Hispanoamérica: Antología literaria.* Boston: Heinle & Heinle.

Cho, John (1995). "The Two-Way Afro-Caribbean Music Connection." In *Señales de humo.* Online. Available: http://www.sdhumo.com/Articles/afro-car.html (1999, February 4).

Clayton, Lawrence A., and Michael L. Conniff (1999). *A History of Modern Latin America.* Fort Worth: Harcourt Brace College.

Cocks, Jay (1986, October 6). "You Can't Stop Dancing: A New Merengue Heats up the Club Scene." *Time.*

Coopersmith, J.M. (1949). *Music and Musicians of the Dominican Republic.* Washington D.C.: Pan American Union.

Considine, J.D. (1999, October 22). "Latin Pop is Spicing up American Charts." *St. Petersburg Times,* p. 24 Weekend Section. Online. Available: Lexis-Nexis Adademic Universe (1999, November 1).

"Court Overturns Conviction in Case of Journalist's Assassination." (2002). Online. *Impunity.* Available: http://www.impunidad.com/pressrelease/iapa_newsll_22_02E.html. (2003, June 8.)

Crassweller, Robert D. (1966). *Trujillo: Life and Times of a Caribbean Dictator.* New York: Macmillan.

Daniel, Yvonne (1995). *Rumba: Dance and Social Change in Contemporary Cuba.* Bloomington, Indiana University Press.

Davila, Arlene M. (1997). *Sponsored Identities.* Philadelphia: Temple University Press.

Davis, Martha Ellen (1994). "Music and Black Ethnicity in the Dominican Republic." In Gerard Béhague (ed.), *Music and Black Ethnicity in the Caribbean and South America* (pp. 119–155). New Brunswick, NJ: Transaction.

del Castillo, José, and Manuel A. García Arévalo. (1989). *Antología del merengue/Anthology of the Merengue.* Santo Domingo: Corripio.

del Castillo, José, and Martin Murphy (1987–88). "Migration, National Identity, and Cultural Policy in Dominican Republic." *Journal of Ethnic Studies* 15 (3), 49–69.

Diederich, Bernard (1978). *Trujillo: The Death of the Goat.* Boston: Little, Brown and Company.

"Dominican Republic." (1999). In *The World Factbook 1999.* Online. Available: http://www.odci.gov/cia/publications/factbook/dr.html. (2000, April 14.)

Duany, Jorge (1998). "Reconstructing racial identity: ethnicity, color, and class among Dominicans in the United States and Puerto Rico." In *Latin American Perspectives* Online, 25(3), 147 (26pp.). Available: Information Access/ INFO-TRAC/Expanded Academic A20757707. (1999, July 23.)

_____ (1994a). "Ethnicity, Identity, and Music: An Anthropological Analysis of the Dominican Merengue." In Gerard Béhague (ed.), *Music and Black Ethnicity in the Caribbean and South America* (pp. 65–90). New Brunswick, NJ: Transaction.

_____ (1994b). *Quisqueya on the Hudson: The Transnational Identity of Dominicans in Washington Heights.* New York: CUNY.

_____ (1992). "Popular Music in Puerto Rico: Toward an Anthropology of *Salsa.*" In Vernon W. Boggs (ed.), *Salsiology: Afro-Cuban Music and the Evolution of Salsa in New York City.* Westport, CT: Greenwood Press.

Duara, Prasenjit (1996). "Historicizing National Identity, or Who Imagines What and When." In Geoff Eley and Ronald Grigor Suny (eds.), *Becoming National* (pp. 151–177). New York: Oxford University Press.

Espaillat, Arturo R. (1963). *Trujillo: The Last Caesar.* Chicago: Henry Regnery.

"Fefita la Grande, La Mayimba" (No date). *Merengue & Bachata República Dominicana* [Online]. Available: http://home-3.tiscali.nl/~pjetax/biografias/fefita.html (May 15, 2003).

Figueroa, Ana, Lynette Clemetson, Pat Wingert, Julie Weingarden, Thomas Hayden & Martha Brant. (1999, July 12). "Generation Ñ." *Newsweek,* pp. 53–58.

Fiske, John (1989). *Understanding Popular Culture.* Boston: Unwin Hyman.

Foucault, Michel (1995). *Discipline and Punish: The Birth of the Prison.* New York: Vintage.

Galíndez, Jesús de (1973). *The Era of Trujillo.* Tucson: University of Arizona Press.

Gardner, Elysa (1999, May 7). "Pop Music's Latin Locomotion." *USA Today* Online, p. 1E Life. Available: Lexis-Nexis Academic Universe (1999, November 1).

Gates, David (1998, January 19). "A Taste of Salsa." *Newsweek* online. Availabl:e Lexis-Nexis Academic Universe (1999, November 30).

Georges, Eugenia (1990). *The Making of a Transnational Community: Migration, Development, and Cultural Change in the Dominican Republic.* New York: Columbia University Press.

Graham, Pamela M. (1998). "The Politics of Incorporation: Dominicans in New York City." *Latino Studies Journal* 9(3), 39–64.

Gramsuck, Sherri, and Patricia R. Pessar (1991). *Between Two Islands: Dominican International Migration.* Berkeley and Los Angeles: University of California Press.

Hall, Stuart. (1992) "Ethnicity: Identity and Difference." In Geoff Eley and Ronald Grigor Suny (eds.), *Becoming National* (pp. 339–349). New York: Oxford University Press.

Hanna, Judith Lynne (1992). "Moving Messages. Identity in Popular Music and

Social Dance." In James Lull (ed.), *Popular Music and Communication* (pp. 176–195). Newbury Park, CA: Sage.

Hartlyn, Jonathan (1998). *The Struggle for Democratic Politics in the Dominican Republic.* Chapel Hill: University of North Carolina Press.

Hayden, Thomas, and Karen Schoemer (1997, November 17). "¿Se Habla Rock and Roll?" *Newsweek.* Online. Available Lexis-Nexis Academic Universe (1999, November 30).

Heilig, Steve (1999). "*Boukman Eksperyans*: Haiti's Real Revolutionaries." *The Beat* 18(2), 42–46.

Heller, Scott (1998, May 1). "Salsa: A Hybrid that Reflects the Globalization of Culture." *Chronicle of Higher Education.* Online. Available Lexis-Nexis Academic Universe (1999, November 30).

Hernández, Julio Alberto (1969). *Música tradicional dominicana.* Santo Domingo: Postigo.

"Historia del merengue." (No date). *Tambora y Güira.* Online. Available: http://www.mindspring.com/~adiascar/musica/merhst-s.htm (1998, December 15).

Hobsbawm, Eric, and Terence Ranger (eds.). (1983). *The Invention of Tradition.* London: Cambridge University Press.

Ikeda, Belkys (1999, December 20). Personal correspondence.

Irwin, Colin (1998, November 8). "Latin Makes the World Go Round." *Music Week.* Online. Available: Lexis-Nexis Academic Universe (1999, December 10).

"JB fue moderado en la oposición." (2002, July 16). Online. *Listín Diario.* p. 1. Available: www.listindiario.com.do. (2002, July 18).

Jiménez, Manuel (1993, June 4). "JB reitera: no va en el 94." *Hoy,* p.1.

Jorge, Bernarda (1982). "Bases ideológicas de la práctica musical durante la era de Trujillo." *Eme Eme 10* (59), 65–99.

Katz, Larry (1995, June 30). "Music; Voodoo Politics: *Boukman Eksperyans* sings so Haiti doesn't burn." *The Boston Herald* Online. Available: Lexis-Nexis Academic Universe (1999, November 8).

Larmer, Brook (1999, July 12). "Latino America." *Newsweek,* 48–51.

_____ (1997, November 17). "Salsa Picante for Sale." *Newseek* Online. Available: Lexis-Nexis Academic Universe (1999, November 30).

Lora, Ana Mitila. "El enigma de un poder." Online. *Listín Diario. Balaguer, Vida y legado de un líder,* n.p. Available: www.listindiario.com.do (2002, July 28).

Malkki, Liisa. (1992) "National Geographic: The Rooting of Peoples and the Territorialization of National Identity among Scholars and Refugees." In Geoff Eley and Ronald Grigor Suny (eds.), *Becoming National* (pp. 434–453). New York: Oxford University Press.

Manuel, Peter, with Kenneth Bilby and Michael Largey (1995). *Caribbean Currents: Caribbean Music from Rumba to Reggae.* Philadelphia: Temple University Press.

Masland, Tom, and Brook Larmer (1998, January 19). "Cuba's Real Religion." *Newsweek* Online. Available Lexis-Nexis Academic Universe (1999, November 30).

Mattern, Mark (1998). *Acting in Concert: Music, Community, and Political Action.* New Brunswick, NJ: Rutgers University Press.

Méndez, Carmen (2000, March 18). "Cuando Vargas Llosa mató al chivo." *Recoletos*

Cia Editorial Expansión. Online, n. p. Lexis-Nexis Academic Universe (2000, September 15).

Morris, Nancy (1999). "Cultural Interaction in Latin American and Caribbean Music." *Latin American Research Review 34* (1), 187–200.

Moya Pons, Frank (1995). *The Dominican Republic: A National History*. New Rochelle, NY: Hispaniola.

_____ (1988). "Modernización y cambios en la República Dominicana." In Bernardo Vega et al (eds.), *Ensayos sobre la cultura dominicana*, (pp. 213–245). Santo Domingo: Fundación Cultural Dominicana.

"Murió Balaguer." (2002, July 15). Online. *Listin Diario*. Available: www.listindiario.com.do. (2002, July 28).

"Music from Cuba." (1997, October 4). *The Economist*. Online. Available: Lexis-Nexis Academic Universe (1999, November 30).

"No hay explicación para la falla del avión." (2001, November 15). *El Ciudadano*. Online, n.p. Available: http://elciudadano.net (2002, July 8).

Pacini Hernández, Deborah (1995). *Bachata: A Social History of a Dominican Popular Music*. Philadelphia: Temple University Press.

_____.(1991). "*La lucha sonora*: Dominican Popular Music in the Post-Trujillo Era." *Latin American Music Review 12* (2), 106–21.

_____.(1989). "Music of Marginality: Social Identity and Class in Dominican Bachata." *Latin American Music Review 10* (1), 69–91.

Padgett, Tim (1991, November 4). "Crossover Dreamers." *Newsweek*, pp. 74–5.

Pasternostro, Silvana (1999, January 10). "The Revolution Will Be in Stereo." *The NewYork Times* Online, Section 6. Available: Lexis-Nexis Academic Universe (1999, November 30).

Pearson, Richard (2002, July 15). "Joaquín Balaguer Dies at 95; Longtime Dominican Leader." *Washington Post*, p. B04.

Pérez, Máximo Manuel (2002, July 24). "Bush incluye a RD en tratado." Online. *Listín Diario. La República*, n.p. Available: www.listindiario.com.do (28 July, 2002).

Pina-Contreras, Guillermo (1997, May). "Colorful language." *UNESCO Courier*. Online. Available: Information Access/INFOTRAC/Expanded Academic ASAP/A19557185 (1999, June 22).

Provencher, Norman (1995, September 28). "Boukman Eksperyans." *The Ottawa Citizen* Online, p. C1. Available: Lexis-Nexis Academic Universe (1999, November 8).

Radcliffe, Sarah, and Sallie Westwood (1996). *Remaking the Nation*. London: Routledge.

Ramirez, Jesse (1999, February 28). "Nightlife in New York." *El Diario*. Online. Available: *LaMusica.com!* and http://www.latinmusiconline.com/jessie.htm (1999, March 2).

Ratliff, Ben (1999, September 14). "Pop Review: Flash and Discipline in the Art of Salsa." *The New York Times* Online, p. 5E. Available: Lexis-Nexis Academic Universe (1999, November 1).

"Reabren juicio contra implicados caso Orlando." (22 May, 2003). Online. *Periodistas Perseguidos*. Available http://portal-pfc.org/perseguidos/2002/096.html. (2003, May 26).

Rivera González, Luis (1960). *Antología musical de la era de Trujillo, 1930–1960.* 5 vols. Ciudad Trujillo: Publicaciones de la Secretaría de Estado de Educación y Bellas Artes.

Rodríguez, Olavo Alén (1994). "The Afro-French Settlement and the Legacy of its Music to the Cuban People." In Gerard Béhague (eds.), *Music and Black Ethnicity in the Caribbean and South America* (pp. 109–117). New Brunswick, NJ: Transaction.

Rodríguez, Tomás (2000). "Dominican Death Squad Sentenced in '75 Murder." *World Socialist Web Site.* Available www.wsws.org/articles/2000/aug2000/domi-a23_prn.shtml (2003, May 26).

Rodríguez, Victoria Eli (1994). "Cuban Music and Ethnicity: Historical Considerations." In Gerard Béhague (eds.), *Music and Black Ethnicity in the Caribbean and South America* (pp. 91–108). New Brunswick, NJ: Transaction.

Rodríguez Demorizi, Emilio (1971). *Música y baile en Santo Domingo.* Santo Domingo: Colección Pensamiento.

Seeger, Anthony (1994). "Whoever We Are Today, We Can Sing a Song about It." In Gerard Béhague (eds.), *Music and Black Ethnicity in the Caribbean and South America* (pp. 1–15). New Brunswick, NJ: Transaction.

_____ (1992). "Performance and Identity: Problems and Perspectives." In Carol E. Robertson (ed.), *Musical Repercussions of 1492: Encounters in Text and Performance,* (pp. 451–461). Washington, D.C.: Smithsonian Institution Press.

Smith, Anthony D. (1992). "The Origins of Nations." In Geoff Eley and Ronald Grigor Suny (eds.), *Becoming National* (pp. 106–130). New York: Oxford University Press.

Stapinski, Helene (1999, July). "Generacion Latino." *American Demographics.* Online. Available Lexis-Nexis Academic Universe (1999, November 30).

Tejeda, Darío (1993). *La historia escondida de Juan Luis Guerra y los 4:40.* Santo Domingo: Ediciones MSC, Amigo del Hogar.

"The blank page." (2002, July 17). dr1.com. [Online]. Available www.dr1.com (2003, May 26).

Tölölyan, Khachig (1992). "The Nation-State and Its Others: In Lieu of a Preface." In Geoff Eley and Ronald Grigor Suny (Eds.), *Becoming National* (pp. 426–431). New York: Oxford University Press.

Torres-Saillant, Silvio (1997). "Diaspora and National Identity: Dominican Migration in the Postmodern Society." In *Migration World Magazine* 25(3), 18. Online. Available: Information Access/INFOTRAC/Expanded Academic ASAP/ A19657004 (1999, June 29).

_____ (1998a). "The Tribulations of Blackness: Stages in Dominican Racial Identity." In *Latin American Perspectives,* 25(3), 126 (21 pp.). Online. Available: Information Access/INFOTRAC/Expanded Academic ASAP/A20757706 (1999, June 22).

_____ (1998b). "Visions of Dominicanness in the United States." In Frank Bonilla, Edwin Meléndez, Rebecca Morales, & María de los Angeles Torres (eds.), *Borderless Borders: US Latinos, Latin Americans, and the Paradox of Interdependence.* (pp. 139–152). Philadelphia: Temple University Press.

Torres-Saillant, Silvio, and Ramona Hernández (1998). *The Dominican Americans.* Westport, CT: Greenwood Press.

"Tulile y Los Rosario ganan con PLD Y PRD." (May 15, 2002). *Diario Libre*, p. 25.

Tumulty, Karen (2001, June 11). "Courting a Sleeping Giant." *Time*, p. 74.

Valdes, Alisa (1996, February 25). "On the Beat: How Proyecto Uno Is Working to Be the Next Big Thing." *The Boston Globe, Sunday City Edition* [Online], p. B27 (1757 words). Available: Lexis-Nexis Adademic Universe (1999, November 5).

Vargas Llosa, Mario (2000). *La fiesta del chivo*. Madrid: Taller.

Vianna, Hermano (1999). *The Mystery of Samba*. Chapel Hill: University of North Carolina Press.

Wilson, David Bertrand, and John Alroy. "Juan Luis Guerra y 440." In *Wilson & Alroy's Record Reviews*. Available: http://home.dti.net/warr/guerra.html (1999, February 2).

Wucker, Michele (1999a). "Race and Massacre in Hispaniola." Online. *Tikkun* 13(6), 61. Available: Information Access/INFOTRAC/Expanded Academic ASAP/ A21248757 (1999, June 22).

_____ (1999b). *Why the Cocks Fight. Dominicans, Haitians and the Struggle for Hispaniola*. New York: Hill & Wang.

Zapata, Nelson (2002, September). Personal interview.

Recordings

Fransheska (1991). "Menéalo." *Menéalo*. RCA International.

Fulanito (1997). *El hombre más famoso de la tierra*. Cutting Records.

Guerra, Juan Luis y 4:40. (1990) "A Pedir su mano." *Bachata Rosa*. Karen Records.

_____ (1990). "La bilirrubina." *Bachata Rosa*. Karen Records.

_____ (1992). "El costo de la vida." *Areito*. Karen Records.

_____ (1995). "Ojalá que llueva café." *Ojalá que llueva café*. Karen Records.

_____ (1995). "Visa para un sueño." *Ojalá que llueva café*. Karen Records.

_____ (1998). "El Niágara en bicicleta." *Ni es lo mismo ni es igual*. Karen Records.

_____ (1998). "Mi PC." *Ni es lo mismo ni es igual*. Karen Records.

Iglesias, Enrique (1999). "Bailamos." *Enrique*. Interscope Records.

Mala Fe (2000). "La vaca." *Con su loquera*. Sony International.

Martin, Ricky (1999). *Ricky Martin*. Sony. Interscope Records.

_____ (2003). "Raza de mil colores." *Almas del silencio*. Sony.

Méndez, Kinito (2002). "¿Qué pasó ahí?" *Sigo siendo el Hombre Merengue*. Sony International.

Morel, Angel (1998). "Mataron al chivo." *Trujillo: El Poder del Jefe I, II, y III*. Sony International.

Proyecto Uno (1991). "Brinca." *Todo el mundo*. 1991. J&N Records/Sony Distribution.

_____ (1996). "Latinos." *New Era*. H.O.L.A. Recordings/Universal Distribution.

_____ (1997). "El Tiburón." *In Da House*. J&N Records/Sony Distribution.

_____ (1997). "Está pega'o." *In Da House*. J&N Records/Sony Distribution.

_____ (1999). "Al otro lado del mar." *4*. H.O.L.A. Recordings/Universal Distribution.

_____ (1999). "25 Horas." *4*. H.O.L.A. Recordings/Universal Distribution.

_____ (2002). "Al otro lado del mar (Versión Bachata)" *Pura Gozadera*. Líderes Entertainment Group.

_____ (2002). "Bajando." *Pura Gozadera*. Líderes Entertainment Group.

_____ (2002). "Holla." *Pura Gozadera*. Líderes Entertainment Group.

_____ (2002). "I Want You to Be My Baby." *Pura Gozadera*. Líderes Entertainment Group.

Shakira (2001). *Laundry Service*. Sony.

Tulile (2000). "La cuca." *La cuca*. Vidal Cedeño.

Vargas, Wilfrido (2000). "Trujillo." *www.WilfridoVargas.com*. BMG/U.S. Latin.

98 Degrees (2000). "Give Me Just One Night/Una Noche." *Revelation*. Universal.

Index